D1542924

The Midnight Special

A Novel about Leadbelly

Edmond G. Addeo & Richard M. Garvin

authorHOUSE®

AuthorHouse™
1663 Liberty Drive
Bloomington, IN 47403
www.authorhouse.com
Phone: 1-800-839-8640

First published by Bernard Geis Associates, November, 1971

Second edition by AuthorHouse, 10/21/2009

ISBN: 978-1-4389-7580-1 (e)
ISBN: 978-1-4389-7578-8 (sc)
ISBN: 978-1-4389-7579-5 (hc)

Printed in the United States of America
Bloomington, Indiana

This book is printed on acid-free paper.

Authors' Note

This book was first published 38 years ago by Bernard Geis Associates, at the time the highest flying publishing house in New York, following a string of smash best-sellers beginning with *Valley of the Dolls*. Needless to say, Dick Garvin and I were near catatonic with excitement; Bernie Geis was the most glamorous publisher we'd had to date, and had elevated the fine art of book promotion to Olympian heights. He practically invented promoting books on radio & TV – we were headed for the best-seller list!

And indeed we were -- the book quickly sold out its first printing! But after a whirlwind promotional tour of the great USA cities, newspaper interviews, bookstore appearances, radio and TV (including one memorable on-air dust-up with Pete Seeger and F. Lee Bailey on the nationally syndicated "The Virginia Graham Show"), Johnny Carson, <u>plus</u> a full-column excellent review in the NYTBR, Bernie Geis filed a Chapter XI in New York. Bankrupt! The distributor and everyone else chose not to do any more business with him.

It was the fastest roller coaster ride in publishing history.

Dick Garvin, a close friend and nonpareil collaborator (we'd had two previous novels published), died in 1980. Over the years since, it has often been suggested that I polish *The Midnight Special* from a perspective of decades later and re-publish it. For example, there has been a resurgent interest in Leadbelly's music in Europe. However, it was difficult to interest a new publisher; traditional publishing today is still mired in the mid-1900s. There are a lot of publishers today who don't even have cell phones, much less are able to tell the difference between a biographical novel and a straight biography. One publisher wanted to re-publish TMS if I'd supply "new" information about Leadbelly. He couldn't grasp the idea that there was no "new" information; Dick Garvin and I had spoken with everyone who had known him, and today they are all dead. And one cannot create "new" archival records or historical documents –– unless, of course, one is a politician.

Now, through the digital miracle of independent publishing, maybe *The Midnight Special* can continue its interrupted journey.

*   *   *   *   *

Leadbelly was not only an outstanding musical talent who achieved the status of a deity in American folklore, he was also a selfish, temperamental rough-hewn ex-convict to whom invention was more interesting than truth. He so loved his own fables that he seldom excluded them from his recollections to folklorists, who often set them down as gospel.

A product of the bruising back country of Louisiana, Leadbelly survived both the prison gangs and the bewildering silverware society of New England suburbs by constantly re-creating himself. Because he was a consummate and imaginative storyteller and not a historian, there remain periods in his life that are either blurred or blank. When restoring an unfinished painting, even the most scholarly expert sometimes must use his own imagination to fill in the missing details. Thus, when we wrote this novel based on the life of one of our greatest folk musicians, we created scenes and reconstructed events in order to provide smooth transitions between known periods in Leadbelly's life. In these few cases, such as the scene with Sycamore Slim, any similarity between fictitious characters and actual persons, alive or dead, is coincidental.

(This idea of a biographical novel was mistakenly overlooked in 1976 when a movie called "Lead Belly" was released by Paramount Pictures, and which contained three distinct scenes, including the Sycamore Slim scene, that Dick Garvin and I had completely made up out of whole cloth. It wasn't a good movie, didn't depict Leadbelly accurately, and bombed at the box office. Somebody should try it again.)

In all scenes, including these fictional restorations, we did our utmost to preserve historical accuracy. We logged three years of research and thousands of miles in retracing the meandering trail of Huddie Ledbetter from his birth in a Louisiana swamp to his pitiful burial in a black cemetery on the Texas-Louisiana border. Many of the places we visited in 1968 -- and the way of life -- were virtually unchanged since the turn of the century: the tattered, deprived prisoners sweltering in the fetid pens of the Angola State farm; the hovels and unbearable poverty in the Deep Elm district of Dallas; the acres of cane, corn and cotton growing from the red earth of the broiling Texas Brazos; the bits of broken glass and crockery that served as tombstones in the graveyard behind the Shiloh Baptist Church in Mooringsport; the bully-tough ghettos of Harlem; the snug and smug security of 1930s Wilton, Connecticut.

At the time, few white men had ever visited the sleazy barrel and bawdy houses of Saint Paul's Bottom in Shreveport, and fewer yet -- none, we suspected -- had waded through the dusty records in courthouse vaults or sat for hours sipping cool drinks and listening to the stories about Leadbelly told with childlike awe by most of his friends and relatives. Dick and I were grateful to have been able to do those things and to see for ourselves what previously we had only read or heard about. And we were privileged to have been welcomed by so many people, black and white.

On the other hand, it sometimes seemed to us that a small circle of Leadbelly's "friends" at the time considered his life their own personal property, to be clutched and guarded like a family heirloom. They were wrong. Leadbelly belongs to no one, and at the same time to anyone who can hum the song that was made popular as "Goodnight, Irene."

An important word to reviewers and critics about dialog. Our editor at Geis at the time was the late Don Preston, who edited a few more books of mine with other publishers and who remained a friend until his death. Don gave us the best possible advice regarding the treatment of Southern black dialect *vis-a-vis* sociological thinking -- at the time -- on racial priorities: "The only certainty about the use of deep-South dialect is that anything you do will be wrong."

The fact is that Louisiana Negro speech in that era was a patois, with peculiar pronunciations and rhythms, and of course it reflects the life of those who speak it. But phonetic spelling would make any accurate dialog read like a foreign language. Therefore, Dick and I compromised somewhere between the extremes of a Stepin Fetchit-like "I'se gwine git dat ol' debbil" and the uncomfortably embellished rhetoric of William Styron's Nat Turner. We kept the "I'se," as in "I'se seventy-two years old," and "I'se known him for ten years," because that particular contraction of "I is" was how people still talked on Fannin Street and Mooringsport in 1968. And we dropped the "g" in all dialog gerunds. It's simply the way uneducated deep South black people spoke in those days, and I'd be less than honest if I didn't maintain historical accuracy. Again, I refuse to make Leadbelly sound a Nobel Laureate in Literature, as Styron so disturbingly did with Nat Turner. (At the time, we were complimented by the way "two white boys" handled the dialog problem in *The New York Times* and several other reviews.)

The use of the word "nigga" is problematic. It was part of the everyday vocabulary of Leadbelly and his black contemporaries, so I've opted to keep it, since it's closer to the actual sound than either "nigger" or "nigguh." Given the intensity of today's political correctness and the sensitivities of minority groups 38 years later, I fully expect to take much more heat about that word than we received when the book was first published.

We believed then, and I believe now, that *The Midnight Special* is the truth about Leadbelly, so far as anyone can ever know it, about a man who spent most of his life either in trouble or on the brink of it. He was -- and still is -- the "King o' the Twelve-String Guitars o' the World" and the "hardest workin', toughest, meanest damn nigga in the state o' Loosiana!"

We pursued that truth long and far, and we had then, and I still have now, the deepest gratitude to the dozens of people who helped along the way, many of whom are probably no longer with us:

Mr. and Mrs. John A. Lomax, Jr., of Houston, Texas; Mr. Edmond Ledbetter, cousin, of Mooringsport, Louisiana; Mrs. Florida Ledbetter Combs, niece, of Shreveport, Louisiana; Mrs. Jessie Mae Ledbetter Baisley, daughter, of San Francisco, California; Dr. George Beto, director, Texas Department of Corrections; Mr. Jack Kyle, assistant director for business, Texas Department of Corrections; Assistant Wardens Hunt and Dickerson, Huntsville and Sugar Land, respectively; Assistant Warden Hayden J. Dees, Louisiana State Penitentiary at Angola, Louisiana; Drs. Milton and Patricia Rickles of the University of Southwest Louisiana, Lafayette, Louisiana; Martin Fox and Lynne Butcher Fox of Mooringsport, Louisiana; Captain Robert Wilkins, Sheriff's Department, Shreveport, Louisiana; Mr. Vel Davis, Jr., postmaster, Wortham, Texas; Mrs. Mildred Watkins, the *Shreveport Journal*, Shreveport, Louisiana; Mr. Grayson Smart, editor, *Shreveport* Magazine, Shreveport, Louisiana; Major and Ernest Lampkins, musicians, Shreveport, Louisiana; Mr. Eddie "Coot" Louis, musician, Shreveport, Louisiana; Mr. Booker T. Washington, friend of Huddie, Mooringsport, Louisiana; Mrs. Cynthia "Buck" Jefferson, friend of Huddie, Mooringsport, Louisiana; Mr. Eddie Baisley, friend of Huddie, Mooringsport, Louisiana; Mr. and Mrs. Alfred Wipf, friends of Huddie, Mooringsport, Louisiana; Dr. Hector Lee, Sonoma State College, Sonoma, California; Mr. Chris Strachwitz, folklorist and president of Arhoolie Records, Berkeley, California; Mr. James McShane, playwright, New York City; Mr. Big Joe Williams, musician, Kansas City, Missouri; Mr. Mance Lipscomb, musician, Centerville, Texas; Mr. Jessie Fuller, musician, San Francisco, California; Mr. William Thorpe, musician, Mill Valley, California; Mr. Jeff Brown, LL.B., Fairfax, California; Mrs. Connie Naitove, friend of Huddie, Hanover, New Hampshire.

And also the many assorted people who helped in smaller but no less important ways, too numerous to name, but prominent among whom are: Harry D. Roffelsen, Patrick L. Murphy, Gerard St. Jovite, Chris Lunn, the staffs of the Dallas Public Library and the *Shreveport Journal*, Tom Glazer, Archie Goldhor, Arnold Caplin, Mike Nevelson, Roderick Anderson, Phoebe Sonenberg, Holly Wood Stephenson, Natalie F. Joffee, Janet Salisbury, Faith Zavon and Margo Mayo. Finally, a special thanks to Shirley and Pete Baucom, Lisa Wash

Railsback, Sandra Haggerty, the Kirschky family and Walter and Ella Forsiak, then of Dallas, Texas and now of Sonoma, California.

God bless you all, wherever you are.

EGA
Mill Valley, California
July, 2009

Caddo Parish, Louisiana: 1887

A tall, goose-necked woman claps her hands and the sacred words pour from her lips. "*Eh! Eh! Romba hen hen!*" she chants in a throaty voice. "*Canga bafe te . . .*"

It is a hidden place, deep within the backwaters of Caddo Lake. The black people are beginning to gather in the ghost forests of towering cypresses long destroyed by some forgotten inlet of salt water. Like gnarled arms, the roots reach out of the brackish water as if seeking solid ground. Elsewhere, tupelo, hackberry and swamp black gums fight each other in a dark, distorted tangle of foliage.

The tall woman, Euphrasine, feels her heartbeat synchronize with the drumbeats. Before her lies a darkly attractive, bulbously pregnant half-breed, stretched on an oily, cotton-stuffed quilt.

She is Sally Pugh Ledbetter, twenty-two years old, the half-Negro and half-Indian daughter of parents she never knew. She had long considered herself barren, and much of her husband Wes's hard-earned savings had been spent with the conjurers. Even now, she cannot believe she is finally about to have a baby.

Old beliefs die hard, and for Sally Ledbetter they will never be entirely buried. Embracing a practice as old as Man, she immersed herself in the magical-religious powers of the "conjure ladies," and spent countless evenings sprinkling the blessed ashes of bobcat fur and the concentrated choppings of wild roots on the doorsteps of Shreveport's brothels.

Among her most sacred possessions are supplies of "Easy Life Mixture," "Black Cat's Oil" and "Lovin' Powder." But the most powerful of all her charms is the "Black Cat's Bone," a relic she knows will keep her husband loving and faithful until he dies.

Out in the clearing, mosquitoes whirr around Wes Ledbetter as he waves a whiskey bottle and coaxes his brother Terrell into a careening cakewalk. They do not participate in the birth ritual.

An old stick of a man, his face as distorted as windswept magnolia, shuffles forward and lights twelve tiny blue candles, inserting them carefully in a barrel full of wet river sand. Euphrasine claps her hands once more, and the believers in this cacaphony of Christ and Congo gather in a circle, their arms linked. Then she reaches upward, and the people fall silent. She whispers to Sally and turns, inscribing three circles in the ground. Deftly, slowly, she removes Sally's gown. The old man puts a bottle of raspberry pop, a greasy jug of cider and a cup of water beside them. Euphrasine places a green candle at Sally's head and a white one at her feet. Upon her sign, the old man extinguishes each of the twelve blue candles by placing them in his mouth.

When he finishes, Euphrasine puts a plate of dried basil near the white candle and a dish containing a mixture of bird seed, cloves and cinnamon at her feet. She anoints Sally on her forehead, her breasts, her belly and between her thighs with a tincture of olive oil and camphor.

It is now time for the priest -- the *Hungan*.

The *Hungan* is a giant quadroon with only one eye. He is flanked by two naked women who grasp and fondle him constantly, encouraging an enormous phallus jutting in front of him. He comes forth and two

2

other women remove his slippers. A bottle of whiskey is thrust at him and he splashes it on Sally's belly. He throws back his head and gulps from the bottle. Then he begins a slow rhythmic shuffle, undulating his hips. Around and around, slowly accelerating, with extravagant gesticulations, he anoints Sally once again with the whiskey.

> *Danse Calinda, boudoum, boudoum!*
> *Danse Calinda, boudoum, boudoum!*

The chanting, a savage and strange minor strain, becomes more gutteral, a mixture of passion and pain. The hands of the *Hungan* sway like fronds, and his feet shuffle to the barbaric measure. By now the two women at his side have done their work and with a hoarse, gravelly moan the *Hungan* spews into their cupped hands. The semen is mixed with sugar and orris powder on an old cracked plate. They make a sign over it and massage the mixture onto Sally, who is now writhing in the advanced stages of labor. Cackling midwives -- the "two-headed doctors" -- stand near her, ready to ease the pain. Their wet faces, rimmed with stringy white hair, glisten from the light of the torches and bonfires. The quilt by now is soaked. A pot of water boils nearby. One of the midwives places her hand between Sally's legs and probes at her. "Everthin' gonna be all right, honey. Jus' you don' worry. Everthin' jus' fine."

Sally cries out suddenly. The pain is so intense it is almost pleasurable. The midwives pull her up to a squatting position and the *Hungan* leers at her, the empty eye socket twitching. He grins and jumps back, soft words of magic tumbling from his lips.

Sally falls, but the midwives hold her tightly. She thinks not of what it will be, but only will it be. The spasms contract her uterine muscles. The hands of the midwives are under her, ready to take the

3

child as if it were an offering. Another shriek. The baby's head is squeezed from Sally, and after another contraction is emitted in a splash of blood and hair. One of the midwives takes the slippery baby, as the eager shrills of the rest cut through the alcoholic haze of Wes Ledbetter. "God A-mighty!" he yells. "I got me a boy!"

His brother Terrell looks up from his guitar. "How you know it's a boy already?"

"We gonna call him Huddie, too," Wes blurts, ignoring the question and lurching his way through the clearing. "He gonna be the bes' damn nigga in dis whole state!"

The men keep guzzling their whiskey through the night. Wes doesn't bother to see Sally or confirm his child's sex. Oblivious to the cries of the infant, the two men fall asleep on the ground.

Muskrats, their darting eyes reflecting the dancing yellow glint of torchlight, scurry fearfully. Motionless alligators watch with detached interest, then slide back into the muddy comfort of the water as bonfires begin to blaze. Above the trees, the black sky is spangled with glistening specks; the moon is just beginning its ascent into the darkness. A yellow-crowned night heron, its wings flapping furiously, heads into the sky.

On a sandy drift the people wait, and the steady and deep-toned booming beat of bones on a skin-covered cask begins. Several of the women have bound their hair with red handkerchiefs and have tied strings of tiny bells around their ankles. On a makeshift altar is an ornamented wooden box containing the *Vodu*, the *Zombi*, the holy spirit. In a jangling procession the people approach the box one by one, then touch it and fall back.

Near the bonfire, Huddie Ledbetter has entered the world -- a world that will never forget him.

4

Chapter One

Sally Pugh Ledbetter sang to herself quietly and watched Huddie bridle the horses and hitch them to the brand new jump-seat buggy from Sears Roebuck. Today was extra special for him, she thought; he had waited a long time for it to come. Five years, in fact. Lord! Five years of badgering, pestering, pleading and begging his papa to take him along on one of the regular Saturday morning trips to Shreveport. Wes, of course, had wanted to take him sooner, but Sally kept refusing. In the tradition of this Southern community, she tenaciously protected her child from the inevitable awareness of being black.

Dawn had barely begun to rupture the sky and tufts of high, feathery clouds were foaming in the sunlight. Swallowtails and bobolinks were fussing in the pines, sycamores and mimosas that dotted the flatlands.

Sally smiled as she sang and looked with pleasure across the Ledbetter farm stretched in front of her. It was 1899, the last year of the century, and it was promising to be the best one yet for the Ledbetters. The harvest of the bountiful cotton crop had perked everyone's spirit, and now the sight of the naked cotton stalks jabbing upward like crooked bristles from the loamy soil was a satisfying one.

At thirty-four, Sally retained the muscular curves of her Indian mother. Her hair was straight and black, tied in a single braid, lending an almost Oriental beauty to her oval face and almond eyes. She was both physically and emotionally strong; the long driving years working alongside her ambitious husband had toned her muscles and given her a determination she had not known as a girl. Yet, with all the work, she retained a certain athletic delicacy and her moves were gracefully deliberate. She wore a simple red print chemise that she had sewn from several yards of store-bought cloth, and her bare feet were spread comfortably on the smooth plank floor.

The Ledbetter farm was tucked into the northwest corner of Louisiana, two miles from Mooringsport and Caddo Lake, not far from the Texas border. It was sixty-eight and one-half acres, half of it cleared for cotton and corn and the other half heavily wooded with long- and short-leaf pine. A dirt road riddled with chuck-holes, slashed the property in two and then swung westward toward Leigh, Texas.

The cabin was built of gray planking and stood on three-foot-high footings sectioned from the thick trunk of an oak. A front porch ran the length of the cabin and supported an overhanging roof of corrugated tin. A flower garden, which Sally tended with meticulous care, punctuated the hard red earth with splashes of yellows and blues. In the back was a well, a rabbit hutch, a chicken coop, two sows, a heifer named Minnie and a vegetable garden -- all Huddie's responsibility. The windows were square openings sawed out of the planks. They were closed at night with shutters. The cabin had two rooms, a bedroom and a kitchen, but five years ago, when Huddie was seven, Wes had added a shedroom in the rear for him.

The kitchen consisted of a massive iron wood-burning stove. And opposite it a flat counter cluttered with chipped pots, battered pans and old bottles. An enormous zinc tub, which served as a bath for children, grown-ups and guests, hung on the whitewashed wall, suspended from a square iron spike. A wooden table stained with indigo dye stood directly in the center of the room. A tattered hooked cotton rug, the color of Spanish moss, lay on the bare floor in the cabin's living area -- a room that served many functions. A wrought-iron bed, neatly covered with a patchwork quilt, was shoved against one wall, and beside it was a screen made of wood and canvas. The fireplace was large, and in it hung a huge cast-iron cauldron. Two rockers and a plain straight-back chair were placed in front of it. Along the front wall, near the door, there were two 20-gauge double-barreled Thomas Barkers; a freshly sharpened sickle; several lengths of hemp rope; an extra pair of heavy boots; an axe; two bridles; a stack of Shreveport Journals; an empty bottle, which had once held expensive bitters and which Wes Ledbetter could not bear to throw away; and three coiled whips nestled like blacksnakes in the corner. Pinned on the wall was a picture of the Statue of Liberty and a yellowed newspaper photo of Abraham Lincoln.

An old dresser leaned against the far wall, and behind it two strips of flowery wallpaper had been tacked to the wood. The dresser was bedecked with a clutter of childhood mementoes, small carved religious icons, the treasured Black Cat's Bone, a collection of celluloid combs and brushes, a hand-decorated perfume atomizer, several barrettes, a silk ribbon and a few lace doilies. A dozen tiny containers of oil, incense and even shells from the delta of the Mississippi were stacked with care along the top.

In the kitchen Sally continued to sing. Her soft voice displayed a gentle clarity that carried it apart from the rest of the Shiloh

Baptist Church choir, and the song was the solo she wanted to sing at tomorrow's services. But she also sang for another reason: thanksgiving. Wes Ledbetter had provided for his family better than most black men in northern Louisiana. Disease and hunger didn't visit the Ledbetter cabin as savagely as they did most of the Mooringsport community. Wes, always a hard worker and a friend of the town's sheriff, Nate Gifford, was accepted as a "good nigga," and he had the largest share of land among his circle of friends.

He reckoned his age at forty. No record of his birth existed. All he could remember of his mother and father were their lifeless forms, laid out in a public building in Kemper County, Mississippi. He was three years old at the time, but the memory of the slaughter of his parents by the Klan was forever lodged in the back of his mind. Perhaps it was because of this memory that he relished liquor and hard work, and lived amid the white man's tight-lipped intimidation.

It had been two years now since Wes's dream had finally taken the form of this fertile land -- some of it hilly and some of it lake level -- that he had purchased for $231.25. Wes now divided his time three ways: mornings were spent clearing and hacking the tangled growths of scrub, thistle and wild strawberries; afternoons were spent tending the crops; the late evenings were spent either drinking with his friend, Big Ted Promise, or listening to the songs of his brothers, or telling Huddie to pay attention to his schoolwork, or making tender love to Sally.

This morning Wes was exceptionally cheerful. He, too, was humming as Huddie finished with the horses and hauled in the water. The two of them sat down, appetites whetted by the smoky smell of frying fatback and eggs. Sally set the food in front of them and sliced off thick slabs of cornbread, frying them to a golden crust in the grease. She heaped them on the plates and covered them with the remaining fat. Wes and Huddie washed down the breakfast with gulps of black coffee. Less than half an hour later they were finally on their way.

Huddie thought his heart would simply blow up from the excitement. Shreveport! The big city! That's where they were going at last! He sat back in the buggy and watched the cypresses slowly disappear, replaced by pecans and mesquite. The morning sun, highlighting the rust-colored mimosa blossoms, warmed them quickly. Squirrels scampered with fluffy speed against the gray black bark of the surrounding oaks.

Huddie tried to relax but couldn't. He kept folding and unfolding his muscular arms, and his fingers fiddled nervously at the ends of his old accordion -- his windjammer. And by the time they were halfway to Shreveport he had played and replayed every song he knew. This was the best day in his life, he decided as he watched a swamp-lizard splash in the water along the Twelve-Mile Bayou. He finally put the windjammer down and sat thinking of the time, almost six years ago, when he decided to become a musician. That, too, was a momentous day.

They had just returned from church, and as they all got out of the buggy, Huddie's Uncle Terrell flashed a package at him, wrapped in newspaper pages and tied with blue string. In the kitchen, they gathered around the table and watched him eagerly rip open the present. "A windjammer!" Huddie yelled. "A windjammer! I got me a windjammer!"

It was just what he'd been wanting. The case was cardboard, stained as imitation mahogany, but that didn't matter. It was shiny and glittering. And it had light green panels with a gilt border wound with white celluloid. Even more, it had ten nickel keys, two stops and two sets of extra quality reeds, triple bellows with nickel patent corners on the folds, and a bright brass clasp. The end straps appeared to be real leather.

Huddie fought to enmesh his hands in the end straps, and the instrument wheezed dissonantly under the pressure.

"Hold on, boy! Took me a long time to make enough money for that thing. Don' go breakin' it right off. It cost over two dollars, so you care for it." Terrell got up and circled the table toward Huddie. Terrell was a well known "songster," a minstrel who rambled throughout East Texas and northern Louisiana entertaining one person or a hundred at a backwater crossroads or a midtown house dance, called a "sukey-jump."

He took the accordion from Huddie and fingered it gently. "If you fixin' to become a music man, you gotta learn it proper right off. This here squeeze box don't like bein' treated like no hammer, you know. More like a lady. Just put you fingers on them keys there, dependin' on what notes you wanna play. Remember, now, each button's a different note, and you push the ends back and forth easy, not like you clappin' you hands at a breakdown."

With that, Terrell began to squeeze the small accordion, demonstrating for Huddie. "Now, here. I'se gonna teach you a first song, and you listen good so you can sing it right off when you play. Now, this here song you could teach all you friends. It's an old song sung by all the poor chiles before they was set free. They'd all go out in the yard and make a ring, and they'd put one li'l chile inside the ring, and then they'd take hold of each other's hands and sing,

> *Ha-ha, thisaway, ho-ho thataway,*
> *Ha-ha, thisaway, then, oh, then.*

"Now, Huddie, they's only two chords to this song and you can play the whole thing."

When Terrell finished the lesson he handed Huddie the windjammer. Huddie held it more gently this time. "Here's you box, Huddie. An' the next time I comes by here for a visit, I want to hear you playin' this old thing like they do down in Shrevepo't."

Late that night, Wes had to get out of bed and go into the shedroom. "Son," he said softly, "ain't you never fixin' to put that thing down and get some sleep?"

Invisible in the dark room, Huddie didn't answer. The music continued, the same two chords of the same song of his long asleep uncle. Huddie had played it all afternoon and evening. "Huddie," Wes whispered again. "You got to go to sleep now, hear? Ain't no good to just play and play without gettin' no sleep."

The music stopped. "Papa?"

"Yes, son."

"Can I go down to Fannin Street with you sometime when I learn me another song and play with the songsters?"

"'Fraid not, Huddie. Youse still too young and you still got too much schoolin' to do. Maybe when youse a bigger boy than youse now, I take you down with me. But right now, you get some sleep or you gonna fall down dead from playin' on that thing."

Wes closed the door gently when he heard Huddie set the box down on the floor and went back to his own bed and Sally.

When he was sure everyone was asleep again, Huddie reached down quietly and picked up his new windjammer. He stroked the smooth side panels and fiddled with the clasp. Then he set it next to him on the bed. Later he picked it up again and held it to the window, hoping to catch another look at it in the filtered moonlight.

He went to sleep, listening to the crickets rubbing dampness from their legs, thinking of the day ending. Huddie Ledbetter had played his first song.

*   *   *   *   *

Since the day of the windjammer, Uncle Terrell became like a second father to Huddie. On Sunday visits to the Ledbetter farm, Terrell brought new music, new songs, new stories around which to weave melodic narratives. Once he even brought Huddie a bell harmonica, and Huddie worked at mastering that for a while but put it away in favor of the windjammer. Terrell had managed to wangle permission from crusty old Reverend Parker to use the ancient upright piano in the church. There, many sweaty Sunday afternoons were spent over the keyboard, with Terrell's strong black fingers making chords for Huddie to memorize. And slowly but determinedly over the next six years, Huddie learned the rudiments of backcountry music in the rear of the old church, with Terrell's guitar and piano and his own windjammer making the old building ring.

Now, finally on his way to Shreveport, Huddie mused about how it seemed as if time had passed so quickly. Yet, when he'd first received his windjammer, he was certain the time would never come when he could go with his papa to Shreveport. Now he could do the things he saw in his dreams, all the wild and wonderful and exciting things he just knew happened every day of the year in the city.

"Y'know," Wes said, almost startling Huddie from the hypnotic, monotonous clopping of the horses. "When we gets to Shrevepo't, we gonna meet ol' Sycamore down where I got to go for the cotton pricin'."

"He the old man what knows Uncle Terrell?"

"That's right. He's a songster, too. I been tellin' him 'bout you and you windjammer, Huddie. He always tellin' me that when you is growed big enough to come on down to Shrevepo't with me, he gonna take you 'round and you two gonna play some songs in the streets. Jus' like all the songsters hereabouts."

Huddie's eyes flashed. "You mean I gonna play with him, papa? He gonna show me how to be a real songster, like Uncle Terrell?"

Wes nodded. "That's right. I got me some business to tend to and ol' Sycamore promise he watch you right careful 'til I gets back. You sure gonna learn some new songs from him, Huddie. An' you pay good attention to him, understan'?"

Huddie looked up eagerly. "What he play on, papa? A windjammer?"

"Oh, he play on all sorts o' things. Mostly on an ol' beat-up guitar. He got hisself a big leather strap he hang 'round his shoulder and he jus' moseys 'round and plays and sings for whatever the folks give him. Jus' like you Uncle Terrell, 'ceptin' Sycamore make a lot more money on account he so popular, and in Shrevepo't they's got more rich white folks what like to hear the niggas sing the old songs. On a Saturday night, all the folks come into Shrevepo't, all the workers what got any money come in whatever they can. Mule, horse and even the railroad. Jus' so they can whoop it up and holler after a whole week o' nothin' but workin'."

"Where they all go to holler? They got a place all themselves?"

"They goes all over the place," Wes laughed. "The niggas has they own places to go, and the white folks go someplace else. They's a district down on Fannin Street they calls Saint Paul's Bottom. Oh, everythin' goes on down there. They's bars and hotels and even a music house. Huddie, they is *everything* on Fannin Street."

"What about the wimmins, papa? Is they allowed to holler and stomp, too?" Huddie remembered yesterday's talk with Hesekie and Billy Coleman at school and tried not to think about what was supposed to happen come Monday with a notorious older girl named Edna Mae.

Wes' eyebrows furrowed briefly, and he kept his eyes straight ahead at the horses. "The wimmins is somethin' you pay no attention to, Huddie," he said, trying to sound casual. "I said they's all kinds o' things happenin' down on Fannin Street, and they's all kinds of wimmins, too. Most o' the things concernin' the wimmins ain't no concern to you till youse bigger. You learn that stuff soon enough, believe me." Wes now chuckled to himself. He dreaded Huddie achieving the age he was alluding to. "Now you just stick with ol' Sycamore and you won't find no concern about the bad parts o' Shrevepo't."

Huddie turned away and grabbed his windjammer. He decided not to pursue the woman question, since the coming Monday with Hesekie and Billy would come all too soon. He spent the rest of the trip talking to his papa and playing his songs over and over again. When the buggy crossed the bridge at McCain Creek the low outline of Shreveport loomed in the distance.

*　　*　　*　　*　　*

The man they called Sycamore Slim hailed from the boggy bayous that sprawled in lush, damp profusion in the Wallace Lake area between Caddo and De Soto Parishes. As best as he could recollect, he was in his late seventies, an ex-slave and ox driver from southern Georgia. Sycamore was a tall, lanky man, bald with his remaining white-wool hair covering part of his ears and lightly touching the back collar of his blue work shirt. He wore coveralls and a faded red bandanna knotted loosely around his neck and his shoes were heavy-duty, rough oxhide, with hobnailed heels and scuffed toes.

Huddie saw him from a half-block away as he and his papa approached the bustling market area along brick-paved Texas Avenue. Huddie had been hoping to catch the infamous name "Fannin," but to no avail. Then he saw Sycamore perched on an iron railing in front of a run-down hotel. Sycamore had his battered old guitar slung casually over his shoulders and he was talking to a group of women, each of whom had a heavy wicker basket of wash balanced on her head.

Sycamore greeted the arrival of the buggy with a display of a full set of teeth that had yellowed like old piano keys. His voice was an epiglottal rumble. "Howdy, Wes. See you finally brought you boy along." He jumped lightly down from the railing and shook Wes's hand. "You boy sure filled out good."

Wes put his hand on Huddie's shoulder. "Huddie's a strong one and the bes' damn windjammer player in Mooringspo't."

"That's what I hear," Sycamore said, still looking at Huddie. "I heard that lots of times. How long you been squeezin' that thing, boy?"

"My Uncle Terrell give it to me when I was six."

"Let's see," Wes said. "That makes five years now I reckon. No six. Six years."

Sycamore's eyebrows jumped upward in disbelief. "You mean you's only *twelve*? Man, you look like you five years older."

"Strong, too," Wes said proudly. "Comes harvest time, Huddie here can pick more cotton in one day than mos' any of the hands."

"Done him good," Sycamore said. "You boy's as big as you an' a damnsight better lookin'!" He turned to Huddie. "Well, now. You daddy, he tells me the las' time he here that you is gonna hang 'round a bit. Sure would 'preciate you helpin' me out, on account it look like today gonna be some good crowds a-walkin' the streets." He shifted his weight and looked up at the sky. "Look like it gonna be a good day, too. You know, I been playin' these here streets for most twenty years and I reckon I ain't never had no one you age play the win'jammer with me. No, can't recollect it a'tall."

"Huddie," Wes said finally, "I gotta get down to the markets before all the orders been took. You jus' stay here with Sycamore and be a good boy and I see you in 'bout four or five hours."

"Okay, papa," Huddie said, and he waved as Wes jumped into the buggy and headed toward the river. Huddie felt Sycamore touch his shoulder.

"Huddie-boy, might jus' as well start right out an' see how much money we can collect 'fore noontime."

"We jus' start playin' right here?" Huddie asked.

"Oh, for a start. Maybe somebody come along and like what we doin'. Never can tell. Day like this bring all sorts of people into town. Ol' sun blazin' up in the sky give a man a terrible thirst, and he jus' has to loosen up in the saloon down on West Center. That's when folks get frisky with the money and sometimes start tossin' it 'round like it don't mean nothin' to 'em."

Sycamore raised the guitar and tucked it under his right arm, holding the neck at a sharp, downward angle. Then, with an index finger *callused* by a lifetime of barring the sharp steel strings, he pressed hard against the second fret. A progression of clear E-flat harmonics jumped from the keyboard, the fingers bleeding the notes, tinting them with discordant, crying tones of the street blues.

"Mr. Sycamore," Huddie said as he sat down and reached for his windjammer. "What we gonna play?"

"Why, that's up to you, Huddie-boy. You jus' start in on somethin' and I'll just sort of follow."

So Huddie began with "Green Corn," a fiddle song and one of the first he had learned. It was a song of the summer corn harvested, of ears roasting in the shuck -- the upbeat of the breakdowns learned from Uncle Terrell. Sycamore picked up the tune, changing the tempo slightly, but Huddie had already established his rhythm, and he began to sing in a high falsetto voice.

Green corn, come along Cholly,
Green corn, come along Cholly,
Stan' aroun', stan' aroun' the jimmy-john,
Stan' aroun', stan' aroun' the jimmy-john.

Huddie rambled the melody and barely noticed when Sycamore began playing softer, finally not strumming at all but simply watching the boy absorbed with the song, oblivious to anything but the music.

Peas in the pot an' the hoecakes a-bakin',
Wake snake, the day's a-breakin'.

Sycamore grinned and drummed his hand on the back of his guitar in tempo with Huddie. When Huddie was finished he was sweating as hard as he ever did in the cotton fields. The old man rapped the box with his knuckles, "Lawd, Huddie-boy! You play that thing like you was born inside it. That the bes' damn windjammer I ever heard in my whole life! You play everythin' that way?"

"Mos' the songs I knows is the fast ones, 'cept for the church music that mamma sings."

"Who taught you that?"

"Mos' of it I learnt myself. But my Uncle Terrell, he was pretty good and helped me learn the chords and all."

Sycamore was still incredulous. He was a man who had spent the past sixty years living with the music of the backwater lands of Louisiana. He had been listening to music and playing his own music for as long as he could remember, yet he had never heard anyone sing and play like that. He knew that, like the guitar, the windjammer was an easy instrument to play badly but a difficult one to play well. Especially a windjammer like that! It was a crude instrument at best, given to leaks and wheezes and cracks, but somehow this boy seemed to command all the wheezes to disappear.

Sycamore, without a word, launched into another tune, one he knew would be -- should be -- much more difficult for Huddie. The boy listened for a moment, picked up the rhythm tentatively and played slowly along for three bars. Then, as if suddenly hitting on the solution to an arithmetic problem, Huddie began to stomp again and play with gusto equal to the previous song.

By now a handful of black men were clustered in front of the railing, watching them play. When they finished the men shouted for more. Huddie grinned and looked up at Sycamore. He was delighted. For the first time, he felt the breathtaking thrill of applause. They liked him. These big sweating men from Shreveport were clapping for *him!*

The impromptu concert lasted for five more songs and, when they finished, Huddie's pocket held three pennies and a nickel. Wait until he told his papa about that! They actually *paid* him to play! And mama! Why didn't she let him come sooner? They could have been rich by now! His fingers jangled the coins again.

"Huddie-boy," Sycamore said, "I do believe we deserves somethin' to douse our thirst. What you say we ramble down to ol'

18

Bo McWhirter's place and I buy you a sody. An' ol' Sycamore jus' might have somethin' a mite stronger, on account o' Huddie-boy, today we's gonna rock ol' Shrevepo't right smack into the Red River! You ever been in a saloon?"

"No suh," Huddie said. "Mama would have a conniption fit. Papa and his friends go to one on Friday nights, and she don't like it none."

"Well, Bo's is a right friendly place, 'ceptin' you gotta watch you manners and you mouth. Sometimes some of the folks get to takin' too much whiskey and they get mean. So you jus' watch me and you do what I do and don't say nothin' less'n someone else say somethin' to you first. You jus' play that there windjammer like you been doin' and we have everybody a-throwin' money at us like it was river sand."

They walked down the street, and a slight swagger crept into Huddie's gait. Down toward the river they went, passing the general store, another hotel, a small bank, a cafe that gave off the pungent odor of red beans and rice, and Pearson's Livery Stable. Finally, there was Bo McWhirter's.

The saloon was filled with men drinking beer. Huddie momentarily hesitated, but Sycamore urged him in.

The odor that hit Huddie's nostrils was a combination of stale tobacco and whiskey, a sour-alcohol stench mixed with cigar smoke. An elaborately carved mahogany bar stretched along one wall and each stool held an overalled rump belonging to someone hunched over the bar top. Most of the men were talking animatedly. At the far end, eight crapshooters were noisily betting their nickels, dimes and an occasional dollar in a mad attempt to "buck the tiger." The wall facing them was lined with wobbly tables of every description. The ceiling was hung with riverboat memorabilia: ropes, broken chronometers, a compass, a rusty anchor, a pinewood replica of a stern-wheeler and a graying life preserver marked, in faded letters, "Penelope." The tables were filled with empty beer bottles, and at one table a doleful man played blues on a harmonica. To the right was a small wooden stage, dark and dusty, on the edge of which more men sat smoking, talking and drinking. In the middle of the floor stood two dozen other patrons, all watchfully waiting for a place to sit, all drinking whiskey or beer.

Before he knew it Huddie was clutching a warm bottle of orange soda pop and Sycamore was taking a gulp of whiskey straight from a bottle. The man with the harmonica stopped and waved a greeting to Sycamore.

"You gonna play for us, Slim?"

Another called, "Hey, Slim, where'd you get the boy?"

"This ain't no boy, Tom, this here's a playin' devil with that there machine." With that, Sycamore took Huddie's hand and they edged their way to the small stage. "Well, Huddie-boy, let's start stompin' for the folks."

Sycamore then ran his fingers lightly over the strings, retuned his E-string, and went right into a song of the Great Flood, improvising the words but telling lyrically how the terrible waters of the Mississippi forced people to leave their homes and farms for higher ground. Then, how a year later, a drought killed everything in sight and how the poor people would go fishing but catch nothing and hunt but kill nothing and come home without catfish, coon or possum. Sycamore told them in song about Old Joe Turner, a white man who would leave meat, flour and molasses for the poor people to eat. The notes hung like tinsel above the heads of the listeners.

Huddie would hear "Joe Turner Blues" again many years later, but now the sound of the blues, a new and different sound, grabbed him. It was different from the hoots and hollers and spirituals of Mooringsport. But he played as well as he could alongside Sycamore, unused to the carefully stretched blues notes and chords, and the leaping, bell-like notes that seemed to spring from the old man's guitar.

For Huddie, the language of the blues was still a strange one, as foreign to him as Uncle Terrell's tales of East Texas. He groped at the ends of his windjammer, trying desperately to match Sycamore's music.

The crowd applauded when they finished, and Sycamore bowed his head. They went right into a faster tune, but this time Huddie dominated the song. He was playing in a more familiar idiom again. The cheerful clapping had started before this one was even finished.

Three hours later, filled with soda pop and fried chicken, Huddie and Sycamore Slim finally left Bo McWhirter's. Huddie had a total of twenty-three cents in his pocket. He had played in a saloon with adults, played alongside Sycamore, alongside the harmonica player, and had even played in a quartet they all formed with a fiddle player who appeared toward the end of the session. He talked and joked with the drinkers and the bums, and had even shaken hands with Bo McWhirter himself!

He didn't realize the radical change this day had made in his life, but he knew he had to do it again. He had to hear the clapping and the jangle of coins at his feet, had to smell the musty, beery air, had to see the smiles and stomping feet of those who listened to his music and loudly called for more.

They went to a spot behind Pearson's Livery Stable, where Sycamore dropped wearily to his haunches and squatted against the wooden wall. Then, with a final wheeze, he sat, stretched out his feet and sank back to rest. Huddie sat beside him, quiet but happy, and looked up expectantly.

"Man, Huddie-boy, we sure showed them a good time! They ain't never heard such music. You havin' fun?"

"I sure am, Mr. Sycamore, I ain't never played so much before, but I sure enjoyin' it."

"You like Shrevepo't, don't you?"

Huddie nodded. "Hope my papa can take me here again."

They said nothing for a few more minutes. "Mr. Sycamore?"

"Huddie-boy?"

"What you call that kind of music we played in the beginnin'? That song about Joe Turner the white man?"

"That's the blues, Huddie. You ain't heard it before 'cause you probably ain't had no occasion to. See, here in the city, there's lots of tough times fo' the black folks. They's children walkin' the streets what ain't got no mamas and whose daddies had to go off somewheres to find some ol' farm to work on. People raisin' cotton what needs lots of black folks to do all the stoopin' and the choppin' and the balin'. An' after the day workin' you hands, they scraped raw and you back feel like you's full o' cranky bones. And you come home, or wherever you livin', an' you jus' sit there an' if you lucky you got some whiskey to take, and a woman to cook you food, and you sit there an' you study 'bout what gonna happen to you tomorrow. The same thing all over agin. An' the blues jus' sorta fall down all aroun' you."

Sycamore's voice drifted off, lost in a reverie, and Huddie suddenly thought about his school friend, Hesekie Coleman. The Colemans worked for a white man, and they were always complaining about it. Did the Colemans feel like what Sycamore Slim was telling him? Was that why Hesekie was such an ornery bastard, and why the family was now almost all killed off? Maybe, Huddie decided, the blues had just fallen down around the Colemans.

Huddie let his head fall back until it hit the boards. He didn't move, thinking Sycamore might be asleep, and simply looked up at the sky, watching a bird and tracing the shadows of the roof across the way. Then he heard a distant laugh, from around a far corner at the end of the alleyway. He heard the hoofs of horses trotting up the alley, and when he lifted his head from the boards he saw two white men, drunk and weaving in their saddles, laughing and shouting. One had a whiskey bottle in his hand and the other was reaching across trying to snatch it away from him. He still couldn't make out what they were saying, but a momentary panic gripped him. He looked at Sycamore, who now had his eyes open but didn't move.

The men looked grisly and unkempt. The tall one had a battered black hat, the flabby one a new white Stetson, probably stolen. Neither had shaved for a long time; guns were slung at their hips. Their shirts were stained and their teeth were brown from chewing tobacco.

Huddie could hear them now. "--fuckin' fat riverhip," one was saying. "Should of slit her throat, that's what. She ain't seen ten dollars since her mother sold her!" The other man laughed again, pulled once more on the bottle and handed it to his companion.

"Funniest thing I ever seen," he said, "when you run outta there half nekkid with your gunbelt slung over your shoulder like a fuckin' Mex!" He laughed again.

The men had a strange drawl; Huddie knew they were the sort of cowboys his uncle had described to him once. From "down Texas way," was how Terrell had bitterly put it. "There they chase cows and have gunfights and take over whole towns just to make themselves look big. Naw, you don't want to have nuthin' to do with Texans."

"Hey, now, Jeff, look yonder. They's a couple of niggers against that wall there." They slowed their horses.

The one called Jeff brought his horse up roughly as he followed the other's gaze. They were about fifty feet from Huddie and Sycamore. "Say, I think you're right. A old one and a young one."

"What do you suppose they're doing here, sitting on their asses behind the stable?"

The flabby one grinned. "You don't suppose they're figgering on hoss-stealing, do you? I hear them niggers steal anything in sight, you let 'em get by with it."

The horses approached closer, slowly, until they almost faced Huddie and Sycamore. "I hear Loosiana niggers are the worse yet, too. You ever hear that, Jeff?"

"Yeah, I heard it. Maybe we can do the community a little favor, eh? Say, save two hosses from being stolen." They reined up right in front of them. Huddie's eyes were bulging but Sycamore seemed calm.

"Hey!" the tall man called down. "What you doing here behind the livery stable, huh?"

Huddie felt Sycamore Slim's hand on his thigh, restraining him. "Jus' restin'," Sycamore said.

"On your feet when you talk to a white man."

Huddie bent his legs under him, starting to get to his feet, but felt Sycamore's hand still restraining him. "Reckon we's jus' too tired, suh. We been workin' all day." Sycamore left it at that.

"You hear that?" the flabby man said. "He's too tired."

"Yeah," the other snarled. "Bet he ain't too tired to play for us, though." The two men got down off their horses. Huddie was panic-stricken. He wondered where his papa was now. He looked over at Sycamore and saw the old man's eyes -- resignation, surrender.

The men stood over them now. "Lazy, that's what they are. Sit around just playin' music. You know what we do to lazy niggers in Texas?"

Sycamore was quiet.

"Answer me!" the flabby man yelled, and reached over and kicked Sycamore's ankle.

Sycamore shook his head. "Ain't never been to Texas, I reckon."

"Well, we cut their black cocks off, that's what. That takes all the lazy right out of 'em, too, I tell you."

Huddie's eyes filled with tears. He began to choke.

"Now, you don't want to get your cock cut off, you stand up and play a little song for us, you hear, nigga? The boy here'll play along, too."

"Play us a song, l'il nigger," the other said to Huddie. "Play 'My Little Texas Buttercup'."

Huddie stood up, holding his windjammer tentatively. He looked down at Sycamore.

Sycamore looked up wearily, eyes unemotional, showing not fear, but sheer exhaustion. He noted the guns on their hips, and decided not to tell Huddie to run.

"Don't reckon I know that one," Sycamore said evenly.

Suddenly the flabby one reached down and grabbed Sycamore by the overall straps and with a grunt jerked the old man to his feet. He slapped him harshly across the face and kicked the guitar on the ground.

"You gonna play that thing or not?"

"No suh," Sycamore said. "I ain't gonna play nuthin'."

Now Huddie was terrified. "I'll play for you," he said quickly. He started to play "Green Corn." "But I don't know no songs about Texas..."

The tall man grabbed the windjammer from Huddie's loose hands, and began to squeeze it awkwardly, making nonsensical sounds, obscene sounds. The flabby man slapped Sycamore again. "No, this one'll play."

Sycamore grunted, and then moaned aloud as the man bashed his head against the wall. "Play, goddam it, you black-assed fucker! Play or I'll cut your fuckin' balls off!"

The filthy sounds from the windjammer grated through Huddie's frightened ears, and the men began cackling like women as they saw the petrified look now in the old man's eyes. Sycamore started slumping, but the flabby man holding him brought his knee up swiftly into his groin, and Sycamore screamed, doubling over.

"Hey, Judy! Snake! Snake!" The tall one suddenly threw Huddie's windjammer under one of the horses, and the startled animal reared, kicking its hoofs and crushing the instrument into the dust.

Immediately Huddie was lunging at the flabby man holding Sycamore. He grabbed him in a stranglehold and tried to reach his gun, but the man elbowed him quickly in the stomach, sending him to his knees. He started pounding on the man's thighs, screaming unintelligible noises, but the tall man came over and grabbed him from behind. "Hey, l'il nigger, you're a brave thing, ain't ya?" He cuffed Huddie hard across the ear, and Huddie fell back. The tall man held him tightly, his hands pinned at his sides, while Huddie kicked and cried and screamed at him.

The flabby man finally let Sycamore slump to the ground, where he kicked him again in the head, hard, and Huddie watched in horror as he saw a dark stain spread over the crotch of Sycamore's overalls. Then the fat man reached down and smashed the box of the fragile guitar over Sycamore's neck. "No playin', no guitar, you hoss-stealing black-ass bastards!"

A piece of splintered wood dug deeply into Sycamore's face; he began to bleed badly. The flabby man leaned over the battered figure and struck with the butt of his pistol. Huddie loosened one of his arms and with the edge of his palm jabbed the man holding him in the groin. When the man crouched in pain, letting him go, Huddie ran as hard as he could. He ran to the corner, expecting a gunshot to tear into his back, but he made it and darted around the corner and down the street as fast as he could. The last sight he remembered, as through a narrowing tunnel, was the two men focusing their beastly rage on the old man lying in a heap on the ground by the wall, his tongue hanging out and his face streaked with blood and splinters of wood. He slowed by a boardwalk post, grabbed at it as he staggered, and then the tunnel closed completely as he passed out.

*   *   *   *   *

Huddie's head was gently rolling and he felt the coarse denim of his shirt chafe against his neck. A throbbing pain pounded mysteriously at the side of his head. When he gingerly moved his body, a soreness in his left side made him wince. His eyelids fluttered and Huddie was staring into the eyes of his father.

Wes spoke to him softly. "What happen, Huddie? You all right?"

Huddie turned his head and looked back down the street. A small crowd was staring from the boardwalk. Wes spoke again. "You all right, Huddie?"

"Yeah, papa."

Wes rocked his son in his arms. "You gonna be all right, Huddie, don't worry. Jus' you take it easy here, and we gets you in the buggy and back home."

Before Huddie could answer, a puny red-faced man with pock-marked cheeks and a badge leaned over him. His hat was too large for his head. "You better get your boy out of here, Ledbetter," he said. "You bring him to this here town, you'd better keep him in tow."

"What happened, Sheriff?"

The sheriff shrugged his shoulders and hooked his thumbs in his gunbelt. "Just troublemakers havin' fun on a Saturday. Had too much to drink, I reckon. Too bad about the old nigger."

"Huh!" Wes's voice cracked. "Where is he?"

"Took him away. Bled to death before anybody came 'round. He was lying around the corner with a gash in his neck."

Wes felt his stomach tighten. Those bastards, he thought, those white bastards! "Huddie," he said finally, "think you can get up all right?"

Huddie nodded and began to cry. "Papa, papa! They killed Mr. Sycamore! They killed him and they smashed my windjammer! They threw it at the horse and the horse stomped it to pieces. We wasn't doin' nothin'! We was singin' and the folks liked my music and they give me twenty-three cents. Look here!"

Huddie reached in the pocket of his trousers but found nothing. "Papa, they took my money. I had nickels and pennies and they took it."

Wes shook his head slowly, then turned to the sheriff. Before Wes could ask, the sheriff shrugged again. "Witness said he saw the two guys ridin' out o' town, but they stopped over Huddie here and slugged and robbed him."

"Ain't you gonna chase 'em? Get a posse? This is murder, Sheriff!"

"Ain't none of my business," the sheriff said. "I got more important things. If you niggers can't take care o' yourselves then maybe you just ought not to come around here anymore."

"Come on, son." Ledbetter threw his arm around Huddie. "Let's go home."

The broken pieces of Huddie's windjammer lay in the dust like wrinkled scraps of colored paper. As they passed on the way to their buggy, Huddie started to go over to pick up the pieces, but his father held him back. "Never mind, son. We get you a new one."

Huddie stared at the pieces and wiped his eyes. The crowd had gone their separate ways now. The momentary thrill of seeing a corpse was gone, but they knew it would happen again soon. Wes Ledbetter, his shoulders heavy, took his son by the hand and walked slowly away.

It was late afternoon and about five hours of light remained before they would reach home. The horses began their slow trot through town, down Texas Avenue and toward the river. Huddie told his father everything he could recall, with Wes listening expressionlessly, only nodding from time to time. "Huddie," he said at last, "you remember a long time ago in the field when you was a little fella? You come out from the house after you had a fight with one of you little friends, and I said you gonna see a lot of mean people? Well, this is jus' what I was talkin' 'bout. When you get off the farm you leaves all the peace behind you. City folks don't care much for black people. They gonna take everythin' you got and never give you nothin' for it, 'cept maybe a beatin'. "

"No suh, papa. They ain't nobody gonna treat me the way I seen them bastids treat that ol' man. No suh, I'd rather kill 'em first!"

"Don't say that! That's what always gets the black folks in trouble. They get mad at the white man and they breaks the law and jus' give 'em another excuse for another beatin'. Now don't you talk like that no more. In fact, we ain't even gonna tell you mama about it 'cause she only gonna get her gimmies on when she hear they been some trouble. No, Huddie, we gonna tell 'er you had a good time as a songster, and I give you some nickels to say you got from the folks on the street."

"But what about my windjammer? She gonna wonder where it is."

"We get you a new one soon. We tell you mama you dropped it in the river water."

Suddenly Huddie thought back to Bo McWhirter's and the strange, almost pathetic music old Sycamore Slim had played. "Papa," he said at last. "You ever hear of a man name Joe Turner?"

"Joe Turner, Joe Turner," he mused. "Seems like I once heard you Uncle Terrell sing a song about that man, but I don't recollect much else."

"Sycamore Slim tol' me he was a white man what done lots o' good for the poor folks during the flood."

"They's lots of good white folks. All I'm sayin' is you ain't gonna be meetin' too many of 'em."

"Papa, I don't want no windjammer."

Wes turned to his son. "You what? You mean you don't want a brand new shiny one?"

"Papa, if you gonna spend you money for a *new* shiny windjammer, can I have instead a *old* guitar?"

"Huddie, you don't know how to play no guitar."

"I think I can, papa."

"What you mean?" Wes said. "You ain't never *had* one."

"Don't make no difference, papa. Jus' don't make no difference."

###

Chapter Two

The other three boys were a few years older than Huddie. Hesekie and Billy Coleman were skinny twin brothers, the youngest of the five surviving Colemans (five others had been taken by lynching, murder or disease). Benjamin Capp was a frail, hare-lipped boy often picked on because of his shyness and lack of physical dexterity.

They met in a frog-laden area near Reddin's Bog, where Hesekie retrieved a bottle of whiskey he had hidden and passed it around. Huddie felt the liquid burn into his stomach. He coughed.

"Ha!" Billy Coleman jeered. "You can't even drink whiskey right and you think you gonna look at Edna Mae without shootin' off?"

"Shit, gimme another swallow!" Huddie took the bottle again as the others, amused, watched him. He threw back his head and guzzled. This time he almost dropped the bottle as he coughed and hacked. Benjamin didn't take any more -- but then, he hadn't made any bets.

"I still say you ain't never saddled up on a woman yet," Hesekie said.

"I never said I been with Edna Mae like you two is always braggin'. But I been with some jus' as good," Huddie retorted.

"He lyin' his brains out," Billy said sarcastically to his brother. "He only twelve, and you knows as well as me he only diddles with the kids an' not with no woman like Edna Mae."

"Shit, you ride Edna Mae you ain't never want no other woman," Hesekie said. "She make a man out o' you, Huddie."

Huddie had seen Edna Mae often as she pulled her baby brothers in a wooden cart outside the pinewood cabin where she worked all day, taking care of the children while her family worked in the fields. He had heard the stories at school about how this older girl would take on anyone for whatever she could collect. He often wanted to ask Benjamin whether he'd ever peeked in through the McJefferson cabin shutters. Huddie had been tempted to sneak down himself and try to get a glimpse of her celebrated body, and now the chiding from his friends was arousing a new curiosity.

"How old is Edna Mae?" he asked,

Hesekie shook his head. "Don't even think *she* knows. She old enough, though. Prob'ly sixteen or seventeen."

"One thing sure," Billy added. "She ain't no baby like you and Benjamin here been diddlin'."

"If she so old, how come she ridin' with the school kids an' not the big guys what got more money?"

"Shit, Huddie, she don't care who she ride with! She jus' likes it. She prob'ly even ride with old man Parker if she could get some of the money he collect in church on Sunday."

Hesekie howled again at his own remark. "Yessir, she take that old Parker an' turn his holy ass upside down an' inside out -- an' the whole choir with him!"

"You mean she ride more'n one guy at once?"

Hesekie grinned. "Man, one time she ride I guess ten guys and they went into her somethin' awful. There was jizz all over the place and all the while them two babies squealin' in the back room wantin' their supper and Edna Mae in the front room bangin' and whuppin' and hollerin' like she got the devil in her. Ask Billy, you don't believe me. He was there, watchin' from the pantry. Got so excited from watchin' he couldn't even wait his turn an' start beatin' on hisself! "

They all looked at Billy, who just sat on the bank and put his hands in his pockets. "Yeah, you jus' wait, Huddie. You gonna do the same thing, you take a look at old Edna Mae."

"Ha!" Hesekie was shouting at Huddie. "We gets you in there, you ain't have no time! You gonna have jizz in you pants before you do anything!"

Huddie was getting angrier. They were taunting him the way they always taunted Benjamin, and he resented it. "Shit," he said to the Coleman boys, not even bothering to see what Benjamin had to say, "This here's one nigga what's gonna ride her ass off!"

Damn, Huddie thought to himself. He remembered the statement as plain as anything and it was what got him into this mess in the first place. Man, those Colemans sure have a way of getting a guy to go along with them. If I told them I haven't even had a girl yet, they'd laughed me right off the road. I ain't even seen a naked girl, much less ridden one.

Don't matter none anyway, he thought. Those two bastids made me bet my windjammer that I wouldn't shoot in my pants.

As they continued down the road Huddie fell silent, listening to the additional tales Hesekie and Billy were obviously making up about their sexual adventures. Huddie was feeling slightly wobbly from the whiskey, and decided not to take any more until it was over, fearing he'd fall down or otherwise lose the bet and have to pay Hesekie with a windjammer he no longer had. He wondered what he'd have to pay instead, wondered what Hesekie and Billy Coleman would do to him when he announced he had no windjammer anymore and, in fact, had nothing at all. He tried not to think about it.

They rounded a bend in the road, and as Caddo Lake loomed at the bottom of a low-rolling hill they saw a small gray shack by the shore. Cypress and gum trees hovered above it like tattered parasols, and the smell of amphibia and musky vegetation hung in the air. The gentle waves on the lake flipped white cusps of foam around a battered rowboat moored at the foot of the cabin. At the back of the place was a line of new wash, the white rectangles of shirts and the long blue work pants and overalls standing out like confetti against the green marshland.

"S'pose she ain't home?" Huddie asked, his voice too loud in the heavy quiet. "We'll have to come back tomorrow."

"Shit, she always home," Hesekie said. "She ain't home she lose some money and she know it. She stay home all the time 'cause she take care o' them babies, anyhow."

Huddie glanced surreptitiously at Benjamin, who was walking along as if in a daze, looking straight ahead and not talking. He felt inexplicably sorry for the boy. Maybe it was because all the other boys were physically normal and Benjamin had that ugly-looking harelip. But Huddie couldn't help Benjamin. He had his own problems. If that damned Hesekie got the better of him, who knows how many of the other boys in school -- and even some of the girls -- would know about his embarrassment by the very next day. What if Parker found out? Or Sally?

In the shack, which was a single room and a pantry no larger than Huddie's shed, Edna Mae McJefferson had just finished feeding the two babies and had put them to sleep in the corner. She hung a blanket between two bent nails, so the late afternoon sun wouldn't shine directly on them.

Edna Mae was seventeen years old and tall. She was a statuesque, lithe woman, with full lips and closely cropped hair, carefully combed into bangs over her forehead. Her shoulders and hips were wide, and her breasts pressed tautly against her knee-length blue print dress. Through her right earlobe was set a gold ring the size of a dime, and she was barefoot.

Edna Mae was saving her money so she could go to New Orleans.

When she saw the quartet through the window, picking their way across the bog behind the shack, she smiled to herself and set down the pan in which she was preparing to cook crawdads. She smoothed her dress, ran a quick comb through her hair, and went to the door. She threw it open and stood, hands on hips, watching the boys. As they drew within earshot, she called out.

"Hesekie Coleman, what you doin'? Bringin' me every coon in Caddo?" She laughed and yelled again. "The way you snowballs walkin', you ain't gonna get here 'til nothin's left!"

When Huddie first heard her voice, he felt his stomach muscles tighten. But he made himself walk on. He followed the Colemans right into the shack, as Edna Mae bade them welcome with an extravagant sweep of her arm.

"Hesekie, who you got this time?" she said.

"This here's Huddie Ledbetter, what lives on the Ledbetter farm. And this here's Benjamin, what's always watchin' the girls peein' but don't do nothin' 'bout it." Benjamin looked angry and scared, but Huddie just stood there, looking at Edna Mae's breasts and the button outline of a nipple under her dress.

"Ledbetter. You daddy got that big place over toward the Texas line, right?"

"Yes, ma'am," Huddie said uncertainly, sending them all into laughter. Edna Mae grinned at him mischievously.

"*Ma'am*? Honey, you don't gotta call me nothin' but Edna Mae, hear?"

Hesekie then went over and put his arm around the girl, squeezing her breast and watching Huddie's reaction. "Edna Mae here is the bes' ridin' gal in the whole state, ain't that right, Edna?"

Ignoring him, Edna eyed the new boys and then looked over at Billy, leaning against a sideboard. "What you doin', Billy, waitin' for me to ask what you got today?"

"We got sixteen cents and some whiskey. That's all we could bring."

"What about you boys? What *you* got?"

Huddie looked at her blankly. "Uh . . . uh, nothin', I reckon," he said. Benjamin shrugged and looked at Hesekie.

"Hah!" Hesekie bellowed. "They ain't got nothin' 'cause we's here on a bet. This here Huddie say he been ridin' gals before, but we don't believe him on account he only twelve. So we brung him here."

Edna gaped at Huddie. "Twelve?" Then she laughed again. "Ain't no twelve-year-old gonna do me any good. Looky that one." She pointed to Benjamin. "Look like he got a bone stickin' out already. How old's he?"

Hesekie looked at Benjamin. Now it was Billy's turn to giggle. "Hey, he does! Hey, Benjy, what you gonna do with that thing, huh?"

Benjamin, embarrassed, turned away lightly and leaned against the wall, as casually as he could. "Shit," Hesekie was saying, "he fourteen like the rest, but old Huddie here, he only twelve. He the one what made the bet he not gonna squirt all over the walls before he get it in."

Edna Mae, still grinning, grabbed the bottle and took a drink before looking back over at Huddie. "He don't look no twelve. You joshin' me, Hesekie Coleman? He look older'n all the rest of you. You really twelve, Huddie?"

"Yes, Ma'am, uh, Edna Mae," Huddie said, summoning his courage. "I'm twelve, but I gonna be better than any damn Coleman."

Edna Mae began strolling around the room, brushing tantalizingly close to each boy, exhibiting her body as best she knew how. Then, when she was nearest to Benjamin, she reached down quickly and flicked at his crotch. He flinched, then stepped back even farther.

"I'se right, he already got one," she giggled. "Let's see it, Benjamin."

Benjamin felt all eyes in the room on him as he folded and unfolded his arms, knowing he shouldn't try to hide himself. "Yeah," Billy shouted, "take it out, Benjamin. Show her what you got -- maybe she won't want no money from us!" He and his brother laughed again.

Edna Mae took another drink and stood in front of Benjamin. The boy looked at her wide-eyed but didn't move. She lifted one leg up onto a chair, and her dress rose to midpoint on her thigh. "C'mon, Benjy," she implored, "won't you show me what you got?"

"N-no, ma'am," he said shakily, "I jus' can't do that right here."

"Oh, come on, honey," Edna Mae said as she drew the chair closer and sat down in front of Benjamin. She began to unbutton his pants, slowly, as the others watched in silence. Huddie was transfixed. Benjamin's arms became rigid and his fists were clenched as he felt her probing fingers.

"God damn!" she roared suddenly, propelling herself and the chair backward with a swift kick against the floor.

Benjamin whimpered and raced out the door. They watched him run crying up the road and disappear.

"Haw! He shot all over the place!" Hesekie shouted in amusement. "Jus' like Huddie gonna do!"

"You see his face?" Billy said. "Worth all the whiskey we got, that was!"

Edna Mae stood up and slumped her shoulders as she wiped her fingers on her dress. "What kinda day this gonna be with you kids, anyhow? Don't got no money an' this here cheap whiskey an' a twelve year old! Shit, then, ol' Edna Mae gonna have some fun for a change!"

She stood up and faced the Coleman boys, then turned and swept her arm toward Huddie, "Hey, boy," she said. "Get you ass over here with the others. All this laughin' an' gigglin' goin' on, we gonna have us a little showin' before we gets down to business. Edna Mae sure gonna get the bigges' first, if not the bestes'!"

Huddie walked over and stood apprehensively next to the others. He wasn't sure what she was going to do.

"Now you boys jus' take it on out here and let Edna see what's on the menu today, hear? Go on, Billy, get it out there!"

Huddie looked at the other two, waiting for the first move. Then Hesekie began to undo his buttons, followed by Billy. There was no choice -- Huddie, fighting embarrassment, unsteadily began to undo his own buttons. He avoided Edna Mae's eyes as he did so.

Hesekie was out first and Huddie looked unashamedly at him. Then Billy, amid Edna Mae's vocal delight in the proceedings. "Hey, looky here," she said as Billy cradled himself proudly in his palms. "Seems like I seen this here fella before!" She giggled and turned to Huddie. "Okay, Mr. Twelve. What's taking you so long?"

Huddie remained silent but in a final fumbling move showed himself to her. He kept his eyes on the doorway at the other side of the room.

"Now I *know* you is lyin' to me," Edna Mae said. "You ain't no twelve years old, boy. You joshin' old Edna, right?'

"Hey, looky that!" Hesekie said. "Huddie's got a big one!"

Edna Mae stood up from the chair and took the bottle again. "This here's the first one, that's for sure," she said. "Don't care how old he is, the new boy's the first one!" Then she added, "You two get outside 'til I call you."

"Outside? How come -- ?"

"Don't gimme no shit-lip, Billy! You get me later an' that's all they is to it! Now get out, hear me?"

The Colemans clumsily buttoned up, shot hard looks at Huddie and stomped out.

"What they mean?" Edna Mae asked when they had gone.

"They made a bet that I'd . . . that I'd. . . ."

"Do the same as that other kid? You mean it's true you ain't never had no girl before?" She grinned at him. Huddie didn't answer,

Edna Mae looked at the closed door, then back to Huddie. "I think I know. Them two always braggin' about what they'd done, Mr. Twelve, but you can tell 'em that I told you the first time Billy there come in to Edna, he do the same as what's-his-name run away. Don't be afraid of me. An' don't worry none, Mr. Twelve, 'cause I gonna show you everythin' you need to know."

Edna Mae guided him to the bed, drawing him slowly by the hand and unbuttoning her dress as she went. She sat him down and pulled his pants off, and then undressed. She leapt on the bed and pulled his head to her, guiding a nipple toward his mouth.

That late afternoon Edna Mae demonstrated everything she knew on Huddie, and in the end it was he who became fiercely aggressive and tossed and twisted her around on the bed.

Later, as they lay beside each other, Huddie asked if he could have some more of her whiskey. When he went over to the kitchen to get it, she exclaimed, "Lawd, you is still *up?*"

Huddie didn't understand and looked down at himself. "Ain't I *supposed* to be?"

Edna Mae threw back her head and laughed, her breasts heaving. "Bring that bottle over here for both of us, boy. We ain't finished yet!"

*   *   *   *   *

Each star was a tiny windmill of light spinning through moist and unfocused eyes as Huddie bounced and lurched along the overgrown path that he hoped led back home. He somehow knew he was drunk, but through his mental haze he worried about the inevitable reprisal soon to come when -- or if -- he reached home tonight.

Huddie realized his father must be out looking for him, and his mother would make good use of the buggy whip as soon as she smelled him. But all Huddie cared about now was Edna Mae. He saw her through the alcoholic fog, dancing naked on the bed above him displaying those hauntingly strange curves and bumps that until now had only been sniggering tales from the older boys. "Guess they was right," Huddie thought aloud.

"Guess gals ain't jus' for teasin' an' lookin', but goin' for a man an' ridin' in the night."

Huddie tried to focus his eyes on the path through the dark, tangled shadows of the trees. He felt himself gag and his stomach convulse painfully, and he vomited raw whiskey on the cypress roots. He steadied himself and wiped his mouth on his sleeve.

Huddie giggled to himself. "Edna Mae, Edna Mae, I loves you!" he called out to the dark weeds. He repeated the phrase, singing it, chanting it and hollering it until he had turned from the path onto the larger road between the schoolhouse and the Ledbetter farm. He remembered the odor of Edna Mae, the musty pungency of her body, and he reached down and felt himself proudly.

He sat down wearily on the road and thought of Sycamore Slim. But Sycamore was dead. A five-year dream to go to Shreveport ended in a pool of blood. They'll never treat me the way they treated ol' Sycamore Slim.

"I loves you, Edna Mae. Whoo-ee!"

Huddie fell back and sprawled spread-eagle in the dust. The stars twirled again and traced a name in the sky. Uncle Terrell, the stars said. Ho! Ho! Thisaway! Ha! Ha! Thataway! Green Corn! "Why that horse stomp on my windjammer like that?" "Better you take your boy home, Ledbetter!" Ha! Ha! Thisaway! Ho! Ho!

*   *   *   *   *

When he found his son an hour later Wes Ledbetter was furious, but, as usual, concern immediately dissipated his anger. He helped the boy to his feet, held the limp form upright with both hands and shook him roughly. Huddie's head bobbed on his shoulders and his eyes opened uncertainly. He moaned.

"Damn it, boy," Wes said, "where the hell you been?"

Huddie wiped his forehead with his sleeve. "Papa, papa."

"Where you get the whiskey, Huddie? I can smell it. It's all over you and you been throwin' up, too."

Huddie shook himself awake, "Papa," he said, "please don' be mad at me!"

"You mama gonna beat you raw, Huddie! She been stewin' about callin' the sheriff and it was all I could do to hold her off. Where you been?"

"I don't have to give Hesekie Coleman my windjammer."

"What you talkin' about? Windjammer? I ask you where you been. You wake up now pretty damned fast. I sick and tired of ridin' around this here road."

"Papa," Huddie said finally. "You gonna whip me?"

"I ain't never whipped you, Huddie, you knows that. But you sure is itchin' for a whippin' right now from your Cajun mama! Where you get the whiskey?"

"Hesekie Coleman brought some to school. Stole it, I guess."

"You mean you been at school all this time?"

"Papa, I been with the wimmens."

Wes sighed and dropped his shoulders, loosening his grip on Huddie. "Let's get you in the buggy, and you 'splain to me everything what happened. We gonna have ourselves a little talk."

Wes helped him into the buggy and snapped the whip sharply at the horse. On a wider stretch of road toward the lake, he pulled the buggy to a stop and loosely tied the reins. He turned to Huddie with a sigh and put his elbow on the back of the seat. The boy lay back languidly, staring straight ahead. Wes looked at him for a moment, thinking, wondering what to say next. He saw the rugged features of Huddie's face and the bulging muscles of his wide shoulders, and once again parental frustration overwhelmed him.

"Huddie," he said quietly, "I ain't gonna whip you, but you mama sure want me to. She been fussin' all afternoon 'cause you didn't come home to do you chores, and we been worryin' sick over you. Now, you jus' tell me exactly what's happened and I try to understand, 'Cause if you been gettin' into trouble, you gonna need you papa to stand by you."

Huddie turned his head to Wes. "Papa," he said, "I been bad, but I couldn't help it. Hesekie Coleman, he brought---"

"Don't tell me 'bout no Hesekie Coleman! I want to know where you got the whiskey and what's this all about the wimmens!"

Huddie told what had happened, hazily avoiding the more grotesque details. When he finished, Wes simply stared straight ahead, trying to think. The boy's confession shocked him at first, but he realized his son was no longer a little boy.

"Huddie," he said evenly, "I always been tellin' you to wait 'til youse bigger, and to wait 'til later when you understand things, but now I reckon the later on I been talkin' 'bout is come right now. Youse bigger than mos' of the boys, and youse smarter, too. Maybe the things you see down in Shrevepo't done make you wanna be a man sooner, but gettin' into trouble ain't no way to do it. Now you drunk some whiskey like the men, and you been with a woman like the men, and I reckon it's 'bout time for me to tell you what you really don't know at all. How you feel now?"

"I sick, papa, an' hungry."

"You is sick and you is hungry. You drunk the whiskey and you been with a woman, and right now you is mostly sick. Huddie, you think that's the way you *supposed* to feel?"

Huddie looked at his father curiously. "Papa, how *is* I supposed to feel? How come you feel so good when you is drinkin' the whiskey, but you feel so bad afterwards?"

Wes shook his head. "Son," he said, "seems like I always givin' you a talkin' to like the Reverend, but that's the question what been botherin' all the niggas since whiskey was invented. If we knew how to drink the whiskey without feelin' bad -- or how to go with the wimmens without gettin' into trouble -- we'd be the smartest men in the world. When you a man, Huddie, everything look good to you until you get it. Then it jus' look the same as before. Same as Shrevepo't. You go down there the first time and you surprised at all the places you can see, but when you goes the second time, it's the same as you seen the first time. You know what I'm talkin' about?"

"No, papa. How come everybody keep on doin' it if they always feel bad after they do it?"

"It's like you fightin'. You always starts the fight 'cause you is mad, and you fights like hell, and even when you win, afterward you is jus' hurtin' and you is sorry you been in the fight."

"Sometime it jus' ain't my fault, papa."

"I know that, Huddie. The fact is you is gonna get in fights whether you like it or not. And as far as the wimmens go, they is gonna come around a-teasin' and a-tauntin' and tellin' stories 'til you feel like you head gonna blow right off. But you go sleepin' with the wrong wimmens, you gets into a heap o' trouble. Best to stay with the good wimmens, like you mama, and then they ain't nobody can come after you or get you in trouble." He sighed. "Huddie, when you gets to be a man, you gonna see what I'se talkin' about. Most o' the wimmens ain't like Edna Mae."

Huddie straightened up and put his hands on his knees. The stars were clearer now, and the tops of the cypresses had stopped spinning above him. "Mama gonna whip me?" he asked finally.

"If she sees you, she is. But if she's asleep, we gonna go straight in and don't make no sound at all. In the mornin' she feel better, but right now best not to rile her. But if she awake, Huddie, I want you to take you whippin' like the big man you is, like a Ledbetter, and I don't wanna hear no cryin'. You done everythin' today like the men, so you maybe gonna have to take you whippin' like a man."

"Papa?" Huddie asked sleepily.

"What's that, Huddie?"

"S'pose I want to see Edna Mae again?"

Wes felt a sudden lump catch in his throat. There was no getting around it, Huddie was hooked. Wes would have preferred it had happened a few years later, but now that was a futile hope.

"Huddie, you want to see Edna Mae again, you goes down there alone, then. And no whiskey. You gotta promise me you won't go down there with anyone else and without no whiskey. It's when too many men hangin' round one gal that trouble come."

"You gonna tell mama about Edna Mae too, papa?"

"I won't tell you mama, Huddie. This here's men business. But you sure gotta start gettin' all the chores done around the place before you go lookin' for the wimmens."

"I promise, papa."

"You know, Huddie," Wes then said with a slight grin, hoping the darkness would shield it from Huddie. "That Edna Mae gal, she pretty well known around this place. She seventeen or eighteen, I reckon. A lot older than you, anyway."

Huddie grinned back at him. "Yeah, papa," he said. "She older."

Fortunately for Huddie, Sally was asleep. They sneaked through the open doorway, and Huddie felt his father's hand gently shove him in the direction of his room. Wes crept toward his own bed, stealthily slipping in next to Sally without waking her.

Huddie went into his shed, shutting the door quietly behind him. Strangely, he didn't feel at all tired. When he'd taken his clothes off, he lifted himself onto the bed. A soft *bungggg* came up from the worn mattress, and he felt a hard, smooth wooden surface near his pillow.

Over the past few days, Huddie Ledbetter had played music on a stage, been paid for it, got drunk, and made violent love to a woman. The pattern was being sketched for his entire future life, but the one missing element now presented itself beside his pillow.

It was a guitar.

###

Chapter Three

Huddie saw Edna Mae only a few more times over the next two years, the last time being the night before she left home at last for the New Orleans of her dreams. But there were many other girls around Mooringsport, and by the time Huddie reached fourteen he had met almost all of them, slept with a majority of them and fought over a few of them. By now, too, there was another love in his life: his guitar. As he had with his windjammer, Huddie played songs over and over into the night, and he pestered every guitar player he ran across to show him something new: a novel song, new chords, bleeding notes, a difficult technique on the strings, elaborate fingering tricks. And Wes Ledbetter, as permissive as ever, took his strong muscular son on his weekly jaunts into Shreveport.

Huddie loved it. There in the bustling river town he met new friends and found new idols. Big Jim Fagin was there, as was Bud Collins, who sang prairie songs in a shrill yet melodic falsetto. Huddie followed the two men whenever he ran across them, studying their techniques and memorizing words and chords. Texas Red, One-eye Thompson and Washboard Willie dazzled the impressionable young musician with their virtuosity on the barrel-house piano, whose rippling and raucous notes Huddie would accompany as best he could on either his guitar or a borrowed windjammer. Bayou Brownie's Jug Band, with its various jugs and makeshift bass equipment, was a particular favorite on Saturday night, and Huddie let its rhythmic simplicity seep into his own music. A new type of music was beginning to emerge in the Louisiana area at that time, something called "boogie woogie," with its rolling, repetitious rhythm. A man called Black Tar would play it incessantly in one of the bars, for anyone who would listen and buy him whiskey. And Chippie Brooks, a huge, Wagnerian black woman with flaming red hair, not only ran a whorehouse but also entertained her waiting customers with ribald banjo songs.

These were some of the people Huddie met, wildly talented men and a few women, innovators, experimenters, unafraid to try anything musically new, however strange or difficult. Piano players, guitarists, banjo players, singers, drummers, trumpeters, tap dancers, jugglers, pool sharks, drunks, brawlers –– all of every shape and color, shades of black and white, octoroons, quadroons, mulattoes, half-breeds, Indians, Creoles, Cajuns, Spaniards, Frenchmen, Mexicans –– Huddie met them all, picking up not only musical tips and tricks, but also words, phrases, curses, although he frequently had to sneak into a barrel house while his father was busy, or be content to spend just a few minutes while Wes hopped from place to place having drinks. On the rare evenings when Wes would hang around until they had to drive home in darkness, he encouraged Huddie to play all his new songs for him.

Huddie couldn't wait for the time when he could go to the bottom of Fannin Street himself and spend as much time as he pleased in that exotic, dirty, bawdy and brawling town.

The days in Mooringsport were filled with school, with work in the fields where his energy and endurance now rivaled those of his father, with endless practice on his guitar and with performing at weekend sukey-jumps and breakdowns for fifty cents an evening.

At fourteen Huddie was large and exceptionally muscular, and that didn't remain unnoticed for long around Caddo Lake. The girls were always after his attention, swarming around him at the parties, inviting him to take them home, to meet them in back of barns and field houses, to play a song especially for them. On the other hand, his newly developed swagger and arrogant self-confidence made him a universal target for resentful insults from frustrated rivals -- a target whose pride and quick temper met any and all belligerence in kind. The respect generally held for the Ledbetter family more than once saved Huddie from Sheriff Nate Gifford's harsh disciplinary hand.

A few exploratory oil wells had been sunk in and around Caddo Lake in recent years under the tentative auspices of the big refineries, and rumors swept through the tiny Mooringsport community daily. Wildcatters, riggers and hard-hatted white men were appearing now, and the word was out that a major new town would be formed somewhere along the lake's periphery if these strange-looking exploratory contraptions yielded what the newspapers and rumors said they would.

As a consequence, Huddie's popularity continued to rise. The whites in the area, many of whom had taken over bars and saloons in Shreveport, Mooringsport and across the lake, would pay Huddie to play exclusively for their own Saturday night socials, and it wasn't long before Huddie was going out several nights a week. Even though Wes and Sally were worried about the fights and the knifings, Wes encouraged his son to learn all he could about his music and to accept all invitations to play.

Huddie was especially admired by a neighbor's daughter, Margaret Judd, who frequently intercepted him as he rode to town for a breakdown and who even followed him into the fields when he went to work. She was also fourteen, and Huddie had often commented to his friends about her soft eyes and full body. He had been thinking of Margaret all day long before one particular sukey-jump and had already decided to see what he could do about getting her alone. He was still thinking about it as he drove along in his father's buggy, his guitar carefully stashed by his side, when Margaret appeared at the side of the road and waved to him as he approached. The sun was almost down, and her orange dress glowed brightly like a solitary blossom against the foliage behind her.

"Hey, Miss Margaret," he called as he stopped the buggy. "What you doin' out here on the road at sundown?"

"Waitin' for you, Huddie. Goin' down to the sukey-jump and hopin' you'd give me a ride tonight." She smiled up at him innocently and waited.

"If I give you a ride to the dance, will you come home with me, too?" Huddie asked.

"Papa says I gotta be home early, though," she said. "How late you stayin'?"

"We come home early enough," he said, smiling at her. "Jump in the buggy and hold my guitar for me."

She cautiously climbed up to the seat and lifted the guitar carefully, cradling it in her lap, Huddie cracked the whip and they started off.

They talked animatedly on the way, Huddie telling Margaret all about his music and his family, she telling about her early life on the other side of the lake before the Judds came to Mooringsport four years ago.

"I seen you workin' in the fields," she admitted at last. "And you sure work hard, Huddie. I seen you pick more cotton than all the rest of 'em one day."

"How come you see me in the field? You been hangin' around?"

She averted her eyes, feigning interest in the countryside. "Jus' passin' by now and again," she said. Then, "Sure is a nice buggy."

"My papa bought it in Shrevepo't. I helped him pick it out, too."

"You go to Shrevepo't with you papa?"

"Lots o' times," he said jauntily. "Sure, I seen lots o' things down there in Shrevepo't. I even play with all the songsters in the saloons."

"People always sayin' how you the best guitar player in Caddo Parish, Huddie. Guess you learnin' good on you trips to Shrevepo't."

Huddie smiled. "We Ledbetters are the best o' everything," he said. "Of course," he added casually, "you gotta be careful 'cause a lot o' people get jealous and start trouble. That's why I always carry this."

He unbuttoned his coat quickly and threw it open. In his belt was a brand new .25-caliber pistol, its dull brown grip intentionally exposed in a soft leather holster. "A pistol!" Margaret said, her eyes narrowing in on the weapon. "What you got that for, Huddie?"

He closed his coat and patted the bulge. "My papa got it for me after I got in a fight over at the lake one night. They was a knifin' and a couple o' guys ganged up on me. My papa said this here gun will protect me, and he told me not to start no trouble, but when somebody tries to meddle with me this here gonna scare him off for sure."

Margaret was impressed with Huddie, who until now had only been the subject of rumors and gossip. She had never before been with a boy who owned a pistol.

"Y'know," Huddie continued, "you is awful young for these kind o' sukey-jumps. They sometimes gets pretty rough."

"I ain't too young," she said indignantly. " 'Sides, I'm as old as you."

"You fourteen?" Huddie asked with genuine interest. The girl on the seat next to him, with her pretty profile outlined against the darkening sky, nodded with a sigh, and he saw the curvature of her breasts bobbing with the horses' gentle trot.

"Well, anyways," he said finally, "don't you go too far away from where I stand when I'm playin'. Maybe I'll get one of the other boys to play for a while and you and me can dance a bit."

"I'd like that, Huddie," she said softly, and he decided Margaret would be easy.

*   *   *   *   *

Allison's barn stood in the flatlands two miles due west of Mooringsport. It was a large, two-story structure, which was still used for the storage of cotton and corn. Old Tom Allison had been dead for three years, and the farm was run by his three sons, Tom Junior, Jack and Howard. Almost every Saturday night the coal-oil lamps were lit and placed around the walls carefully, chairs and benches were set out on the hard dirt floor and enormous buckets of sweet cider were put out for the guests. Usually at these affairs six or seven musicians played one- and two-steps, cakewalks and barn-dance tunes. There were a lot of teenagers, some men and women in their early twenties and a few of the more agile and less weary older folks. Almost all the men wore overalls, and the women wore cotton print dresses of their own manufacture, with their hair tied in brightly colored ribbons. The men laughed and talked while the food was being roasted. Some would drink whiskey and dance the reels and cakewalks, or cluster, talk and tap their feet. Outside, the roughest and drunkest of the local boys would be telling dirty stories and throwing obscene comments at any girls who ventured out for a breath of air.

Huddie helped Margaret out of the buggy. She held his hand tightly as they walked to the dance, Huddie holding his guitar by its neck, resting the box on his shoulder. Laughter and music drifted out from the open doors, and Huddie was immediately greeted from the porch by Howard Allison, who took them inside.

"You want some whiskey, Huddie?"

"Yeah, and some o' that cider here for the lady," he said with affected casualness. Someone handed him a bottle and Huddie took a long pull, letting the green corn whiskey burn into his stomach.

"Okay, Huddie, we ain't payin' you fifty cents for standin' around drinkin' and makin' eyes at that gal. Give out with a tune."

Huddie strode to a small platform at one side of the barn. He propped one foot up on a straight-backed chair, and the holler rang with his shout:

Hoday! Hoday! Hoday!
Hoday! Hoday! Hoday!

He sang this boyhood whoop for three minutes straight, never changing the words, its 6/4 measure swinging freely. Then, without changing tempo he switched to a field holler. The dance had begun. Dresses twirled in the flickering pumpkin-colored light, and work shoes thumped and stomped in the hard-packed dirt.

By the third tune, Huddie's forehead was beaded with sweat. His fingers flew furiously over the guitar, his right hand picking and thumbing the steel wire strings, hammering down the notes and letting the discordant harmonies melt into the fabric of the song. It was times like these that Huddie Ledbetter, fourteen years old, was in his glory. There were other musicians there, of course. Another guitar and a fiddle, two windjammers and a mouth organ. But there was no doubt who was the king of the stage, the focus of all attention. Huddie Ledbetter reveled in the applause and the smiles of envy and admiration that looked back at him from the flickering orange dimness.

The breaks and the subsequent stinging gulps of whiskey were many, but the energy he expended burned away the effects of the alcohol, and before he knew it, it was eleven o'clock. Margaret was nowhere to be seen. He played a few more reels and work songs, then saw Margaret come back inside. She looked over at him and he smiled to her, motioning with his head for her to stand near the stage and wait for him.

"Didn't get no chance to dance with you," he said to Margaret when he was finished. "Where you been?"

"Out on the porch talkin'," she said coyly. "Gettin' late now, too."

"Yeah," he said. "Lemme finish my whiskey and we go home."

They stood around inside the barn for a while longer, talking to friends. One girl was especially friendly, Margaret noted, and she insinuated herself into the conversation at every opportunity. Margaret, however, carefully took Huddie's arm and said, "It's gettin' late, Huddie." She made certain the other girls heard her.

Huddie nodded to her and said goodbye, agreeing to play again next week and saying he'd see his friends at church the next morning.

He put the guitar over his shoulder and walked with Margaret out onto the porch.

"Man, that breeze sure feel good," he said.

Margaret started to say something, but suddenly a large man approached and started yelling at her. Huddie recognized him as an older worker from somewhere down along the Caddo Lake shoreline. "Hey, come along with me, Margaret! I'll take you home on my new horse."

Huddie glared at the man. "She goin' with me," he said evenly, and took a step in front of Margaret.

The man ignored Huddie. "Come on, now, girl," he said, and staggered toward her again. "This here nigga ain't takin' you home tonight."

"No thank you, mister," Margaret said politely. "I'se goin' home with Huddie tonight."

The man guffawed. "This here farm nigga? Now, what you want him for? He gonna play music for you all night long?"

Margaret now stepped back, for she saw Huddie relax his grip on his guitar and slowly shove it in her direction. Below the porch, buggies and horses began to leave.

Margaret took Huddie's guitar and held it firmly. Then, before she could move, the man reached out and grabbed her arm. "Why don't you come with a *big* nigga, girl? C'mon, I take you home the long way," and he continued to grin.

Huddie inserted himself between the man and Margaret, and chopped down hard on his forearm. The man winced and glared at Huddie.

"You bastid, you take your hand off'n her! She comin' home with me," Huddie said.

The man lurched past Huddie again and quickly grabbed Margaret by the waist, forcing her to drop the guitar. He began pulling her off the porch, but she grabbed Huddie's arm. The three of them tugged almost comically for a second, then Huddie jerked the man toward him with his free arm, pulling him off balance. Margaret let go suddenly and Huddie swung, catching the man square between the eyes. He reeled backward, shouting curses, and Huddie leaped on him, pummeling his midsection and head until the man fell down.

Huddie jumped down and straddled him, taking his gun from under his coat. The barrel flashed in the dim coal-oil light as Huddie crashed the gun against the side of the man's head. He yelled and Margaret screamed. Cursing violently, Huddie pointed the gun into the man's throat and pulled the trigger.

Click!

Somehow, it didn't fire. Huddie pulled the gun away and looked at it, puzzled. As he loosened his grip on the man's throat to check that the gun was loaded, the man's eyes bulged with fright. With one Herculean surge of power, he flipped Huddie to the side, leaped to his feet and ran toward the edge of the building. Huddie pointed the gun at him, still swearing. The man disappeared around the side of the barn just as Huddie fired, and a plank at the corner splintered. Margaret screamed again, and Tom Allison ran out onto the porch.

"Son-of-a-bitch, Huddie!" he yelled. "What the hell you doin'?"

"That bastid! I catch him again I gonna kill him right now!"

Allison suppressed his own panic and calmed Huddie down. Margaret was now sobbing, clinging to Huddie's arm and holding his guitar by her side.

"I kill anybody what touch my gal like that again!" Huddie said contemptuously to Allison, as if Allison himself represented a second threat. "I blow his no good brains all over the floor!"

"But she ain't your gal," Allison said. "I never seen you with her before."

"She's my gal tonight," Huddie said angrily.

Allison gave Huddie another drink of whiskey, and the three of them sat down on the porch. "Man, youse crazy," Allison said. "An' youse lucky that cartridge didn't fire. That's one nigga what's gonna get you into a heap o' trouble if he takes it in his head to report this to Gifford."

"Don't guess I care none," Huddie said. The dire implications had the gun fired were completely lost on him. "You see him again, you tell him the next time I see him 'roun' this here gal, he gonna get his head mashed in."

Huddie handed his bottle to Allison and took Margaret's hand, "He hurt you arm when he grab you?"

"No," she said. "But it's late, you know. You gotta gallop that horse!"

Huddie nodded and said goodnight to Allison. Then, as if in afterthought as he stepped down from the porch, Huddie turned around again, an unfamiliar sheepish look on his face. "I sorry about that, Tom. I guess I jus' got so mad I got myself blinded. Hope the gun didn't scare anyone none."

"It's all right, Huddie," Allison said as he waved goodnight a second time. "But you oughtta leave that thing home. Gonna get you in a lot o' trouble someday, you keep packin' it."

On the way back from the dance, Huddie put his arm around Margaret and she snuggled close to him, nestling on his shoulder. There was a full moon, and fireflies sparkled. It was still warm and the earth radiated heat from the late summer day. The hoofbeats of the horse and the perpetual rocking of the buggy lulled them into silence, and Huddie felt a strange new sensation slowly creep into him.

Margaret stirred at his side and nuzzled her head against his cheek. She was in love. Watching Huddie that evening at the sukey-jump, her sweet brown eyes had clouded over with admiration. To her, he symbolized everything she wanted: a handsome man who could stand his ground against anybody, who could make people happy by his antics and heart-pounding music, and who could be gentle and loving.

The road back to the farm was not much more than a dirt path. Like a water snake, it twisted and wound through the cypresses and gums. Huddie pulled the buggy to the side of the road and leaned back against the wooden seat. Margaret stirred at his side and opened her eyes. "Are we home?" she whispered.

"Another mile yet," he answered. For the first time Huddie was groping for an approach. There was something about Margaret Judd that bothered him. Perhaps it was her coyness or the shy, innocent smiles she flashed at him during the evening. Subconsciously he had set her apart from the other girls. Margaret, he decided, would be his girl, and someday they would get married and he would be a famous musician in Shreveport.

"We should hurry," Margaret said. "I promised papa I wouldn't be too late."

"Ah, hell. He don't know what time it is. Jus' as long as youse safe. 'Sides, you folks probably all asleep by now anyway."

She sighed. "I know but---"

Huddie interrupted her. "If you want to go home, we go home."

"I didn't say I *wanted* to. I jus' said I promised papa."

"Then make up you mind. You want to stay here for a little while?"

"Well, a *little* while, maybe." Margaret felt Huddie's arm around her again. She felt his hand on her cheek and he gently turned her face to him. Huddie kissed her on the lips, opening his mouth slightly, letting his hand stray from her face to her breast. She shoved his hand away. "No," she whispered. "Please, Huddie, no."

Huddie let his hand drop. "Don't you like to be touched?"

"I jus' don't think it proper, that's all. Papa told me I could get in a lot o' trouble if I let boys fool 'round with me."

"No boy ever gonna fool 'round with you, Margaret, 'cept me."

Margaret nodded silently and stared straight ahead. She reluctantly followed when Huddie helped her out of the buggy and led her from the road into a grassy field. The two shadowed figures made their way into the woods, paused at a clearing, listening as some furry animal rustled in the undergrowth. In the seductive dimness Huddie dropped to the ground and lay back, pulling Margaret down beside him. He looked at her in the moonlight. She was the prettiest girl he could ever remember. Huddie kissed her again. He heard her breathing increase and she squirmed slightly, moving herself closer to him.

"Margaret," he whispered. "I love you."

"An' I love you too, Huddie. I ain't never met anyone like you."

"Then let's do it."

"I can't."

"Why not?"

"I ain't never done it before. I ain't never been with no boy."

"That's all right."

"I'm scared."

"Nothin' to be scared of."

"What if I get a baby?"

"You ain't gonna get no baby. I be careful."

"But what if I *does*?"

"Then I'll marry you."

Margaret shook her head, "You ain't gonna marry me, Huddie. You ain't old enough and besides you ain't got no money."

"My papa got lots of money. I promise I marry you if you get a baby. But you ain't gonna get no baby."

Margaret sighed. "I jus' don't know."

Huddie bent over and kissed her again. He felt her quiver as he touched her breasts, pressing them, feeling her nipples pop into hardness and her body tense. He opened the front of her dress and kissed her hard on the breasts. She pulled him down to her and his hand groped between her legs. He took her hand and placed it on his crotch, moving her palm against him.

"It's so big, Huddie. It gonna hurt me."

"I be gentle."

Huddie knelt before her, opening her legs and guiding himself slowly into her. He felt Margaret clutch at him and raise her hips slightly. Then she cried out, "Lawd, Huddie! It hurts!"

He pressed harder.

"Huddie! You hurtin' me!"

She lay back, breathing heavily. Huddie kissed her again and touched her gently. "I love you, Margaret."

"Oh, Huddie. You said you wouldn't hurt me."

"That's only 'cuz it was the first time. I ain't gonna hurt you no more. An' we gonna go everywhere together."

"You mean I gonna be you gal?"

"That's jus' what I mean. Ain't nobody gonna touch you 'cept me. An' if I catch any fella hangin' 'round you, I gonna bash his head in."

Happiness swept through her like a windstorm. The girl friend of Huddie Ledbetter, she thought. His woman! The pain between her legs stung her now, yet it was not an unpleasant sensation. She was relieved, in a way, and glad he had not prolonged it as she thought he might.

Huddie let his hand play down her back. He touched her hair, toying with it idly, letting his thoughts wander back to Edna Mae. How different Margaret was from her. How tiny and gentle she was, with skin as soft and as brown as pudding. A girl with a quiet and lilting hoarseness to her voice, and laughter that tinkled like rain in the forest. He imagined Margaret now, at the bottom of the long mahogany staircase, in a dress of silver and gold. He took her by the hand and bowed to the excited applause.

*   *   *   *   *

Word reached Wes Ledbetter the next day that his son had tried to murder a man named Sammy Cox, who was a known troublemaker from Natchitoches, and after church Sheriff Gifford met Wes and Huddie outside with a warrant for Huddie's arrest. But it didn't take long for Wes, with the help of ten dollars, to convince Gifford to drop the charge. He promised on Huddie's behalf that it wouldn't happen again, self-defense or no. Gifford was placated, but Wes took Huddie's gun away from him and promised his son the money would be sweated out of his hide.

For the balance of the summer, Huddie did the work of two men on the Ledbetter farm. The fields were harvested and new land was cultivated for planting the following spring. Huddie barely had time of his own. He split wood, chopped cotton, loaded bales, cleared land, and when it seemed there was going to be time to rest, Wes would send him on errands or make him dig a ditch.

By now, a cousin of Huddie's, Edmond, whose familial ties never were too clear to Huddie, lived with the Ledbetters. He and Huddie became close friends. Edmond was four years younger and enjoyed hearing about Huddie's exploits in town. Huddie showed Edmond how to play the guitar, and the four of them would sit around in the chilly evenings, in front of a fireplace crammed with thin pine logs, singing spirituals. Sally's voice rose above it all, and she taught the family each new song she learned.

Winter came quickly and suddenly. It rained hard that year, and flooding hampered travel between Mooringsport and Shreveport. Firewood was scarce, and most of Huddie's rabbits and chickens perished. But the hardship the harsh winter inflicted on the people of Caddo Parish paled the following spring with the sudden and clamorous announcement of young Margaret Judd's pregnancy.

The news, as is always the case, was more traumatic to the families than it was to Huddie and Margaret. Margaret was thrilled when she first realized her condition, but Huddie took the news dispassionately. He told Margaret he would marry her and left the handling of the delicate details up to her. But the calm was short lived. The night the Judd family rode up to the Ledbetter farm was the most cyclonic Huddie could remember. As soon as he heard the buggy along the path, he knew there was going to be a showdown.

"It's the Judds," Sally said as she peeked through the opening above her pan of dishes.

"Wonder what they want," Wes said, cleaning his shotgun. Huddie sat still as he watched his father go to the door and throw it open.

"Hey, Frank!" Wes called. "What you doin' out so late tonight?"

"You gonna find out right goddam quick what I'm doin' out, Ledbetter!" Huddie heard the gruff voice of old man Judd, and braced himself against the approaching hurricane. Edmond retreated to the shedroom and closed the door.

Sally watched apprehensively as Frank Judd, the veins on his neck bulging, led his wife and daughter into the room. "Howdy, Mae," Sally said tentatively. Mae Judd, a plump woman with a huge birthmark on the side of her neck, glowered back at Sally.

"What's goin' on, Frank?" Wes said. "What you so riled about?"

"About that damned boy of yours!" Judd yelled. "Ledbetter, you so blind you don't know what these two been doin'?" He waved at his daughter and continued to glare across the room at Huddie.

Wes stifled a rising anger. His eyes went from Huddie to Frank Judd to Margaret and finally to Sally. "What you talking about?" he said.

"This gal carryin' that sonofabitch's baby, that's what!"

Margaret began to weep at her father's words. Sally gasped. "Oh, Lawd" was all she said, and she looked at Wes.

"That bastid been sneakin' around my place takin' advantage of my daughter," Judd said. "He ought to be strung up and whipped!"

"Now, you hold you tongue, Frank," Wes said, automatically siding with his son. "Let's be a little calm about this. You say you daughter's carryin' a chile and Huddie's the one what made her that way?"

"You damn right he the one, Ledbetter! Ask him."

Wes turned to Huddie, who had shuffled silently toward the middle of the room, now standing next to Margaret. "Huddie, you hear?"

"Yes, papa," he said evenly. "And it's true. I'se gonna marry Margaret."

Sally nearly swooned, and she grabbed the edge of the sideboard firmly. "Oh Lawd," she said again. "Oh, *Huddie!*"

Judd was ranting. "You damn right, you gonna marry her and youse gonna provide for her proper!"

"Hold on," Wes repeated. "How we know Huddie's actual the one?"

Judd's eyes widened. "What you sayin', Ledbetter? You accusin' my daughter?"

"I ain't accusin' nuthin'," Wes said quickly. "But youse makin' a serious charge here, and I ain't gonna see Huddie forced into nothin' he don't want."

Margaret was crying loudly by now, and Sally and Mae had launched into a shrill debate in the kitchen. Judd and Wes stood face to face, in the center of the room, their voices rising steadily. Huddie stood behind his father, slightly taller than both men, glancing compassionately at Margaret.

"That's one troublemaker gonna take the blame this time, Ledbetter! My daughter says he the father of this chile and he damn well gonna marry her and take care of it!"

"You don't stop rantin' at my son like that, Judd, I'se gonna throw you out o' this house!" Wes shouted. "You come 'round here makin' these accusations like youse Reverend Parker, and you 'spect me to say 'Howdy, Frank, go right ahead and take my son'?" Wes said. "Jus' like that?"

"You ain't throwin' me out, Ledbetter, 'til you face up to what he done!"

Wes turned his back on Judd, angering the man more, and grabbed Huddie's shoulder. "Huddie, what you got to say for yourself?"

Huddie's voice was quiet. "Nothin', papa. Me an' Margaret gonna get married and move to Shrevepo't."

Wes waved his comment away. "The hell you is. Youse only fifteen years old and you ain't goin' nowhere. Marryin' this here girl is plain out of the question."

"Ledbetter!"

"Frank, they's still schoolin' to be done for both o' them, and they is too young to move down to that place by themselves. If you calm down you get some sense comin' back to you."

"Ledbetter!" Judd screamed again. "Shut you mouth with them fancy words! He gonna marry my daughter and you ain't got nothin' to do with it!"

"Margaret," Wes asked, trying to soften his voice. "You want to marry my Huddie?"

"Yessir, Mr. Ledbetter," Margaret said. "Reckon me an' Huddie love each other."

"Oh, Lawd," Wes said and looked at the staring women in the kitchen. "They jus' babies, but they in love," he said mockingly.

Judd took Wes's arm roughly and spun him around. "They not too goddam young to *make* babies you mule-head!" he screamed. "They old enough to sneak around, they old enough to get married."

"Huddie ain't done no sneakin' around," Wes said. "It takes two people to make a baby, Judd."

Mae Judd objected at the implication, and Huddie himself started to interrupt, but Judd beat him to it. "I gonna beat his black hide myself, you keep sayin' he ain't the one, Ledbetter! She ain't been with no other boy since they been goin' to the sukey-jumps together, and you know it. Never liked them parties no how, with all the drinkin' and fightin' what goes on. An' you boy always seem to be right smack in the middle of it."

The two men stood toe to toe, staring angrily.

Sally broke the tension briefly when she called from the stove. "When's the baby comin'?"

"Two months!" Judd yelled back, not taking his eyes from Wes. "He got two months to marry her before I go right to the sheriff and have him put in jail with all them other whiskey-drinkin' ponies!"

Wes grabbed Judd's shirt collar. "I gonna push you nose right into you skull, you keep talkin' that way about my son, Judd!" Sally screamed. Judd began to flail away at Wes, swiping at his face and trying to wrest himself away from Wes's grip.

Huddie stepped quickly between them and pushed them apart. "Papa!" he said. "Don't make no sense to start fightin' right here."

"That bastid gonna get thrown right out on his ass!" Wes yelled.

"Wes!" Sally shouted.

"You go ahead and start right in, Ledbetter!" Judd said.

"Wait!" Huddie yelled, holding them apart. "It's me and Margaret's baby and we gonna take care of it! All the shoutin' and the fightin', and they ain't no trouble a'tall. We's gonna do the bes' thing."

Wes tried to relax, and looked around Huddie at Judd. Margaret stared admiringly at Huddie. The women in the kitchen were still clucking to each other. By now, Mae Judd was crying too.

"Now look here, Frank," Wes said finally, as calmly as he could. He walked into the kitchen, avoiding Mae's and Sally's look, and grabbed a bottle of whiskey. Returning to the main room, he began his proposition. "We been friends a long time and we been in our whiskey together and rode to Shrevepo't together. And we both got fine children and they ain't nothin' a'tall to be ashamed of. This here thing happenin' all the time, and we jus' one o' the families what got caught in it. The important thing is the baby, now, don't you agree?"

Huddie looked at his father and saw the familiar pattern begin to repeat itself one more time. He decided to listen and hold his peace a while longer. He could still learn a lot from his old man. He watched Wes offer Judd a drink, and Judd accepted reluctantly.

"An' my daughter?" Judd said.

Wes nodded. "An' you daughter. Now, Huddie here is only fifteen years old, and he ain't got no money and no way to make any."

"But he the best guitar player in the parish. He could make money doin' that."

"No. He ain't old enough and he ain't good enough yet."

Huddie started to argue but resisted the temptation.

"Now," Wes continued matter-of-factly. "'Spose the Ledbetter family sees to it that you daughter's baby is taken care of proper?"

"Only one who can take care of a baby proper is its father and mother."

"How much money do you think a father would have to earn every month to take care of a baby?"

Judd scratched his chin and pulled at an ear. "Twenty dollars."

"What you talkin'? Food an' clothes is all."

"It still take twenty dollars."

"I pay you, Frank, to take care of the baby, about ten dollars every month. You can buy baby things and food on half of that and you know it. But I'm being generous 'cause I'se a fair man and I understand how it is on you daughter. They jus' ain't no sense in letting Huddie marry her now, but later, if they still want to get married, they can. Next year Huddie be sixteen and can do what he want."

Frank Judd knew immediately he was trapped. He realized, but refused to admit, that he could not really force the marriage. The Judd farm was a poor one, scarcely four acres.

"You sure that's the bes' thing, papa?" Huddie glanced in the direction of Margaret and then back at Wes.

Wes nodded emphatically, "It's the bes' for everybody, son. It's the bes' for the chile an' it's bes' for Margaret here an' it's bes' for you. Next year, if you feel like you love this here gal and you still feel you want to hook up with her, then you can. That right, Sally?" He turned in the direction of the women.

Sally touched Mae Judd lightly on the arm. "You understand, Mae?"

"I reckon." She shook her head sadly.

"Then it's settled," Wes said, and he poured the rest of the whiskey into Frank Judd's tin cup.

"The Ledbetters always look after their responsibilities," he said once again. "The Ledbetters is always fair."

*   *   *   *   *

The baby came with the summer, and it provoked a community outcry that disrupted the Ledbetter farm forever. Sally Ledbetter was no longer invited to sing at church, and Wes and Huddie stopped attending altogether. Better to stay on the farm and work, they said, than to listen to the gossip and feel the icy stares of indignation. People stared at Wes when he went to town; Sheriff Gifford stroked his chin and prowled around, waiting for a new chance to get at Huddie. Reverend Parker spoke out about the rising delinquency of the Mooringsport youth, and even mentioned Huddie by name one particularly vitriolic Sunday.

The Allisons, although they permitted Huddie to continue playing his ever-present guitar at the sukey-jumps and breakdowns, no longer paid him much. A few friends would take up a collection, but the few pennies hardly matched the fifty cents of old. Huddie took to leaving Mooringsport to go across Caddo Lake, where the oil explorations were being carried out, playing in honky-tonk hangouts and local temporary housing units for the prospectors. He earned money, which he brought home to Wes or sometimes gave to Margaret during their assignations, which continued after the baby was born. The Judds didn't speak to the Ledbetters, but Huddie would deliver Wes's monthly allotment to Margaret, who would turn it over to Frank Judd.

Huddie's friends in school were leery of him, and he was suddenly overburdened with schoolwork. Wes noticed that prices seemed to go up when he and Sally shopped in town. Rumors were rampant. The women of Mooringsport gossiped that Huddie was sleeping with every available single girl and a few wives. They said he and his father went to the red-light houses in Shreveport. They said Sally was a voodoo witch. It was whispered that Huddie went across the river to tote for the white Texas oil men. Huddie did this, Huddie did that. And the people of Mooringsport all but isolated the Ledbetters.

Through it all, though, Huddie Ledbetter learned. He learned about rumor, about hatred, about the lot of black people in black or white environments. He dropped out of the meager schooling he'd been receiving, and he learned that his music could wiggle through the social barrier. But he also learned that when his fingers stopped, so did his popularity. When Huddie played, Huddie was king, but when Huddie did anything else, he was damned. The girls still chased him, unseen by their watchful parents, and there were knifings, shootings and beatings. Huddie reveled in it all, laughing and drinking and playing his way through the summer in sweaty splendor.

And he grew. Huddie was acknowledged as the strongest among the local boys, even those a few years older. Above all, Huddie was the "best damn guitar-playing nigga in the world!"

The summer drew to a tumultuous close, and autumn cotton harvesting came. Huddie toiled in the field alongside his father and mother, brawny back bulging with steel muscle. He chopped more cotton than anyone, split more wood, toted more bales, worked longer hours, hefted more tools and felled more trees. And when he was through working, Huddie played. He carefully stayed away from Margaret but Rachel came out to the cornfields at night, and Bessie came out too. Mary Julia Powell appeared often before the sun was down, and frisky Ida Hamilton one evening tapped on the wall of his shed. The parade of girls, young and old, seemed endless.

And then autumn, too, ended. The clock moved fast through the winter, for the hours of youth were dwindling. Winter nights were spent lingering for hours over his guitar. He fought with his mother often this year, for Sally was tired and Wes was drinking hard. The money diminished rapidly after another heavy snowfall virtually blockaded the road to Shreveport. Huddie began having drinking bouts with his father, and often they would yell in tandem at Sally. Huddie sensed that the family was breaking up. In the dark hours while everyone else slept, Huddie wondered whether his father would even stay at home come spring.

Huddie sang spirituals in more tender moments, bringing a rare smile to Sally's face, and he sang stomps and hollers when his father felt like singing. The clock kept spinning into spring at last, but it seemed no better than the last one.

Huddie despaired of Mooringsport and longed for Shreveport. Then one day the news spread like a vicious forest fire that Margaret was pregnant again, and the accusing fingers of the community once again aimed at Huddie. He made his decision. This time he was innocent; he hadn't laid with Margaret since the confrontation at Wes's house. But Frank Judd wanted to kill him and Sheriff Gifford was hounding him. He spent a week hiding out near the lake, where Edmond brought him food. He finally sneaked home one sultry evening to gather his things. Not even his parents believed him this time, and the signal flashed in his mind like a warning beacon: Huddie Ledbetter had grown too big for Mooringsport.

He was a man and a musician. Nearly six feet tall now, with a massive frame and hands as strong as wolf traps, he had everything he needed. Mooringsport had nothing but trouble.

When he turned sixteen, Huddie asked for and received two pairs of long pants, a canvas sack for his guitar, a horse and saddle, forty dollars in cash and his freedom.

Fannin Street and the red-light districts beckoned.

###

Chapter Four

Shreveport smelled like an overworked horse.

In 1903 it was largely confined to a twenty-block business and

nightclub matrix, and the chief commodities were cotton, sugar cane, whiskey and women. Within the quadrangles bordered by Cypress and Crockett streets, men, women and children tried to eke out a living selling wares, whiskey, opium and themselves. Lynchings happened often.

Texas Avenue split the town in half, its brick streets recently inlaid with shiny new rails for trolleys. Two blocks north was Fannin Street, a twelve-block conglomeration of wood frame buildings, brick hotels and warehouses. And at Saint Paul's Bottom, where Fannin Street terminated, dance halls, bawdy houses, blood-drenched bars and sleazy boarding houses provided round-the-clock diversions for the town's struggling black population.

Fannin, stretching southwest from the Red River wharves, became the center of young Huddie's activities in the ensuing years: Bo McWhirter's saloon, with its constant stream of transient drunks and broken-down songsters; the Red Mud Cafe, where the rich, greasy-sweet smell of rancid pork fat formed a pungent background for guitars and fiddles, harmonicas and windjaminers; Bessie Vinson's art house, whose half-dozen fancy and gilt-framed paintings formed a seductive tapestry for the prostitutes upstairs and the cacophony of the barroom below; Aunt Pearl's boarding house, less expensive than Bessie Vinson's, where the rotund Pearl herself regaled her guests with ribald stories of her incredible past; The Caddo, a nondescript two-room saloon that showed off the best piano in Shreveport and served the best food; the Market Street Hotel, an ill-designed building without a plumb column or level board; and the Salt Box, known throughout the town as the most dangerous place for the timid, the non-fighter, and which was Sheriff Tom Hughes's first and last stop when he made his infrequent rounds. And there were seven other rooming houses, catering primarily to the riverboat trade, where transient work seekers and surreptitious slave traders could find room and board without attracting the attention of the law.

When Huddie arrived in town, he headed directly for Bo McWhirter's in Saint Paul's Bottom, where Fannin intersected North, and had no trouble talking the beet-cheeked McWhirter into letting him play his guitar for tips and a tiny room with a cot upstairs. Huddie was delighted. It would be easy, he decided, just doing what he liked best. In a year he would be rich and famous. Then there would be other cities -- even larger ones -- clamoring to hear him play.

His music caught on immediately, and before long the young man was no longer known as "old Wes Ledbetter's boy," but as Huddie Ledbetter, who could "out-whoop, out-stomp and out-play any nigga in Shrevepo't."

Wes, on his visits to Shreveport, had no trouble tracking him down. The two would have a few beers together, and then, with a wink, Wes would wander over to Bessie's or Pearl's to do some "cotton pricin'."

Huddie grew more and more at ease in his new life, and

at seventeen he was strutting around The Bottom "greetin', jokin', sassin' and shit-lippin' every riverhip on Fannin." But most of all he liked to talk to the songsters. He met Blind Sonny Jackson, whose milky white cataracts etched his face into an eerie bas-relief. Jackson tried to escape from the guitar's tonal confines by re-tuning his instrument and barring with the neck of a medicine bottle stuck on his index finger. Huddie experimented with this technique for a few weeks and liked it at first. But he finally abandoned it because it retarded his speed.

Roy Dickey, a "black butt" player from the emerging oil towns north of Caddo Lake, had blur-fast fingers on a bell-shaped guitar to which he had added two extra strings.

Claude Cook was a tall and rangy "fast western" piano player who sang in a twangy imitation of Southern guitarists while rolling eight-to-the-bar rhythms in the bass and blues variations in the treble. He would play, flashing a metallic smile as his mouthful of gold teeth caught the lamp glow in the corner of the Caddo Bar. Along with a man known as Big Maceo, a large, barrel-chested dandy who had been a successful riverboat banjo player and who still wore six gold rings on his strumming hand and two on his left, they often played as the Lakeside Three, and became a regular Friday night attraction at the Caddo.

During his first year on Fannin Street Huddie divided his time between the music, the whiskey and the women. The pageant of prostitutes and bloody fights, the drunken late nights and the early morning carousing through the waterfront alleyways continued week after week, month after month. His money came and went.

At a husky eighteen his popularity soared and his pockets jingled with more cash than he had ever dreamed of. He bought himself flashy clothes and a wide-brimmed Stetson. But with all his flamboyance, Huddie shied away from the crap games and numbers rackets and the card-playing, deciding his money had been too hard-earned to toss away at the fall of a pair of Memphis Dominoes.

Then, one evening in a back alley off Fannin St., he was set upon by three drunken seamen from one of the river ships, and before he could draw his gun one of them cracked him over the head with a rock-in-a-sock and slashed him in the neck. They robbed him of his last dime. He was found by Maceo several hours later, nearly dead from loss of blood. Maceo had trouble finding a doctor who would take the time to treat him, but finally Bo McWhirter produced an old horse doctor to dress the wound.

Huddie was unconscious for three days. A week later, though, the healing scabs were nothing compared to Huddie's chief concern. True, there was an ugly slash under his chin. But even when the vet redid the dressing on the cut, those pains were nearly pleasures alongside the agony Huddie felt when he urinated. He thought there might be something terribly wrong with him, but the old vet merely prescribed warm compresses and a mild mustard poultice. For the next few weeks, Huddie simply endured the pain. Then one night Maceo appeared with an Indian crone named Lil Giroux, who brought a mixture used by the French during the war, purported to have magic healing powers for afflictions of the genitals. It was called "Lafayette's Mixture," and it was a blend of potassium hydroxide, copaiba, tincture of lavender, spirits of nitrous ether and mucilage of acacia suspended in a sweet syrup. It was a primitive cure for gonorrhea, a disease just as foul as the taste of the medicine itself, but it worked.

In February of 1905, Huddie got tired of Shreveport and decided to go home. He packed his things -- including a bottle of the bitter brown elixir -- slung his guitar over his shoulder and headed out into the morning sunshine. He was happy now that he was heading home. And, for once, he had been sober for an entire week. He enjoyed the crisp, river-flavored air and watched the boats and crews beginning to bustle along the wharf.

Then he saw the little girl. As aware as he was of the poverty and the constant struggle that went on unseen in the houses and back streets of Shreveport, it still got to him. She was blind and ill-clad in a worn red cotton dress. She sat on a small stool on the corner, near the curb, begging with a chipped enamel cup. He noticed her right leg was scarcely thicker than a stick and twisted sharply inward at the ankle. She couldn't have been more than eight years old.

He approached her slowly and then stopped, watching her. Four men passed by, eyeing Huddie curiously and totally avoiding the child. Then the lonely sound of a single coin clanking drearily in the cup made him reach into his pocket and carefully take out all his loose change. When he put it into the cup the girl turned her head and sightlessly sought the source of her new money.

"Thank you, mister," she said.

"What you doin' out here so early, l'il gal?" Huddie sat down next to her on the edge of the boardwalk. "Ain't you got no place to go?"

The girl shook her head. "No, mister," she said quietly, a bit afraid. "I got to get the money home to my mama for dinner tonight."

Huddie frowned. "Missy," he said haltingly. "It's early in the mornin'. Mos' children are still home in their beds now."

The girl's eyebrows fluttered up as her eyes desperately sought Huddie's face. Bewildered, she groped for an answer that wouldn't be embarrassing. Then she broke down in tears, and Huddie reached out and held her shoulders. She had thought it was afternoon.

"Now here, don't you cry. Maybe you papa buy you somethin' with the coins I give you."

"I ain't got no papa."

Then he pulled her to him and wrapped his arms around her for a long while.

Huddie succeeded in stopping her tears and holding back his own by taking his guitar and letting her touch its smooth and satiny surface. She plucked two strings and finally smiled.

"Tell you what," Huddie said. "I gonna sit here for a while and make up a pretty song for you, and maybe the people will put some more money in your cup." Softly strumming the guitar, Huddie began to sing:

> *Pretty li'l gal wit' the red dress on,*
> *Pretty li'l gal wit' the*
> *red dress on.*

The girl smiled and bobbed her head with the melody, and Huddie looked up at the sky as he sang, glad she couldn't see the tears forming in his own eyes.

An hour and twenty cents later, after almost all the soft ballads he knew had been sung, he suddenly felt the steadily warming rays of the sun turn cold on the back of his neck. The shadow flowed past him onto the girl's arm, and he stopped playing. The girl turned as he did.

The deputy had his hands on his hips and his hat was tilted back over his sunburned forehead. "What do you think you're doing?"

Huddie smiled up at him. "Jus' helpin' this here li'l gal get some money for her mama," he said. "She blind."

"You just get her outta here. Ain't no begging allowed downtown."

"But she don't know. She don't realize where---" Huddie was still smiling as he was cut off.

"I ain't gonna ask you again. Now, get your ass and hers outta here, I said."

Huddie remained seated, but it was getting more difficult to keep smiling. "Can't we jus' finish up this here one little thing, sir? She almos' got enough now to go on home."

The deputy brushed past Huddie quickly and hefted the girl up from the stool by her arm. "You're outta your neighborhood, kid," he said brusquely. "Get on home and let your mama do her own begging." With that he kicked over the stool and seized the girl's cup. Before the stool had rolled to a stop, Huddie was on him, and the little blind girl was screaming.

It didn't last long. By the time the deputy was unconscious, two more had appeared and were pointing their guns at Huddie. Someone hit him on the back of the head and he fell to the ground.

He woke up in the Shreveport jail. He was stretched on his back on a wooden pallet, a single flickering bulb dangling above him. The stench of feces made him gag. He thought of the little girl. Where was she? Where was his guitar? Or his horse?

He got up and lurched to the heavy iron grate in the door and called a guard. The guard looked at him vacantly and disappeared down the hallway. Hours later, Sheriff Tom Hughes appeared on the other side of the grate.

"Ledbetter, you sonofabitch! I'm gonna let you rot here until you settle down."

Huddie moaned. "All I remembers is the deputy takin' the li'l girl's money."

"You were beggin' downtown and you know better!"

"She was a li'l blind cripple gal, Sheriff. She didn't know where she was. She thought it was afternoon, even."

"You should have told her and taken her out of there before the trouble started."

"But the deputy took her money. That ain't right, Sheriff."

"An' it ain't right to beat up on no officer, neither! Sorry, Ledbetter, you're here for six months this time." Hughes walked off, and when his footsteps were gone Huddie shuffled back to his pallet and sobbed aloud. Not at the thought of the six foul months ahead of him, but at the thought of the little blind girl.

*   *   *   *   *

Huddie's weight dropped considerably during the ensuing months on a diet of cornbread and water, with occasional beans, but no meat. They had taken his guitar and locked it up. He grew sullen and morose and spoke to his cellmates in bitter, monosyllabic grunts. After a month he was tossed into solitary confinement for a week when he almost choked another prisoner to death for making a sexual advance.

Hughes refused him visitors, but one day Huddie did receive a letter from his father, who was waiting downstairs for a reply. It was scrawled in a childlike pencil script:

> *son I just now heared about your*
> *trubble. I aint tellin you*
> *mama nuthin no need for her to no. I*
> *made a promis to sherif*
> *huse when you gets out you cum bak*
> *home and wuck. They been sum fells from*

the oil company and they has alreddy start to
dril in the lake. Lots of money they
say and lots of the boys
in town wuckin for the oil man makin
lots of money. You could
too huddie and make a lot of money Im
waitin down the stairs
for you anser. Edmond is wucking for
the gulf people too.

Papa

Huddie read the letter and carefully folded it and put it into his pocket. Again a feeling of utter frustration descended upon him. Papa was downstairs and he had two more months to spend cooped up in this dreary old jail. He leaned back against the grimy wall and tried to compose his reply. He thought about the oil drilling in Caddo Lake, remembering the rumors that had been sweeping through the parish. Edmond must be making good money. Maybe even as much as the oil men in Texas he had heard about. And he, Huddie, who was the best worker in Mooringsport, could probably make even more than anybody else.

His mental vision slowly focused. You're the best there is, he told himself. The last two years had been wasted. He had drunk too much and had let the whores give him the clap, but he was better than that. Why, he could outplay any songster in Shreveport. Why stick around here for nickels when he could go out and sing to bigger audiences? The thought soared immediately, and he saw himself riding a brand new stallion and giving Wes and Sally enormous amounts of money to buy more land. He saw himself and Edmond striding into the best saloons and the best stores, buying silk dresses for the women and the sweetest pecan divinity for all the children in sight.

No. No more of Shreveport and the beer-fattened bitches and the harsh green whiskey. He decided to get a job in Mooringsport, to work hard, save his money, and then seek his fortune somewhere else.

He called the guard. "Tell my papa that I'se gonna come right home when they let me out and do whatever work he want."

The guard stared blankly at him, nodded and turned away. Huddie called back to him. "An' tell him to give my mama a kiss for me!"

###

Chapter Five

Oil had invaded the backcountry of northern Louisiana. For the past several years prospectors from the major companies had been examining deep core samples. They set up rigs in the northeastern section of Caddo Lake, and soon dozens of black geysers spewed skyward and spread the greasy crude oil over the surface of the lake.

It seemed as though everyone flocked to Shreveport and Mooringsport to exploit the fields. Derricks sprang up overnight in the piney forests around Mooringsport, and with the oil men came new saloons and new women. Automobiles lurched along the dusty streets belching blue gray smoke behind them. From Pine Island to James Bayou, the smell of petroleum saturated the air.

But the strikes, as it turned out, had a polarizing effect on the life of people long dependent on farming, lumber and some general commerce. The discovery of oil sucked people from every part of the nation into Shreveport. The newly rich moved from their modest homes into the more "exclusive sections" along the Red River. But the Caddo Parish farmers, who knew nothing except cotton, didn't give up traditional livelihood for the enticement of oil. Wes Ledbetter was one of these men.

Sally was shocked at her son's appearance, but she kissed him gently on the cheek and scurried into the pantry to fix him something to eat. The six months in the Shreveport jail had left him weaker than he could remember. He ate voraciously, worked long days helping Wes chop wood or clear a new patch of field, and stayed close to the farm. Edmond, now fifteen, wanted to hear the lusty stories of Fannin Street, and Huddie told them, suitably embellished. Edmond told him about Margaret, about how she had married Heseki Coleman and moved to the Mississippi lowlands.

Huddie's voice was steady and sure; the eager, untrained one of his school years was gone forever. He sang the ballads and blues of Arkansas, Texas and Louisiana with a new knowledge of their meaning.

Summer passed for the most part without incident. More than once, Huddie was nearly provoked into a fight, but he succeeded in either avoiding it or talking himself out of it. He began to realize that he could talk his way out of just about anything unless he let his temper cross that invisible line.

He tried not to think why, but he dreamed often of Sycamore Slim. On such mornings he woke depressed and bothered and on those days he worked hardest in the fields, sweating under a broiling sun, trying to erase the sharp images of broken windjammers and blood-stained dust.

He eventually took a job with Gulf and volunteered for the most strenuous chores -- even looking forward to moving the oil drums from wagon to flatcar. In the evenings, he rested and played his guitar.

The girls of Oil City and Mooringsport were as willing as ever, but only occasionally would he go to the saloon, usually on a Saturday night. He played for a sukey-jump now and then, but found he no longer enjoyed his Mooringsport contemporaries. After a year of working for Gulf, he began to yearn once again for the nightlife of Fannin Street and the gaiety of Texas Avenue, for Maceo and the others. But his goal was now New Orleans and that was that.

One evening, Wes Ledbetter's old friend Big Ted Promise crashed into the house insisting they drink a bottle of whiskey to celebrate his new daughter. They had named her Martha, and Ted wanted Wes to stand up and be her godfather the following Sunday at Shiloh Baptist Church. In the evening the men wanted to drink alone, so Huddie and his cousin wandered into town.

"Hud," Edmond said later, as they started home, "how long you s'pose this oil business is gonna keep up?"

"Don't know," Huddie said. "Mos' people seems to be makin' a heap of money out of it, but seems I just can't gather me up no big savin' bundle. Guess it's gonna stay for a while, though."

"You gonna stay, too?"

"Don't know that either, Eddie. Sometimes I gets to thinkin' 'bout N'Orleans, an' I starts wonderin' what's Mooringspo't got for me. Don't seem like none but a few of the guys care much for me -- specially the old folks around here. An' jus' goin' home every night ain't much fun no more."

"I know," Edmond said. "I don't think I like this dirty oil work no more, either. Uncle says I can come back and jus' work on the farm for a few more years, and when I get to be a few years older he gimme some acres."

"You want to be a farmer?" Huddie asked, mildly surprised. "Why don't you come on down to N'Orleans with me and we can play us some good blues and maybe make more money than we's gettin' from the Gulf?"

"Nah, Hud. Don't guess that's the kinda life I want. You can get into trouble down there, and I don't want to spend no time in that jail you talk about. Goin' to stay in Mooringspo't and stay with the farm."

"Well, not me," Huddie said, making up his mind on the spot. "I'se gettin' sick of liftin' oil drums when all the white people makin' all the money. I reckon I'll jus' go on down the river and stay outta trouble this time. N'Orleans! That's the spot for me, yeah."

Edmond traced a wiggly line in the dirt with his foot and slung his guitar over his shoulder by its neck. "I think you ought to stay around, Huddie. You got all the wimmins you need here, and you papa and mama gettin' kinda old to see to the farm all by theyselves. 'Sides, you and me gonna have the whole place someday, and we could put out a helluva lot of cotton and corn, workin' together like we do."

"Not me, Eddie. You can be the bes' cotton farmer in the world if you want, but I'se gonna be the bes' damn guitar-playin' nigga in Loosiana before I gets through. They's people down in N'Orleans payin' good money jus' to hear some guy named Buddy Bolden play a horn. Shit, I can play this here thing better than he can play his horn, and everybody in Shrevepo't know it."

"You never heard him. How you know?"

"I jus' know, Eddie. I feel it under my skin. Sometimes I get to playin' a good fast cakewalk and I try to play it faster than my hands can move. But I jus' know someday I be able to play jus' as fast as I hear it in my head. Jus' you wait."

"You tell you papa yet you leavin'?"

Huddie shook his head. "Guess I should soon. He won't mind, I don't guess, but mama sure gonna be mad again."

"Sometimes I hear her cryin' in the bedroom when you gets into trouble. You papa, he don't say nothin' 'cept you still has the ramblin' urge. But you mama, she sure pray up a storm you don't get hurt bad someday."

"That's what I say. Mama gonna worry anyways, and at least if I'm gone she won't get no sass from those ol' biddies down to the church. Everybody look at you, they say, 'Ain't he a good boy, Eddie Ledbetter.' But when they look at me, they say, 'Looky that no-good Huddie, always fightin' and gettin' the girls in trouble.'"

That night Huddie told his parents he wanted to leave again, and, as Edmond predicted, Sally began to cry and left the room. Wes just sat back in his chair and nodded, punctuating Huddie's reasons with an occasional grunt, signifying neither approval nor disapproval. A thin slice of Mooringsport moon was high in the sky when the two men finally shook hands. An hour later, Sally heard her son saddle his horse and spur it in the direction of town. *He couldn't even wait 'til morning*, she thought. *Sweet Jesus, take care o' him now.*

When he arrived in Shreveport, he couldn't resist the temptation to take one last ride through Saint Paul's Bottom. The first thing he learned was that Bessie Vinson's place had burned to the ground three weeks ago and the fire had taken seventeen lives, including Bessie's. Bo McWhirter's was now called "Sammy's," and Huddie didn't like it. The new influx of oil men and their exploiters had brought about considerable change, most of it for the worse. No one knew the whereabouts of Claude Cook or Big Maceo. The Salt Box had become a den for homosexuals -- mellow boys, as they were called -- and Aunt Pearl's had been closed by the health department. She had been arrested for selling bootleg rum and sentenced to five years at the women's outcamp at Angola State Penitentiary.

He looked in at another place. An aging singer with heavy breasts and a loose fold of skin under her chin was screeching off-key. She reminded him of a frighterned chicken and he left immediately. No, Shreveport ain't for me, he thought.

It had to be New Orleans.

He intended to cross the river into Bossier City and then ride east to Vicksburg. From there he would follow the Mississippi down to New Orleans. But he rode no farther than Bossier City.

The Black Ace was a dingy strip-joint that smelled of bacteria and bathtub gin. A painted sign boasted of twelve girls. Inside, a half-dozen electric lamps were strung along two walls. Tables and chairs were crowded closely alongside a makeshift stage. Twenty or thirty men were at the tables or lined up at the bar. Guitar in hand, Huddie ordered a whiskey, then changed it to a glass of beer. Fifteen minutes later the lights were shut off and the stage was illuminated with a pinkish glow. A terrible comedian began a series of off-color jokes and was booed away by the audience.

A man next to Huddie poked him in the ribs and leered at him. "Wait till you see these gals, man. They got a fat ol' cow here that I'd jus' love to play in-and-out-the-window with." He laughed and wiped his mouth on his sleeve.

The men began whooping and wise-cracking when a series of crude and blatantly unprofessional strippers paraded across the stage amid the shouts and obscenities of the drinkers. Huddie ordered another beer and decided what he needed was a woman. The man next to him pounded the table and laughed.

Then she came out, the main attraction of the Black Ace. Dressed in a white sequined gown, she smiled sexily down at the men. That girl couldn't be more than nineteen or twenty, he thought, and a high yellow! She was beautiful. Long straight black hair, big brown eyes and a complexion smooth as honey. She began to remove her gloves and Huddie's eyes were riveted on her taut breasts. He started sweating.

She was now stark naked and Huddie stared at the softness between her legs. He couldn't hear the music anymore, and the whoops and shouts of the audience were muted. The girl spread her legs and dared the audience.

The man next to him staggered to his feet and approached the stage. He stuck a silver dollar between his teeth and laid the back of his head on the floorboards, holding the coin up to her. The girl moved her hips over him, and slowly, arms out straight for balance, bent her knees and gently plucked the coin from the man's mouth. The place went wild. She rose quickly, the metal glinting in the dark triangle, and held out her arms to the frenzied applause.

Huddie was transfixed; he had never seen anything like it. He fumbled in his coat and found a dollar bill and headed toward the stage. He saw the girl wink at him. The piano began to play and he held the bill out to her with his lips. As she got nearer, the girl laughed. He could smell her. He suddenly grabbed out and went crashing down on top of her. She screamed as he tried to bury his face between her legs.

Somewhere a whistle blew and five huge bouncers appeared from the side. In an instant, a fight was in full flourish. Huddie whipped his knife from his pocket and shoved the girl behind him, against the wall. A chair splintered off his shoulders; he felt his knife plunge into something soft. The mass of throbbing, shouting, bleeding bodies blurred in a fleshy vortex.

He seized the girl and dragged her toward the rear door. She was shaken, speechless. He grabbed a coat and threw it at her. "You go outside, gal!"

She hesitated.

"Move you ass!"

He whirled and ran back into the melee, shoving and punching his way to the bar. His guitar lay on the floor, like a butchered animal, a hole gaping from the box. He grabbed it up anyway and ran.

Outside, the girl still cringed against the wall, afraid. He took her wrist and pulled her toward the street. They ran several blocks before she fell, scraping her knees and cutting her free hand on the gravel. "Oh, Lawd," she cried. "Don't let him find me! He'll kill me! "

Her name was Lethe Massey and she was eighteen years old. She had run away from her husband because he beat her and forced her to work for his drinking money. Lethe had come to Bossier City from Baton Rouge and had taken a new name. The money she had been offered for stripping was irresistible. She hadn't liked it at first, but after a short while she learned the ropes, discovered that she had a unique talent, and began cashing in on her obscene act.

They made love on an old stained mattress in a room in the Market Street Hotel. "Y'know," Huddie said at last, "youse too pretty a gal to be doin' stuff like that."

She shrugged. "Don't matter now, anyway."

"Jus' as well. I don't like you workin' there."

"Why should *you* care? You don' know me. 'Sides, it's none of you business." She turned her head and stared at the wallpaper. Huddie reached over and stroked her shoulder.

"I care on accounta I like you."

"Don' give me any of you shit-lippin'."

"Baby!"

She reached over and jerked his face down to hers. Then she bit his lips hard and hungrily as she pulled at him with both hands.

"That's what you want," she said. "You don' give dog shit for me. All you want is lovin'."

Huddie stared at her. What am I doing here? he thought. I should be on my way to N'Orleans. But this gal . . . Her eyes flashed knowingly at him in the dimness. "Why you talk to me like that?" he said.

"I'se heard that before, I tell you."

"Honest. I even got some money. What say you and me travel together?"

"Shit."

"No, I play the music and you do the dancin'. What you say?"

"I say youse crazy."

Huddie cupped her face in his hands. "I ain't crazy. They's real money down N'Orleans way. I hear musicians really clean up down there."

Lethe laughed. "Now I know you crazy! Them poor niggas in N'Orleans ain't makin' nothin'. Half of 'em are on strike anyway 'cause of them Jim Crow law-passers. And I know, believe me. I worked in some of them claptraps with all them clay-faced ponies. Shit, them ol' wormy moneyboots ain't got nothin'. Nothin'!" She spat the words at him.

"On strike? What's that?" A term Huddie had never heard.

"That means nobody do any work on account they disagree wit' the boss."

"What's dat Jim Crow mean?"

"That's what the strike's about. Jim Crow law says niggas can't eat or even piss where the white folks do."

"Well," he said. "That ain't what *I* heard."

"You jus' never been in a big town where the whites outnumber the niggas." She got out of bed and started to dress. "Oh, what's the use!"

"What you mean?" Huddie examined her body. He wanted her again.

"I jus' mean we in the same boat, that's all. You headin' down to N'Orleans tryin' to get somethin' what ain't there, and I'se tryin' to make a livin' catchin' quarters and silver dollars. So what the hell am I hurryin' out again for? My old man sure as hell gonna find me and beat the livin' hell outta me, now you fixed me up so good over in Bossier an'---"

Huddie sat up in bed. "He ain't gonna find out! We gettin' outta here together, an' that's that!"

Lethe looked at him coldly, "He'd just as sure kill you, too. My old man's a mean bastard."

"Well, we head out. Trouble been followin' me most of my life anyway."

"It's this stinkin' rotten state! Loosiana ain't no good for niggas. Never has and never will be. Whitey just use you like youse an old cow, that's for sure. And the governor sittin' signin' Jim Crow bills like they is nothin' else for him to do. An' all the while them little babies got their bellies stickin' out from bein' hungry. Lawd, they can't even bury people right in this damn state!"

"Bury people?"

"Yeah. Down N'Orleans, land is so low, them dead bodies just pop right back up again. Scare the shit right out of you." She laughed again. "You sure you want to hook up with me?"

"Yeah," he said and had his palms on her backside, urging her down to him.

"Then we goin' to Texas! We gonna haul our asses out o' this shit-hole and go to Texas. Dallas is where we goin', and you know why? Because Dallas is where you can earn some good money. Everybody I talk to says they's makin' the bes' music in Dallas."

"Come here, gal. Just lookin' at you jigglin' makes me want more of that sweet lovin'."

She tilted her head. "You take me to Dallas?"

He nodded. "Yeah. Yeah, Lethe, I take you to Dallas."

"Promise?"

"Come here, you!"

She hopped on the bed and leaned over him. He reached up and fondled her breasts. "Oh, you my man, Huddie," she sighed. "We go to Dallas and maybe gets us a real nice place with runnin' water and a kitchen and some flowers growin' outside."

"That's right," he said. "That's right, gal. We go to Dallas." Then he pulled her down and began again.

Once and for all, his Fannin Street days were over.

###

Chapter Six

When they reached Dallas, both Huddie and Lethe were surprised to find a strangely different culture. There were black ghettoes, like the big one in the Deep Elm section of East Dallas, but it wasn't like Mooringsport where there were fewer whites than blacks. In Dallas, whites and blacks mingled in an indefinable way to Huddie. The only word he could think of was *civilized*.

But they had second thoughts about teaming up as an act. After two weeks they found the competition was too much for them and their income was virtually nonexistent. Lethe wanted to return to stripping, but Huddie wouldn't permit it. She took a job as a waitress at a run-down barbecue and Huddie worked on a cotton farm out toward Terrell. They were renting a shack in the Deep Elm section for eight dollars a month.

Working hard in the summers in order to survive the winters, Huddie soon found himself in demand. The local farmers wanted the man who could pick more cotton and work more rows in a single day than any three other pickers. The pay got better, and Huddie found he could stash away a few coins while still drinking and rambling several evenings a week.

The first year went quickly and was relatively trouble free. Huddie went into town, Lethe remained home and cooked his meals. In the summer of the second year they were legally married by a justice of the peace, and Huddie was made a leadman on one of the largest cotton farms in East Texas. At first, marriage seemed good for Huddie. Evenings were spent making love to his guitar and his woman; days were spent sweating, working, fixing the house, chopping and picking cotton, and even nursing the bougainvillea vines into blossoming health. Rambling nights were few, all-out drunks only once- or twice-a-month affairs. All in all, it was one of the calmest periods of his life since his early school days, when the only trouble he'd had was an occasional fight behind the church.

In 1909, Dallas was the chief marketing center for all the farm crops on the vanishing frontier. Placid, dusty and humid, it was a sweltering terminal for the farmers and workers of Terrell, Mesquite, Corsicana, Denton, Wortham and Tyler, the chief surrounding communities. Nightlife for the blacks was mainly kept along Elm -- a street that began with ramshackle buildings and plank boardwalks and ended in a cluster of the ever-present bawdy houses, bars and dimly lit cafes where the local musicians entertained all who could afford the price of whiskey.

For the most part, the houses along Elm were wooden hovels, their sloping roofs riddled with rot and hastily patched with cardboard, tar paper and tin, and their window shutters hanging askew on rusty hinges. The dust and dung in the streets clung like talcum, and when it rained the roads ran brown and slippery.

Throughout these years, Huddie, as always, was a man of extremes: when he drank he stayed drunk for days; when he tended to his job or household he was the perfect worker and husband. His music took second place to nothing, and he started performing with a boisterous vigor. His popularity quickly rose and he eagerly pursued dozens of sexual adventures. He became a flashy dresser.

The marriage finally began to decay. More than once he found Lethe with another man, and more than once he found himself in knife fights because of her. The first time, after his rage drove him to cutting the man seriously and beating Lethe, he went out of the house with his guitar and didn't return for two months, during which he bedded a long procession of women and drank and fought his way from one end of Elm to the other and back again.

He finally returned to Lethe and forgave her, explaining that he was going to try to make even more money than they made before.

The next year, in February, 1915, he announced he was going to Wortham to work for the railroad, and Lethe reluctantly consented to stay home and wait for him.

The land southwest of Dallas was forested with a lush blanket of piney woods, and the country around Wortham was a rolling farmland bordered by spruce, pine and scrub oak. The railroad had wedged its way through from Houston to Dallas, through plowed cotton fields and heavy brush. Huddie got a job as a brakeman -- a "stinger" -- for the seventy-mile railroad spur between Wortham and Dallas-Fort Worth. He frequently had a two- or three-day layover at one end or the other, and when in Wortham he would stroll the three-block Main Street, running alongside the tracks, past the dozen brick buildings shielded from the sun by eaves of corrugated tin. Anything that happened in Wortham happened on Main somewhere along these three blocks -- and one of the things that happened to Huddie was the son of Alec Jefferson. He was seventeen years old and weighed almost two hundred and fifty pounds. He was called Lemon. And he was blind.

It was early in August, and Huddie had spent a free afternoon drinking beer and chatting with friends about the women of Houston. The growing war in Europe was of little interest to them -- East Texas was their whole world. Later that evening Huddie was walking, trying to decide where to eat, when he saw an obese figure grope for support against a boardwalk lamppost in front of the post office. The man wore rimless glasses and a tattered pair of faded blue trousers, and his face was round, with thick lips that curled back on themselves. His eyes squinted, and behind the glasses little crescents of light shone on sweating cheeks. He carried a guitar.

Huddie stopped and regarded the figure for several minutes, waiting for him to play. Huddie had heard about Blind Lemon Jefferson, the fat boy who made his living singing for picnics and breakdowns in the farmland between Wortham and Mexia, but he'd never seen him before.

Huddie took his own guitar and sat down beside him, strumming a few tentative chords. Lemon whirled and groped at him harshly. "Who's that?" he said.

"Mind if I sit in?"

"Get outta here! I don't need no help!"

The boy's attitude surprised Huddie. He swallowed slowly and rested his guitar between his legs. "Sorry," he began, "but I---"

"Get you ass outta here! You ain't gettin' none o' my action!" The boy's breath smelled of sour whiskey, and a facial tic made his jowls quiver.

Huddie tried to placate him. "Don't want none of yours," he said softly. "I jus' heard you and thought I'd play along."

"Well, you start thinkin' different," Lemon said curtly. "I always play alone. Who the hell are you?"

"Name's Ledbetter. Workin' for the railroad and stayin' down by the barracks."

"Well, get on back down there, Ledbetter, before I break you neck. Fuckin' snakes crowdin' the whole town!"

Huddie frowned. This boy's got a lot of sass, he thought. Fat, blind and barefoot, and he's telling me he'll break my neck. His frown turned to a bemused grin. "Hey, there," he said. "You gotta be careful how you talkin'. Youse the bigges' and softes' target for a knife I ever seen."

Before Huddie knew it the fat boy was on his feet, his guitar in the dust, and his right hand swinging a long cane knife like a horizontal pendulum.

"Okay, snake!" Lemon was yelling. "I maybe can't see you too good, but I can smell you! Come on!"

Huddie saw the mask of sudden hatred on the boy's face, his lips parting grotesquely, revealing pointed brown teeth. Lemon seethed his defiant words through a trickle of saliva. Huddie stood up, guarding against a quick lunge. This was ridiculous. Here he was, one of the strongest men in the area, getting into a fight with a fat blind boy. No use arguing, he thought. This kid won't even admit he's *blind*!

"Okay," he said finally. "Don't want no trouble. Jus' thought you could teach me one of you songs. I thought I knowed 'em all." And flinging his instrument over his shoulder, Huddie walked away. He turned back once, and Lemon was again sitting on the boardwalk, strumming softly as if nothing had happened. Huddie shook his head and went straight back to the barracks for some food, a woman, a few drinks and a good night's sleep.

He got everything but the sleep. With his belly full and still a half a bottle of whiskey left, he sat against a wall near his bed in the darkness and strummed a soft song to himself. As he did, he thought about Mooringsport and wondered what his father was doing. He hadn't been home for more than five years, and the irregular correspondence between him and his parents when he lived in Dallas had stopped. The last he'd heard was that Edmond was working his own small place across the lake at Plum Point. His mother stayed at home, for the most part, and his father, as always, was saving as much money as he could to buy another plot of land on the other side of the Cushman place. He got dreamy, and he fell asleep against the wall thinking of poor little Benjamin Capp. Wonder what happened to him?

*   *   *   *   *

Huddie exploded awake and had his gun in front of him in less than a second. There was someone in the room. The massive shadow filling the doorway cut off the night's silver light. It was the blind boy -- what was his name? Lemon.

"What you want?" Huddie asked, remembering the long blade flashing in the Wortham sunlight that afternoon.

"Mr. Ledbetter?" The fat boy's voice was softer this time, almost respectful.

"What you want? You gonna get you head blown off you come in here with that knife."

"Ain't got my knife," the boy said. "Jus' came to say I'se sorry. Folks in the bar tol' me who you is. You *Huddie* Ledbetter? Heard you name once."

Huddie stashed his gun back into his deep overalls pocket. He was mighty pleased someone had known his name. "That's okay," he said. "You don't has to say nothin'." Huddie struck a match, and in the yellow glow he saw the eyes staring at nothing. Lemon stood in the doorway holding his guitar as Huddie touched the tip of the match to a coal-oil lamp.

"What song you want to learn?" Lemon asked.

"You want some whiskey?" Huddie asked, pointing at the half-empty bottle. Lemon didn't follow his finger, but for the first time a glimmer of a smile came to the flaccid face.

"Yeah."

Huddie guided Lemon's hand to the bottle and the boy took a long pull on it. "Where you from?" he asked at last.

"Loosiana. Mooringspo't."

"I ain't never been up there. I ain't never been north of Corsicana. Spend most of my time in Mexia. Don't 'spect I'll ever get there."

"There's a lot goin' on in Dallas. Down on Elm you could make money, 'stead of sittin' in front of the post office down here for pennies."

"Don't need nothin' much more. My folks feed me and give me a bed and don't make me work. They think I'se blinder than I really is."

Huddie smiled, took a drink from the bottle and passed it back to Lemon. The boy's stomach was so large that when he played his guitar it rested on top of the bulge, just beneath his chin. He began to sing:

> *I stood on the corner and almos' bust my head,*
> *I stood on the corner and almos' bust my head,*
> *I couldn't earn enough money to buy me a loaf*
> *of bread.*

Huddie didn't touch his guitar that early morning. In a high-pitched nasal voice, Blind Lemon Jefferson sang the backcountry blues of

East Texas. It was a new sound to Huddie, the repetitive lines and notes, the screeching field hollers telling of the dried-up land south to the Brazos, the poverty and loneliness and disappointments that echoed through the songs like distant train whistles.

After that, Huddie looked forward to his layovers in Wortham. With every visit he learned more about Lemon's music. New guitar techniques, song inflections and variations, how to command different and better sounds from the stringed box held tightly under his massive arms. He drank and sang along the Wortham streets, learning the blues of Blind Lemon Jefferson.

Huddie played his spirituals, his cakewalks, the folk tunes from his youth, but Lemon was unimpressed. Huddie lacked the suffering, he said, and Lemon insisted that he couldn't play the blues unless he learned to feel them. He told Huddie pathetic stories of suffering, horrible tales of disease and drought, stories of sore-ridden black men, of women in the fields whose bloody fingers stained the cotton, of whips in the hands of sadistic men and of children who died every day from rat bites. There were images of exposed bone and absent eyes, of crippled old men and lifeless babies and mothers who sold their milk.

And somehow during these months of Wortham layovers, while Huddie was walking the ties or nailing the rattlers, while he was greasing the bearings or riding the blinds, even through the grime and smoke of the roundhouse, Lemon's message got through.

And the blues began to close in on him.

###

Chapter Seven

At the end of the summer Huddie decided to quit the railroad and get back to Lethe and his music in Dallas. The railroad work offered him nothing but calluses on the wrong fingers and sweat for the wrong reasons. He went back to Lethe and resumed a marriage too-long dormant to be revived, and amid the battling and the cursing and the infidelities, Huddie rambled along Deep Elm. He sang his new blues, nurtured and nourished by frequent returns to Wortham. He picked cotton during the day and at night, when lesser men would be stretched out exhausted at home, he drank, sang and jellyrolled whoever was nearest at hand. He tried to persuade Blind Lemon to come up to Dallas, but the fat boy couldn't break away from his poor parents. And as Huddie hammered and banged his way to wider celebrity, he fell in love again.

It happened on a sultry evening in Rockwell. Huddie was staggering back from a party. He had started drinking early, and he walked uncertainly, his mind a blank and his guitar slung casually over his shoulder. A pint of whiskey gurgled in his back pocket.

The scented air was alive with fireflies and he grabbed out and caught one. It squished in his palm, leaving a tiny fluorescent puddle. He wiped it off on his shirt.

He saw the tent as he turned from the dirt road. Yellow light was seeping through the canvas flaps and he heard faint clapping and then the sound of a spiritual. He headed toward it.

The revival was in full sway. Huddie stood outside, drinking from the bottle and tapping his foot along with the singing. And then he heard it.

Someone was playing a guitar, but it was unlike any sound he had ever heard. The notes and chords seemed fuller and more complex, almost as if two guitars were playing simultaneously. Nothing he had ever played, no peak of frenzied strum or rampant run had ever sounded like the guitar he now heard. He shoved the bottle in his pocket and headed directly for the rectangular netting of the entrance. Quietly, he entered the meeting and stood motionless beside the last row of wooden chairs.

There, in the glaring light from the unshielded white and yellow bulbs strung in a flickering network above the congregation, a young girl dressed in a long white gown was singing:

> *There's a man*
> *goin' 'round takin' names,*
> *There's a man*
> *goin' 'round takin' names,*
> *He has taken my*
> *mother's name and has*
> *left me*
> *here in vain!*
> *There's a man*
> *goin' 'round takin' names.*

But it wasn't the girl or the song that transfixed Huddie. It was the guitar she held. It was larger than Huddie's and its neck was thicker.

And it had twelve strings.

When the song was over, the girl put the instrument down delicately beside her and sat attentively as the preacher implored the heavenly hosts to spew down upon the tortured earth their everlasting glory and divine salvation. Then she picked it up again and sang another spiritual. The congregation clapped and yelled. Huddie moved not at all.

He couldn't remember exactly how many songs she'd sung, but when the congregation began shuffling from the tent, he emerged from his trance and strained to keep his eye on the girl. She had put the guitar on the floor and was talking to the preacher.

He walked forward but ignored them. His gaze was fixed on the guitar. Twelve strings, he counted quickly. And twelve tuning keys. He remembered that many street musicians had played double-string instruments. Even Blind Lemon played the mandolin sometimes. It was not uncommon to nail extra strings onto a guitar. But this was new. Store-bought, the chrome keys glistening.

" 'scuse me, m'am. Can I see you guitar?"

"See here, mister," the preacher interrupted. "I said the meeting's over. Now what do you want?"

"That's all right, papa," the girl said. "He's just asking about my guitar." She held it toward him, and he took it like it was a newborn infant. He held it out across his massive palms, cautiously. "Go on," she said, "you can play it if you want."

Huddie sat down and ran his thumb experimentally across the strings. Then he grasped the neck in his left hand and strummed a simple chord progression. C, F, G7...

103

"Y'know," he said, "that first song I heard you play, 'bout the man goin' 'round takin' names. That's the first song my mama taught me when I was little." Then he sang it for her, tentatively at first, not believing the sound he himself was producing, and then burst into a gusty second verse and tapped his feet hard against the floor. The girl's expression visibly changed, and the preacher came over from his chair. It was their turn to stare.

When he was finished, the preacher looked at him with new respect. "Son, when you come to us here I thought first you were just some tramp looking for a handout. Now I think you got yourself a special gift in them hands. That's what it is, a gift from God."

Huddie mumbled something, a trifle embarrassed. "I been singin' a good deal, sir. Ever since I can remember, as a matter o' fact. But I ain't never seen or played a twelve-string guitar before. It's the bes' instrument I ever heard."

*   *   *   *   *

"You bastid! You ain't takin' that money jus' to go buy yourself that guitar!" Lethe screamed as she stood in the doorway. She was haggard and tired, her face drawn from late nights and hard work. Huddie continued to scour the house for money.

"You can yell there all you want," he said. "I got to get me a twelve-string guitar. I can make us more money with one o' them!"

"An' spend it downtown with those bitches," she said. "That's money we been savin' and now you want to go spend it on somethin' we don't need."

"I *do* need it," he said, peering into a coffee can. Finally he gave up the search and counted the bills. He had thirty-six dollars and some change.

He turned toward Lethe, who still barred the doorway. "Now, you don't move away from there I gonna come on right through you. Get outta the way, Lethe."

"I ain't movin' till you gimme at least half o' that money back," she said. "'Cause I earned it, too, workin' with you in those goddam fields. It's half mine!"

Huddie paused. She was right, he thought. Besides, he should be able to get one for eighteen dollars if he threw in his old guitar. He reluctantly counted out eighteen dollars and tossed it on the bed. "Okay. Here's you part." Then he left and headed toward town.

Three hours later he found a twelve-string in a music store near the railroad tracks. It cost him fifteen dollars and his old guitar. He gladly paid it. He spent the rest of the money on a bottle of whiskey and sat for the rest of the day in a back corner of Milo's Bar, practicing.

And so it went. Evenings, he played in Milo's for money. Days were spent sleeping and practicing. He saw nothing of Lethe and continued to have nightly affairs with the women of Deep Elm. He took a room in a boarding house and eventually forgot about her completely. One day he went to collect his things, but she was gone.

On a drizzly morning in December, 1916, Blind Lemon Jefferson tracked him down, and they decided to combine their talents. They played where they could, Huddie sometimes shuffling and dancing to Lemon's harsh music. Still, there wasn't enough money to keep them going for long. Night after night the two played together. Lemon drank too much. He would shove his battered guitar under his chair and make a clumsy attempt at love with one of the women. Huddie watched him sadly. Lemon was only twenty years old and already looked twice that.

Early in February, Lemon accepted an offer to wrestle in town. It was a novelty act in which two blind men would wrestle each other for three falls, groping and grunting around the ring like bewildered animals. Lemon was large and soft enough to avoid serious injury, but it was a degrading, brutal way to make a few dollars. The wrestling promoter gave him a meal, which he ate with his hands.

Meanwhile, on the nights when Lemon was wrestling, Huddie sang and played on Deep Elm. He was making more money now and trying to save some for a down payment on a used Ford, though most of it still went for women and whiskey. He slept in many beds, fist and knife fights were weekly events, and no one could keep up with him when he was rolling fast. When he was drunk he would sometimes physically force a woman to ride with him or a bartender to pour him another drink. He was feared by the most hardened Dallas prostitutes.

But he had a plan: he and Lemon would buy that Ford and play for every dance within a hundred miles. The word coming in from the outlying towns of Marshall, De Kalb, New Boston and even Texarkana was that people had heard of Huddie and Lemon and wanted them for special events, breakdowns and sukey-jumps. They even had one request from the Salvation Army in Ft. Worth to play at a fundraising picnic.

Huddie and Blind Lemon began to rely on each other more and more. They even worked out a routine for when a fight broke out -- Huddie would hustle Lemon under the nearest sturdy table, where he would protect the guitars while Huddie cracked skulls.

Huddie began calling himself "The King o' the Twelve-String Guitar." Blind Lemon finally gave up his grotesque life as a novelty wrestler, and the two of them bought a Model T Ford. With everything they owned in the rear seat, Huddie drove the automobile like a maniac while the moon-faced Lemon squinted ahead and insisted he could take a turn behind the wheel.

On the roads between the towns their conversation most often consisted of Blind Lemon's pronouncements of his hatred of white people. "They's out to get every nigga in the fuckin' world," he said one day between Tyler and Longview. "Can't see how you puts up with it."

"Don't make no difference to me who's handing over the money, black or white, jus' as long as I get my share."

"You ain't never gonna get a fair share, that's for sure. Shit, them white bastids almost killed my mama and papa."

Huddie just shrugged. "Don't know nothin' 'bout that. My papa always got along real good with the white men up in Mooringspo't, 'cept when I got into all the trouble."

"That's what I mean. They robbed him by threatenin' what they gonna do with you. They don't ever give you a fair share of what you got comin' to you. You work for them and you wife and children work for them when they should be in school instead of workin' their fingers raw in the sun. Ain't right to have them little bitty babies all dusty and thirsty when they should be havin' fun and learnin' somethin'. All you mean to them is you is jus' a workin' machine and nothin' else. I hate the white man, Huddie, and I ain't that blind. Sometimes I can't stand it when you goes lickin' around them. Ain't gonna get you nowhere."

"My daddy once told me that you ain't never gonna get nowhere in the world unless you work among the whites, an' I believe it."

"Shit!"

"That's what I mean, Lemon. You say 'shit.' That's all you say. What does it hurt to say 'thank you' when they give you the money? If that's lickin' at 'em, I'se gonna lick. I ain't gonna spend my life jus' fightin' with the whores. No, man, the 'King o' the Twelve-String Guitar' is gonna get rich on the white people's money. Don't want no trouble. Jus' want to play the music they want to hear."

Lemon pointed to the fields outside. "I can't see too good, but I see 'nuff. You try to tell that to them folks."

Huddie looked where he pointed and saw that they were passing a decrepit wooden shack whose brown and sooty planks were falling away. Huddie pulled the car to an abrupt stop. "Lemon," he said, turning in the seat. "I'se gonna prove what I say to you." He got out of the car and, as Lemon squinted after him, strode to the front yard where two bloat-bellied, grimy children were playing with a chicken. After inquiring where their mother was and discovering that both parents were out in the field picking cotton, he gave the older of the two children a five-dollar bill. When he was back in the car he turned and with a half-sneer said, "Lemon, that was white men's money I gave those hungry children. You think they gonna throw it away?"

Blind Lemon just grunted.

That evening in Longview, Huddie and Lemon made twenty dollars.

The summer went quickly and the money came faster. Huddie worked constantly on the twelve-bar stanzas of the backcountry of East Texas. His singing became textured with the expressions and inflections of the rural areas. He began to use the falsetto more and experimented with unorthodox techniques. In honky-tonks, in tenements and windowless rooms, with banjos and fiddles, with washtub bases and "spasm bands," the music went on.

That is, the music went on until the first day of December, 1917. Huddie and Lemon were playing in a sporting house in Marshall, Texas. It was run by two sisters, and their establishment was one of the best. They had even printed up a broadside advertising "The Mahogany Mansion."

MADAMES POLLY & BESS WHITE
No One Is A Stranger
The Mahogany Mansion–1585 West Houston

There are few places where the stranger and the friend can find
handsomer women than at The Mahogany Mansion. Madames
White are
beautiful octoroons and have employed the twenty-two
"entertainers
from the East." Among a collection of costly paintings and
priceless pearls, diamonds, rubies, emeralds and other rare gems,
the girls give you the "goods right from the spring." To visit
Mahogany Mansion is like witnessing a dazzling electrical
display on the Cascade. Anyone who knows yesterday from today
will agree the Mahogany Mansion can put the stranger on the
"proper path" away from hold-ups, brace games and loneliness.
There is something always new at the Mahogany Mansion,
where
the best musicians of Texas and Louisiana are invited to
entertain. "A good time" is our solitary purpose. PHONE 456

Underneath, scrawled with a quill pen, was:
Now playing weekends, Mr. Huddie Ledbetter from
Louisiana and Mr. Lemon Jefferson from Texas.

It was the first time he had ever seen his name advertised. They had been playing at Polly and Bess's for two weeks, and early one morning, when Lemon fumbled his way upstairs with a quadroon named Shirley Tender, Huddie's whiskey-fogged eyes wandered to Polly White herself.

He remembered that a long time ago he heard his father sing about a girl by the name of Becky Dean. Becky had made her living dealing Monte, playing Coon Can and shooting craps. She worked on the levees and was as hard-bitten as any man. But Becky was tender-hearted, in her own way, and would spend her last penny on her lover. Employing a device he had found to be almost foolproof, he altered the title and began to sing to her.

> *Polly White, she was a gamblin' gal,*
> *She win the money, and she win it fair.*
> *Polly White, walked all the way from East*
> *Saint Louis,*
> *When she didn't have but one thin dime,*
> *Didn't spend it for whiskey, honey and*
> *neither for wine,*
> *She spent it all on the sake o' that*
> *man o' mine.*

He noticed the flattery take effect. She turned to him. "Well, that's a fine old song, Mr. Ledbetter. I thank you for singin' it. But right now, I gotta close up."

Huddie frowned, "Hey, I didn't make up that pretty song for nothin'. Come on upstairs for a while."

"You've had too much whiskey."

"Nah, youse so pretty." Huddie reeled back and accidently knocked a bottle of gin from the table. It crashed to the floor.

"Damn it, Ledbetter! You is drunk! Get yourself outta here."

"C'mon, baby!" He grabbed at her. Polly took a hatpin from the sleeve of her dress and stabbed him hard on the arm.

"No!"

He tried to pull her to him, but she screamed. He hit her, hard, and she fell to the floor. He tore at her skirt, cursing, holding her hands tightly over her head and forcing himself into her.

The last thing Huddie remembered, before something crashed down on the back of his head, was that Madame Polly White, co-manager of The Mahogany Mansion, the fanciest cathouse in town, was a virgin.

*　　*　　*　　*　　*

He awoke in familiar surroundings. The cell was almost identical to the one in Shreveport: cement floors, a hard wooden pallet, heavy iron bars painted yellow. He tried to piece last evening together. He remembered Lemon disappearing up the stairway with one of the girls. Where was he now? He recalled spilling the gin, but between that and his surprise when he was on Polly was a blur.

He felt his head. There was a knot behind his right ear. He supposed someone had knocked him out from behind -- probably Sam Cole, the club's bouncer. And as he lay there, the only conclusion he could come to was that he had tried to rape Polly. He rebelled against the realization, but there was no alternative. He also remembered giving up the idea when he discovered she was a virgin -- he had decided in a flash there on the floor to just pick up his guitar and get out of there for good instead of getting into trouble again -- but he knew it no longer mattered.

He turned on the hard pallet and moaned. Jail again, when one more minute would have avoided it. He considered what the charges would be. Rape? Beating up a whore? But she wasn't a whore.

Robbery, then? But he didn't rob anything. An enormous remorse swept over him. He knew the procedure. The sheriff would come in a while, tell him what he was being held for, probably curse at him or otherwise let his hatred be known, and he'd be brought to trial. Who knew what would happen next.

As he thought about it, Huddie began to weep. The toughest, strongest cotton-chopper in the state seemed to fill with tears more frequently than his image dictated. And he prayed. For long minutes he prayed for the power to bring back the evening, to do it all over again, to be allowed to show someone – anyone -- that he wasn't going to go through with it. That he was drunk and disorderly, yes, but that he intended getting out of there and not causing any further trouble. And he wept a long time. Contrition was a new emotion to Huddie.

That afternoon he was informed by the sheriff, a weasel-faced type who made it very clear that he and the White girls had a very tidy arrangement in Marshall, that he was being officially booked for assault with intent to commit murder, and that Polly White had insisted charges be brought and trial date be set as soon as possible.

Murder? Huddie's protestations went unheeded. No one, of course, would believe his version of the incident, and the sheriff wouldn't listen to more than a few words.

He wondered again about Lemon. What had they done with him? Probably nothing. He couldn't know what Huddie knew and he probably got off with just being fired and told about Huddie's fate. He'd go back to Dallas somehow, in their Model T Ford, finally getting his turn at the wheel. And where was his guitar? Would there be a note from his father -- would his family even be informed?

Huddie supposed not, and wept again.

He was transferred from the jail to the courthouse in New Boston, Texas, nearly a hundred miles north. His defense attorney was better than he expected, though, and after hearing Huddie's version of the incident, he entered a plea of guilty to the second charge of assault to commit rape but not guilty to the first charge of assault with intent to commit murder. Cross-examination, though brief, showed that Huddie never actually did more physical damage than slap Polly, and the judge, who turned out to be a devout Baptist with strong anti-vice predispositions, seemed impressed by defense counsel's summation. The trial was a brief one, lasting only thirty minutes. When it was over, Huddie's effects, including his new guitar, were retained by the Harrison County clerk. On December 13, 1917, the thirty-year-old Huddie was sentenced to one year of hard labor on the Harrison County chain gang.

###

Chapter Eight

On his first day on the Harrison County chain gang Huddie Ledbetter saw things that would have aged any other man forty years. The conditions to which he was exposed would indelibly stain his mind. Nothing he had ever seen before -- neither the vilest mistreatment of men or the filthiest living conditions -- could even approach life on a Texas chain gang.

On that first day he was locked up in a stone cell that measured three by seven feet. His bed was a pile of rotting straw, clumps of fetid feces surrounded him and flies as big as fingernails swarmed everywhere. By mid-morning the temperature was more than a hundred degrees, but at the end of the day he was glad to be back in that hovel.

Since 1902, the number of prisoners had far exceeded the available camps in the state of Texas, and overcrowding had become a horrendous problem. The solution was simple, one that would provide more revenue to the state: the prison would simply lease out convict gangs for use on state projects. Shackled together, the convicts could drain the swamps, work the quarries and build roads through the woods and marshes. Under armed supervision, men, women and even children worked as much as sixteen hours at a stretch. As many as three hundred convicts were chained together, sleeping at night in the ditches, the chain secured at regular intervals with a twenty-pound iron ball.

At one point seventy-three girls barely in their teens were shipped to Georgia to work in the phosphate mines. The law ruled that the most trivial offenses were enough to send a man to the work camps for months. Inability to prove means of support, or a card game played on a Texas train, were evidence enough to sentence a man to six months of hard labor in the broiling Brazos bottomland. The gangs were, for the most part, black. Any rebellion, no matter how insignificant, was met with extreme punishment. The bastinadoes -- beatings with a heavy cudgel -- were delivered indiscriminately, and the "red heifer" whips snapped out at the workers with clock-like regularity. At the base camp a series of "sweat boxes" were used to curb any rebellious spirit; as many as fifty recalcitrant blacks were packed and left to fry in less than a hundred square feet. Even though most of these conditions and punishments had long since been outlawed by Congress, the rebellious nature of Texans defiantly ignored it. The Ku Klux Klan wielded enormous power over the prison heads, and in many cases the officials themselves were Kleagles and Grand Wizards. Floggings with the "bat," a fourteen-pound leather strap, were daily occurrences, and lynchings and castrations were frequent. Men and women were burned to death, hanged from cottonwood limbs, their mutilated corpses charred with blowtorches and torn to shreds with corkscrews. In the town, men were constantly reminded of Texas justice when the fingers of lynched corpses were displayed in butcher shop windows.

Prisoners were forced to wear leg irons to which were welded the heavy heads of sledgehammers and picks. The day before Huddie was admitted to the Harrison County office, he heard that forty blacks on a chain gang nearby had hamstrung themselves to avoid further work and torture. Naked women were flogged mercilessly in front of all, and when they finally died, their bodies were left to rot.

In the ditches, cries of hunger, pain and disease rang through the night. A whimper was treated as a curse, and the guards were quick to reprimand. Almost every form of medieval punishment was practiced: heavy iron straps were used to bind children; mace-like clubs were demonstrated to inspire terror; it was even rumored that some camps used stretch racks when someone tried to escape. When whole families were sentenced to the chain gangs and other labor camps, the youngest offspring was often beaten to death in front of the parents as an example, or else the heads of infants -- useless as workers -- were bashed in with rifle butts. When a man collapsed from sheer overexposure in the sweltering Brazos, he was often buried alive as work continued uninterrupted and the roads and railway right-of-way were laid. Twenty years later the Japanese would invade China and commit what would infamously be called "The Rape of Nanking," and the atrocities reported would seem no more harsh than those perpetrated in the name of Texas justice in the early twentieth century.

The food was nothing but stale bread and piles of grits, washed down with swamp water if one were lucky enough to survive the wolfpack battles to get some. Men and women bit and kicked each other to get the smallest scrap, and human excrement was eaten by children too young to know better. Open, festering wounds were packed with mud to coerce yet another day's work from a man. Skulls were found as new dirt was overturned, and the hard objects struck with shovel tips were frequently identified as human bones. The prisoners slept in heaps, stacked like cordwood, and when it was time to go back to the roads, they were shipped in horse-drawn boxcars with five tiers of bunks, with only eighteen inches of headroom. When the work site was reached, often only half the load was still alive.

The stories of these conditions were somberly relayed to the new prisoners by the guards: about the thirty women and girls who dug a building foundation with forty-pound balls slung around their necks to keep them stooped low to the ground; about the man who tried to escape and was recaptured in an hour, only to be strung by his heels in the living quarters with an axe-handle forced deep into his rectum; about the small gang near Houston who were stoned to death by another gang when the latter was told the first had stolen food from the supply shack; about the little boy who was quartered with a machete before his mother's eyes because the mother refused to dispose of the child herself.

Huddie didn't see this, of course, but he realized what the system was like just by crossing -- or being led across -- the road from the cell blocks to the headquarters building, an L-shaped, wood plank structure set on brick pilings. He thought it would be a relief to get out into the air, but the area around the cell block was putrid.

At headquarters, he was pushed toward a long oak counter. "Okay, off with your clothes," the guard behind it said indifferently. At Huddie's blank look, he repeated the order more roughly. "You get your stripes here," the guard said. After Huddie slowly undressed, the guard threw a set of stripes at Huddie. "Put these on and get to the next room."

Huddie obediently dressed and shuffled to another door, behind which a porcine man with a whistle around his neck sat behind a large desk, dipping snuff. Huddie stood before him as the man reached out and took a paper in one hand. He scanned it briefly and looked up in contempt at Huddie.

"Another rapist, eh?" he said. "Well, they ain't no black pussy here. All they is, is work. And all's you gotta know right now is that if you don't do your share, you won't get out alive. Obey the rules and keep your nose clean and you won't end up like this." He picked up a dry, sausage-like object and held it toward Huddie. "Know what this is?"

Huddie looked at it and knew, but said nothing.

"I'll bet you do. From a guy who thought he'd run away. Another one of those dumb fuckin' brothers of yours. Understand?"

Huddie nodded.

"Now, it says here," the guard went on, throwing the object aside on his desk, "that you got a good medical. Pretty strong looking, too. We can always use good strong bucks here." He looked up and grinned through brown teeth for the first time. "Except they usually don't stay strong for long. And sometimes they don't stay bucks, either." Then he chuckled as he indicated the sausage again with his head.

"Now, we're gonna try you as a gang-guard first. See how you make out. Down here we got maybe a hundred on a chain, working straight across a field breaking rocks for the railroad, and a shotgun on horseback watching 'em. One of the inmates gets to wear only shackles so he can move around. He don't have to break rocks, but he's got a lot of other muscle work to do. He watches and makes sure it moves along without being held back by some laggard who won't do his share. He gets leftover rocks, too. Get me?" The guard spit on the floor beside his chair, and a brown goo oozed down his chin. He wiped it off with a finger.

"Yessuh," Huddie said.

He was taken to a far-off field where a gang was working its way along a stretch of bedrock extending into the distance. His feet were

118

shackled with an eighteen-inch chain, and he was given a long, sharp machete. He wondered why, since there were no crops evident that had to be chopped. The guard motioned for him to follow and rode off down the long line of workers. Huddie saw women chained beside men, children tied with wire to their mother's chains. They were all linked to a long, heavier chain of more than five hundred feet, and as those at the front finished their work and moved ahead, the others were forced to step along to the work that was left unfinished.

"Sometimes we get a chunk just too damn big to get all crushed before we move along," the guard said as Huddie hobbled along next to his horse. "When that happens you take a hammer from the last man and finish it yourself. Easier for you to catch up with the gang than have the whole line stopped because one nigger couldn't make it."

As he looked down to see whether Huddie understood, Huddie watched the chain gang. They were heading toward the end of it, and it looked like there were at least a hundred on the chain as the other guard had said. Huddie hadn't seen anything like it. Emaciated, diseased men and women, struggling with hammers and picks too heavy to lift, to break rocks too large to be broken by any but the strongest. He realized his work would probably be the hardest of all, and not as easy as it first had seemed. Not many on the chain could finish their own work before the gang moved on.

But he was completely unprepared for his next assignment. The guard picked up his horse's pace, noticing something farther down the line. "C'mon," he said abruptly. "There's one, now." Huddie tried to hop and hobble more quickly but couldn't. When he finally caught up to the guard, the man was pointing down with his Winchester.

"This happens too goddam often," he said disgustedly. "One of 'em dies or just plain falls down for good, and the others get slowed up. And we can't get 'em off the chain so we have to chop 'em off. That's your job, with the machete."

Huddie could only gape at the man. The man laughed briefly. "Yeah, it's a bad job, but they's welded on and I'm not getting down on that ground for nothin'! You just cut 'em off at the knee. The rest of the leg stays on. The next gang'll roll the guy over to the side or bury him, don't worry." Then he laughed louder, enjoying what might or might not have been a joke. "Besides, it'll probably get eaten before sundown. Fuckin' cannibals!"

Huddie's stomach turned. The man was a savage. He was worse than all the names he called the blacks on the gang! Huddie stood there, staring unbelievingly.

"Okay," the guard said. "May as well get your feet wet. Cut him off." Huddie looked down at the prostrate man and a gag came to his throat. After a while, with the guard chattering down at him unheard, Huddie looked up again.

"What..." He felt his throat tightening. "What if he ain't dead?"

"If he ain't workin', he's dead. Now chop him off so we can get back to the head of the line."

Huddie was paralyzed. He held the machete limply at his side, staring down at the man.

The guard edged his horse a few yards away from where Huddie stood and aimed the Winchester at him. "You chop him off that chain or your head gets blown off, you understand? They's lots more that want to be gang leaders around here."

Huddie still couldn't move. He was petrified, his mind refusing to accept the command.

"Listen, you black-ass bastard! I'll count to three and pull this fuckin' trigger! One!"

It was sheer self-preservation that moved Huddie's feet, the basic drive that forces humans into inhuman acts. He moved to the prone man's side, looking fearfully down at him, his fist clenched tightly around the handle of the machete.

"Two!"

Huddie raised his hand to stop the count. The machete's blade gleamed in the sunlight. Huddie saw the faces of the other prisoners watching without emotion.

In a fitful slash of the gray metal, in one blow Huddie severed the man's leg at the knee, and then vomited as he heard the guard's horse gallop back to the front of the chain.

Huddie could only take two more days of it. As usual, he had devised a plan.

On the third day, his gang was working near the Sulphur River, clearing the woods for a road into Cookville. Huddie made certain that a large stump of oak was left behind for him to chop to bits as the gang moved farther southward. After the first day the guards had paid Huddie little attention, and he had worked hard and kept his mouth shut. He spoke to no one, not even to the other prisoners. The mounted guard was at the head of the column yelling instructions. Huddie tested his chained legs and judged just how much of a stride he could take. He decided to risk it. At the first opportunity he was over the fence and racing through the wooded area as fast as he could. He made a hundred and fifty yards before he heard the loud report of the Winchester and the yelling of the guard. He didn't stop to turn around. He reached the denser part of the woods and raced through the trees and brush until he thought he would pass out from exhaustion. He knew they would probably send dogs after him, and his only hope was to put as many miles between him and the dogs as possible.

He ran for another hour. When he finally stumbled into a barn belonging to a poor black farmer, his legs were bleeding. He persuaded the farmer to help him chisel off his chains and give him something to eat and drink. The old man was sympathetic. He gave Huddie a pair of overalls and told him which way to head for the best chance to beat the dogs. In a half hour Huddie was heading north toward a wide stretch of the Red River.

A day later he made it across the river into Arkansas, and a day after that he was in Foreman, hitching a ride down into Texarkana. There he washed dishes for three days, and with his pay he made his way to Mooringsport -- and home.

It had been nine years since he'd seen the farmhouse, but it was still the same. The porch had never been fixed, and the old rabbit hutch that he used as a boy was now a woodbin. As he stood in the waning light, he thought about what he would say. It didn't take much debate to decide to tell the truth. His family would have to hide him, give him some money and help him get away. Then he saw Sally. She was coming out of the cabin carrying a tub of water. She splashed it on the porch and began scrubbing with a broom. But the broom dropped from her hands when she saw him.

"Hello, mama," he said.

"Huddie!" Sally ran toward him, and Huddie lifted her up as if she were a toy. She began to cry, hugging him and kissing him and clutching him tightly. A few minutes later Wes came in from the fields and repeated the scene. And a few minutes after that Wes was firing questions at Huddie while Sally busied herself with dinner. Her prayers were answered and her son was home. That was enough for now.

Huddie noticed sadly that his father was strikingly older. At fifty-nine, his hair was gray and he had lost weight. There was a slight trembling in his hands when he sipped his whiskey, and it took him a little longer to answer a question. Sally, on the other hand, looked as young as ever. Her long hair was still coal black, and only around the eyes were there any hints of wrinkles. She was still as trim as she had been when he was a boy.

Huddie finished explaining his latest escapades in a relaxed, almost matter-of-fact manner. He was in trouble and he needed help. "If I can stay here for a while until the heat's off, then I'll start all over again. Don't want no more of that chain gang, papa."

"When you gonna stop that ramblin' around, Huddie? You been gettin' into trouble since you was a kid."

"Jus' don't know, papa. All the time I'se gettin' cheated, and it jus' make me mad as the devil."

"You always had a bad temper," Sally called as she came into the room. "How come Edmond ain't never like this? How come he can settle down and get married and you jus' keep runnin'?"

"Sorry, mama," Huddie said. "But I can't stand jus' workin' on the farm my whole life. Jus' a born rambler, I guess. I dunno."

"Ain't no such thing as a born rambler, Huddie," Wes said. "You should have a nice farm for yourself right here in Mooringspo't or a good job with the Gulf."

His mother agreed. "Make a right good livin' workin' out on the lake. Now you is jus' a convict."

Huddie shook his head contritely. "I ain't never gonna get in trouble no more. Gonna change my name and start all over again. Maybe down in N'Orleans."

"What you got to change your name for?" Wes asked. 'Shamed of Ledbetter?"

"No, papa, it's jus' that they is lookin' for Huddie Ledbetter. And besides, I cause you enough problems already. No, jus' gonna start all over again."

"The Lawd said in the Good Book, Huddie, that it ain't never too late to be born again. That's the way back to salvation."

"Oh, mama," Huddie said. "I didn't bring all that trouble on me. It jus' seems like everybody always doin' me bad, and I jus' can't stand to see that. Remember the trouble in Shrevepo't with the li'l blind girl? That's what I mean."

Sally eyed him suspiciously. "Shrevepo't? What trouble in Shrevepo't?"

"Now, Sally." Wes was on his feet and offering Huddie a drink. "That's jus' somethin' what happened a long time ago and we jus' didn't tell you. No matter now, anyhow. Huddie, how long you gonna stay here?"

"I dunno. I got to get some money somehow. I don't even have my guitar no more. They took it from me up in New Boston. Like to stay for Christmas before I go away again. Then maybe I'll write to Lethe and ask her if she don't guess she'll take me back and we start all over again. Maybe even have babies."

Wes looked intently at his son, then sighed. "If you make that promise to me and you mama to settle down and stop you ramblin', I give you some money for a right good start. We sellin' ten acres o' the farm, and we was gonna give Edmond up in Plum Point most of the money for his new spread, but you can have a share of it."

Huddie looked toward his mother to get her reaction, but her face showed only resignation. He turned back to Wes and nodded. "I promise, papa. Don't want no more trouble with the sheriffs."

During supper Huddie told them of his years in Texas with Lethe, and of the misunderstanding that had landed him on the chain gang. He chattered on about Blind Lemon Jefferson and the music of East Texas, and Wes and Sally ate and listened in silence.

By seven o'clock Huddie was sleeping deeply in his old shedroom. Wes Ledbetter and Sally rocked by the stove until well past midnight.

###

Chapter Nine

It was a sorrowful parting when Huddie got on the train for New Orleans. Wes sold his acreage, and the profits had been a Christmas gift to his two "sons." Edmond, his wife of one year, and their new baby, Florida, had come up for a special supper at the farm, and the entire family had enjoyed a few days of relaxation. But now, on January 2, 1918, it was time for Huddie to leave again. Armed with a new guitar, he was finally going to New Orleans, where he hoped to get a new musical start under a new name.

But there was no home in New Orleans for Huddie Ledbetter, alias Walter Boyd. Storyville, the official red-light district, had been closed the previous year, and many of the musicians had headed north. Besides, emerging from the mainstream of Storyville was the music of jazz and rhythm bands -- a sound far different from the songs of Huddie Ledbetter. Vocals and solos were rare, and Huddie was definitely a solo. Not many people paid attention to him. Reluctantly, a disappointed Huddie headed home again.

Much to his surprise Lethe was there in Mooringsport to meet him, begging forgiveness. Huddie took her in his arms and made promise after promise that he, too, would settle down and get a job. They decided to try to live a normal married life.

"The sheriff was out here lookin' for you," was the first thing Wes said when he saw Huddie. "Was the day after you left. I tol' him the last I heard was you was in Dallas pickin' cotton. Don't think he believed me, but he rode off and ain't come back since."

Huddie stayed around Mooringsport for two weeks, just playing his guitar and greeting old friends from his boyhood. His manner was guarded, as if he were trying to assure everyone that he was no longer the battling, roughhousing Huddie of ten years ago, but a more mature, more sensible man of thirty-one. He met little Benjamin Capp, now a foreman for the Gulf and married, with three children. A few of the girls he used to see were still single, and they all turned out for the one breakdown where he played. There were a few touchy moments, when other girls' husbands became apprehensive about their wives' attention to Huddie, but nothing serious occurred. He even saw his father's friend, Big Ted Promise, who had moved from Shreveport to Mooringsport and had also taken a job with the Gulf. His daughter, Martha, whom Huddie had first seen as a tiny baby, was now thirteen years old and one could tell she would develop into a stunning woman.

Lethe told him about the small rent-farm she and her brother had been working in De Kalb. It was dangerously close to the chain gang headquarters from which Huddie had escaped, but she assured him that the farm was remote, and that the "Boyd family" could live there safely as long as they remained quiet and Huddie didn't create any disturbances. They could get a good financial start, then move to wherever Huddie wanted. Against his better judgment, he decided it might be worth the risk.

He had the cotton completely planted by the end of February.

*　　*　　*　　*　　*

Before the sprouts were visible, Lethe became ill. To Huddie's confusion, she developed a thick, greenish discharge from her vagina, and her labia became tender and inflamed. She urinated frequently and painfully, and Huddie was alarmed when the doctor told him she had gonorrhea. He rushed out and bought his old cure-all, Lafayette's Mixture, which he administered to her in massive doses. Then, during an examination, it was found she had an abscess, possibly a tumor, on her cervix. It wasn't known then as cancer, but they realized she might not live. Lethe was taken to a black clinic, where she would have to stay for at least three weeks.

The old voodoo superstition crashed again on Huddie. He was certain he had transmitted the affliction, and began to drink heavily. He loved Lethe now, and in one of his rare nonmusical conversations with God, he asked why this had to happen when he demonstrated his good faith by ceasing his rambling.

There was no answer, so Huddie composed his own. The message was to ramble, to drink, to forget, to cast it all out.

He got drunk the evening he heard the news and stayed that way for two weeks. During this period, he went to Dallas often and, while careful not to let word of his antics spread too far, he rambled and caroused, trying to blur Lethe's image with whiskey and women. To prove to himself that he had lost none of his sexual strength, he rolled with every woman he could, regardless of how she looked -- always with Lethe's illness in the back of his mind. With the profits from his music and what he'd got so far from the small farm, he spent money lavishly.

When he came home, Lethe was dead. She'd been buried outside of De Kalb in the Harrell Cemetery. Huddie spent an entire month alone in the farmhouse, by turns brooding, crying and drinking. He saw no one and did no work. By the end of the month the weevils had ruined the entire cotton crop, but he didn't care.

What was left of his life? He could go back home again, but he had caused enough sadness to Wes and Sally. He could go back to Dallas, or maybe he could try a trip up north to Chicago, like he'd heard his old friend Blind Lemon Jefferson had done. He couldn't decide.

He began to make brief, tentative appearances in public around De Kalb, along the Red River in the northeast corner to Texas. One of them was a big dance in a schoolhouse. He carried his new gun and guitar with him and walked slowly, thinking of the songs he was going to sing. As usual, he toyed with lyrics and melodies of new songs he wanted to compose.

As he strolled along Mud Creek toward the Bethlehem schoolhouse three miles away, night birds began their twilight chirping and a soft breeze squirmed through the mesquite and chaparral. For the first time in almost five weeks, he felt relaxed and confident. He looked forward to a pleasant evening, and reminded himself to drink only a little or, better yet, nothing at all. It would be a long walk back home, but perhaps he could get a ride with someone. If he stayed sober it would be easier.

The Bethlehem schoolhouse was a dingy cube in an untended field of deer grass and scrub. Inside, the benches were shoved against the walls, the lanterns were lit, and the corn whiskey was plentiful. It was a loud and boisterous dance, but many people extended their condolences to Huddie as he played, or during short breathers outside on the veranda.

There were two surly men at the dance whom he knew to be tough types from Oak Grove, and he tried to avoid them throughout the evening. But as he was chatting on the veranda with a group of eager young women, the two men, now drunk, stumbled through the doorway and came up to him. Alex Griffin was a short, wiry cowboy-type with a drawn face and eyes so black one couldn't distinguish his pupils from his irises. Will Stafford was taller, and he was said to have a nasty disposition when he drank.

"Hey, you finally come outta hidin', Walter?" Stafford grinned at Huddie. He staggered to the railing and pushed a girl aside for space.

"Howdy, Will," Huddie said politely. "Howdy, Alex."

"Where you been?" Griffin asked. "Heard you went back down to Dallas."

Stafford laughed sarcastically. "Yeah, to pick up some more clap, that's what!"

Huddie knew they were asking for trouble, but avoided antagonizing them. "Now, don't you go talkin' that way around the wimmins, Will," he said, not looking at the girls. He tried to smile.

Stafford took a swig from his bottle and raised his arm, waving Huddie's words away. "Shit, don't bother me none," he said. "These here pretty gals oughta know what they gonna end up with, they go with you tonight."

"Will, I don't guess I'd talk like that any more. Why don't you jus' go back inside and have youself a good time." Huddie forced his smile this time.

"Stay where I want to, Boyd," Stafford said. He tried to put his arm around the girl next to him, but she wiggled away and stood with a friend behind Huddie.

Griffin jumped in. "That true you got the clap down in Dallas, Walter?"

Before Huddie could reply, Stafford blurted, "Shit! He got it somewhere, 'cause everybody sayin' he had it for years. The bastid, even his wife had it!"

Huddie stood up. "Now I'se tellin' you, Will. You shut you mouth right quick or you gettin' into mighty big trouble. I ain't lookin' for no fight. I jus' come here to play some music."

"You ain't no bigger'n me, Boyd," Griffin said as he noted Huddie's height. "What's all I hear 'bout you bein' the bes' fighter in the county? Man with the clap, and not even six feet?"

The taller Stafford grinned, towering over Huddie. "Yeah, don't go with this nigga tonight, girls, else you get it like his wife done."

Huddie reached out and grabbed Stafford's shirt tight in his fist and shook him twice. "Shut you mouth, Stafford," he seethed. "I'se warnin' you!"

With both hands, Stafford shoved him back, breaking his grip. "Get you fuckin' hands offa me, clap-man! That whore of yours died from it an' you know it!"

The last vestige of control left Huddie. He lunged at Stafford, knocking the bigger man off the porch with one punch. As Stafford fell, Huddie turned and crashed his foot into Griffin's groin, and then came down hard on the back of his neck. Griffin fell into a heap, but Huddie saw Stafford take a small revolver from inside his shirt and aim it at him. Before he knew what he was doing, Huddie kicked out and knocked the gun from Stafford's hands, then kicked Stafford hard in the side.

His own gun was in Huddie's hand, and Stafford's filthy face was cursing at him, and then the face had a bloody hole in it, just above the bridge of the nose, and everyone was screaming. Huddie stood rigid, staring unbelievingly at the widening red splotch and the now-vacant eyes of Will Stafford.

*   *   *   *   *

Wes Ledbetter's reply to Huddie's only permitted message from the De Kalb jailhouse was that he had sold twenty-three acres of his farm and was hiring two lawyers named Mahaffey and Keency to defend him. A few days later the three of them appeared, and Mahaffey and Keeney interviewed Huddie extensively while his father listened and fumbled nervously with a roll of bills.

In the following week, the two lawyers worked patiently with Huddie, attempting to construct a plea of self-defense. Huddie never mentioned his real name or his chain-gang sentence, and as far as anyone but Wes was concerned, he was Walter Boyd.

The trial was held in March, 1918, in the county courthouse of New Boston. It was a brief but noisy one. The eye-witnesses called in by Mahaffey and Keency verified Stafford's bad reputation. But the prosecution was brutal. Yes, Stafford was very drunk and undoubtedly would have been a very poor shot. Yes, Boyd carried a gun himself, illegally. Yes, he had been in a lot of fights in Dallas and De Kalb. Yes, Boyd had been unfaithful to his wife.

The judge, while agreeing with the self-defense verdict and dismissing the possibility of capital punishment, sent the jury to its deliberations with a sharp admonition that a man of the character of Walter Boyd constituted a potential menace to the citizenry of De Kalb.

The jury was out for only thirty-six minutes. The foreman passed a note to the judge and, after Huddie was told to stand, delivered the verdict: Guilty of assault with intent to murder.

With a sigh, the judge put the paper down and looked at Huddie. "It is the decision of this court that you, Walter Boyd, be sentenced to thirty-five years at hard labor at the state penitentiary in Huntsville, and that you be remanded to the county jail in New Boston until such time as you can be transferred by state authorities."

Mahaffey and Keency lost their appeal. The "King o' the Twelve-String Guitar" was in jail again, gray steel bars containing him, holding helpless the body and the mind that yearned to ramble and roll.

A short time later Huddie overpowered a jailer and escaped, but be was captured in three days and flogged with the "bat." With a physician in attendance, Huddie received thirty-eight lashes before the first trickle of blood appeared on his back and the whipping was ordered stopped. Security was increased, and shortly thereafter "Walter Boyd" was scheduled for transfer to the Huntsville unit of the Texas prison system.

Ahead of him were thirty-five desperate, wretched years.

###

Chapter Ten

On June 7, 1918, Huddie was taken to Shaw State Prison, ten miles away, where he was issued fatigues and confined. Two months later, in leg irons and handcuffs, he was escorted to Dallas and, from there, one hundred and fifty miles south to Huntsville.

It was a savage trip, on the rails he had ridden as a free man so many years ago. But now the details had faded and the towns swirled by dispassionately: Wilmer, Ferris, Alma, Corsicana. The train stopped in Wortham, and Huddie squinted from the window to see if he could catch a glimpse of the boardwalk along the storefronts where he had first met Blind Lemon.

All that was gone, Huddie thought. His life was over. He felt an aching throb in the pit of his stomach. The train jolted forward and passed the very barracks where he had listened to Lemon sing all night long.

Then southward again, through the piney woods, past fields lush with cotton, cane, soy and corn. From Mexia to Buffalo and from Buffalo to Centerville, to Leona and Midway and finally to Huntsville. It was four-thirty in the afternoon of June 8, and the moon was passing the sun in a total eclipse. Hens were going to roost in the premature darkness; birds were chirping back to their nests.

The prisoners were unloaded and marched eastward past storefronts until the brick facade of the seventy-year-old prison loomed ahead. Huddie could see a tall, brick watchtower where men with highdomed Stetsons walked casually about, shotguns and highpowered rifles slung across their shoulders. The facade itself was twenty-five feet high, and the iron-barred gates in its center were flanked on each side by two false archways.

Huntsville, the receiving prison for the Texas penitentiary system, was about ten acres: the buildings, old and shoddy, housed factories for the manufacture of wagons, stoves and textiles. There were less than 500 prisoners confined at Huntsville, in buildings filled to overflowing. The cells were cramped and had full-grated fronts. Toilets were at the end of a corridor in each cell block. The beds were straw-filled ticking, and fire was an ever-present hazard.

Most of the buildings were brick and had fallen into disrepair. The main cell block was dilapidated and overcrowded. It smelled of sweat and excrement. A string of dim light bulbs hung from cracked ceilings.

Huddie was given a casual physical and assigned a number. He was handed bread, crawling with weevils, and rancid pork. He ate it, weevils and all.

Huddie found the daily life hardly better than the chain gang in Harrison County. Self-mutilations to avoid work were common, and starvation and disease were rampant. He gagged the first time he went to the shower room, seeing the cement floor caked with dried blood from the lungs of tubercular prisoners.

His two cellmates were a man named Sawtooth, sentenced to life at hard labor for raping a twelve-year-old boy after cutting off the boy's penis to simulate a vagina, and a man named John who had robbed a grocery store of seven dollars and was sentenced to five years.

Huddie got along as best he could, spending the days picking cotton on the farms six miles to the south and returning late in the evening to a cold, greasy meal and sleep. For twelve hours each day, row upon row of convicts stooped and picked the cotton from the bolls, dragging heavy canvas sacks behind them. There were five prisoners for every guard, and the officers were mounted, rifles resting confidently across their saddles. But even these workers, who caused relatively little trouble, were whipped with bridle reins, bullwhips, blackjacks and clubs if they didn't work as fast as was demanded. The law, which dictated that whipping was to stop as soon as blood appeared, was ignored at Huntsville. It was not uncommon, when coming back from the fields at sundown, to see a bleeding convict strapped to the railing in front of the machine shop, hanging unconscious.

Before long Huddie got the reputation for being one of the strongest and best hands in Huntsville. He worked like a demon in the cotton rows, picking more cotton in a single day than any three inmates. On the hoe squads he "rolled" more than anyone, and at the end of each day had performed more work than anyone else. Huddie had decided, when he first entered, that hard work would help him avoid the daily beatings and whippings and would also keep him in good physical condition to avoid disease. From time to time he thought about escape, but he could see no way.

He requested permission to have his guitar sent to him, so that he could play in the evenings and entertain the rest of the prisoners after supper. It was granted, and Huddie played every evening, sharpening his skills and learning more songs.

Throughout the first year at Huntsville, Huddie continued to develop his style, singing with his eyes tightly shut, one foot keeping the beat. He began to sing old-fashioned songs, fully and softly, as if he were mellow on green corn whiskey. He sang old jugs, ragtime struts, backsteps, and double shuffles and pigeon wings. He sang of the people he knew, inventing new lyrics as he went and altering old lyrics to suit his current surroundings. Often he turned to work songs, hollers, chants and blues, songs of the broiling Brazos, low-down barrel-house blues with a series of magnificent runs on his twelve-string guitar. Then there were the knife blues, tunes learned from his pal Blind Lemon on forgotten street corners, in urine-soaked doorways, in the saloons and red-light houses of Dallas and Fort Worth. Kiln-hot notes sizzled from the old guitar. Rambling minor progressions danced out on the midnight air, on the black levees and murky, muddy waters.

Huddie sang and worked. His reputation for both was known by every inmate and every guard. Soon the mask of Walter Boyd slipped away and vanished forever. He was Huddie, Wes Ledbetter's son from Mooringsport. And because of Huddie's iron-hard constitution and incredible physical endurance, his name was soon corrupted. "Ledbetter" slowly became "Ledbella," which evolved into "Ledbelly," and finally "Leadbelly." Huddie liked the half-admiring, half-insulting nickname and so he became "Leadbelly" to the men at Huntsville and would remain "Leadbelly" the rest of his life.

The months peeled away slowly, and his frustration was only relieved by playing his guitar. He had no women, and his yearning for one turned frequently to physical pain. More than once he had to fight the temptation to join in homosexual activities at night, and often a fight broke out in the shower room where he had to defend himself against an especially ferocious "freak," "mellow" or "sissy."

More than once, he lay awake long into the night thinking of Lethe, Margaret, Edna Mae and the rest.

The accumulating frustration culminated one evening into a decision both impetuous and foolhardy: he would escape. He would to try to get away from Huntsville once and for all, and, with two others, he concocted a plan. A week later the three of them were over the fence and running west in the direction of the railroad and deep into the piney woods. Late that night, they split up and Leadbelly went his own way. When he was sure the others were far enough away to divert attention from him, he lay down near a pond and went to sleep.

In the early morning he was roughly awakened by a tall white man with two bloodhounds and a shotgun. "Come on, Leadbelly," he said with what Leadbelly thought was unusual gentleness. "Let's go back to camp, now. Leadbelly sat up and blinked awake, looking at the dogs and then up at the man. "No suh," he said, shaking his head. "I ain't goin' back there. Not nohow."

"I said come on! Am I going to have to shoot you?" The guard sounded as if he felt sorry for Leadbelly.

Leadbelly sat there. "Yessuh, I reckon so." Then he got to his feet slowly. "I ain't goin' back with you."

"Listen to me. You're a good worker and well liked. If you come back peaceable, there won't be any punishment. I promise you."

"No suh," Leadbelly said. He turned slowly and walked away. "You goin' to have to bring me back to that rathole dead. Those damn dogs got a better place to sleep than I do." His voice broke as he said it.

The man let him walk ten yards and then fired a shotgun blast into the air. "You're giving me no choice, Leadbelly. Come back with me now or I'm goin' to have to do my job. I'm askin' you nice."

"Let me go, mister," Leadbelly said without turning to face him. "I ain't no killer. I ain't no murderer. I jus' want to play my music and let everybody be. I ain't no mad dog what has to be whipped every day and starved every night. Please. Let me go. Jus' say you couldn't find me nohow."

"Can't do that. But I'll tell you what." The guard walked up to Leadbelly. "I don't want to shoot you, so you come back and I'll see you get made leadman on the first hoe squad. That's a good job and you'll get to be outdoors more often. Come on."

No reply.

The guard approached him cautiously.

"Leadbelly? Are you *crying?*"

*   *   *   *   *

"Leadbelly, there's something we ought to talk about." Captain Franklin grinned across the desk and lit a cigarette. Franklin was second in command at the Huntsville facility, a college graduate with loftier goals than prison administration. He was a pleasant man with a reputation for treating the inmates decently. That is, as far as he could control his guards. Incredibly, he actually didn't know about many of the beatings.

At first, Leadbelly was puzzled and suspicious of the friendly tone of Franklin's voice. Was another beating awaiting him? Sweet Jesus, he thought, why was all this happening to him? Why had he been singled out? "I ain't a killer, Cap'n Franklin," he blurted out. "I jus' got in a fight with someone who wanted to kill me. That's all. I ain't no killer. I don' belong here at all."

Franklin nodded slowly. "I took the trouble to get the record of your trial. Just between us, the penalty was too severe." He watched for a reaction but there was none. "But that's something we can't do anything about. However, the warden has agreed to ignore your escape. It will not be entered in your file. Now I'm doing that because I want you to know how we feel, or at least how I feel, about the difficulties here at Huntsville. I think the Texas prison system is a disgrace and I want to see it changed. I want to use you as a start to my own private campaign to get things cleaned up. So I'd like to make you a leadman on the first hoe squad in return for your cooperation in starting up a recreation program on Sundays. You're the best damn guitar player I ever heard."

Franklin sat back again, and took a puff on his cigarette. He eyed Leadbelly carefully. "What do you think so far?"

Leadbelly stared at the captain. He sat hunched over, his hands intertwined in front of his chest, his elbows resting heavily on the wooden arms of the chair. He had never heard this kind of talk. Could there actually be a white man in a Texas prison whose sole existence wasn't dedicated to whipping blacks?

"I…" Leadbelly groped for words. He wanted to sound intelligent. He tried desperately to remember the way Reverend Parker spoke at Sunday church back in Mooringsport. "I…I think that's mighty decent," he stammered. "Didn't seem like nobody ever knew that I didn't deserve no thirty-five years for jus' keepin' myself from being killed. I think that's mighty fine, yessuh."

"Well, Leadbelly, the hoe-squad work should keep you in good physical shape, and I can promise that a pardon is not out of the question in a year or so, if everything goes the way I hope it will."

Pardon!

It hadn't occurred to him. Pardons were almost unheard of. A pardon? How soon? He would do anything to get out of Huntsville!

Franklin stood up and offered Leadbelly his hand. "Is it a deal?"

He stood, nodding and grinning in confusion. He looked down at Franklin's hand clasping his. White in black. Black in white. It was the first time he had ever shaken the hand of a white man.

*   *   *   *   *

The change in Leadbelly was rapid. He became "the best white man's nigga in the whole camp," as Sawtooth referred to him, and tried to stay out of trouble. But trouble was as ubiquitous in Huntsville as the oppressive heat, and there were close calls. Once, word went around that over by the textile factory a man named Redwine was making whiskey out of apricots he had stolen, and Leadbelly managed to get some. But he saw that Redwine was courting trouble by being too stingy with his booty, and it wasn't long before someone crept up behind the man and decapitated him with a cane knife. Leadbelly saw the event from afar: Redwine's headless body still sitting erect, a cigarette smoking between his fingers.

There were other, equally risky things going on, but Leadbelly was careful not to get associated with them. Prisoners smuggled water moccasins and rattlesnakes into the camp by taping them to their legs. Inside, they would put the snakes in the water tanks, so when the guards searched for bootleg liquor, they'd be bitten. Mutilations were a daily event, and convicts cut off their fingers and toes and hamstrung themselves in protest against the conditions. Through it all, Leadbelly worked hard as a leadman.

By the end of the year, when the area was blanketed by an unusual snow six inches deep, forty-five prisoners froze to death. Franklin decided to try for Leadbelly's parole. He assembled his records and wrote an eight-page argument for Leadbelly's full pardon. When he finished, he called Leadbelly into the office and read him the report.

Even though Franklin was careful to point out the possibility -- the probability -- that he would be turned down, Leadbelly remained overjoyed and, as usual, superbly confident. Franklin asked question after question about his background, his musical ambitions, his frequent scrapes with the law in Shreveport and Dallas. He anticipated every argument the Pardons Board could possibly find, and he presented the report to the board the following Monday.

A week later he was summoned back.

"I'm afraid we can't accept this, Captain," Major Bond said to him. Bond was a former Texas Ranger, a mustached man in his fifties, a somber, rulebook type. "After just two years of a thirty-five-year sentence, we'll have to have more evidence of extraordinarily good behavior."

"But my point, sir, as you'll note, is that the thirty-five years was far out of line in the first place. One has to view the two years against, say, a ten-year sentence."

"We're not the magistrates, Franklin. He received thirty-five years in a court of law, and we're here to see that that sentence is carried out."

"But exceptions can be made, sir, and we all know it. Isn't that what the Pardons Board is for, after all?"

The other four men sitting beside Bond remained silent, unmoving. Bond shuffled papers. "What about this business of escaping the chain gang in Harrison County and assuming an alias? Is that the behavior of a repentant criminal?"

"In this case, yes sir, it is. Have you seen what goes on up there in Harrison? Have you ever really taken a look, even, at what goes on here in Huntsville? I submit that each of us would do exactly the same as this man Ledbetter. We'd get the hell out as fast as we could and by any means we could!"

"Now, Captain," Bond said. "Let's not let our own feelings color the facts. We realize you've been the most vocal of the correctional officers about present conditions, and steps are being taken to improve them, I assure you."

Franklin decided patience was ineffective. For six years he had been hearing the same words.

"Let me explain myself further," he said, facing the long table. "No reform we could ever possibly initiate would be of any real value unless we start trying to analyze the men -- the inmates, not just their routine or food or tools. We have to start placing more importance on motives, not a past crime that can't be erased. Why do you think inmates cut their own feet off, Major? Not because they're lazy, as everyone seems to want to think. It's because they've given up altogether. They've lost all hope of ever being considered as deserving just the smallest break, and they decide they'd rather spend the rest of their lives as a cripple than in a place you wouldn't keep your hogs in."

"We're getting astray here---"

"No we're not! Pardon me, sir, if I'm being too blunt, but we're not astray. The point is that we're not treating these people as human beings, and no physical comfort we give them is going to change our mental attitudes. We've got forty-five guards here at Huntsville, and the majority take joy in whipping a man with the bat. In the case of this man Ledbetter, I've discovered him to be docile, hard-working and a very talented musician. He plays the guitar, as I've noted in the report. And sings. This man killed another in self-defense, as was proven at his trial, and some judge who had a bad breakfast that morning gave him thirty-five years at hard labor. Would you want the same justice? I wouldn't. I'd have every lawyer in the country appealing that decision."

Bond dropped the papers. "As I said before, Captain, we're not the judges. We carry out the decisions; we don't make them. Ledbetter is a convicted killer, has been convicted before, has had numerous run-ins, and after just two years and a runaway at that! After just two years of a thirty-five-year sentence, we can't parole him. The public wouldn't stand for it, and the governor would fire both of us."

Franklin held out his hands to Bond. "Major, I've interviewed this man extensively. I've listened to the spirit in his singing, the hope in his voice. This man wants to reform! He's fighting for self-control. In almost every instance where he's broken the law, he's been provoked, and some inborn anger comes out quickly when he thinks he's being wronged. We all have it, for God's sake! Something inside he can't control when he sees a little beggar girl knocked down or an old man in Shreveport murdered before his eyes. He just goes wild. And he knows it! That's the wonderful first step! He knows it, and he's trying to tame it. He wants no trouble. He wants nothing but to play his music. I've studied some sociology, Major, and I know something about music. This man is a great musician, and with our help, he can bring his talent to the world. I believe that's what we're here for. Not to whip him and beat him and starve him, but to help him reach his full potential."

Franklin sighed and lit a cigarette without asking permission. His face was wet and dripping, and his hair tousled. He looked at the members of the board; Bond was looking at the paper again.

"Okay, Captain, you've made your point well," Bond said at last. "All of us here on the board have many more years experience at handling our…uh…our undesirable citizens, than you. And we're all proud of the work you've done here at Huntsville, and we hope we can all continue to work as a team at alleviating some of the trouble spots at the outcamps. We'll keep this case open and consider it further at our next meeting." He looked up at the clock and then around at the other board members. "Meanwhile," he added, "I'm hungry. Didn't get anything to eat this morning."

*   *   *   *   *

Exactly four weeks later, Leadbelly was elated when he was told to report to Captain Franklin's office. "Lawd, it's the pardon!" he yelled as he leaped from his bunk. "Lawd, I'se gonna be free again!"

He was escorted across the yard and into Franklin's office. His spirits were at new heights as he waited for the captain to arrive. A pardon! He'd be a free man again and go back to Mooringsport. He'd stay away from Fannin Street and fights and drunken men. He'd patch things up with his family and friends and settle down, maybe with Edmond on his farm, or else buy a place of his own. Maybe he'd even try going up north where the best musicians went, and become famous. Maybe get married. After all, he mused, he was thirty-three years old now and should decide what he would do for the rest of his life. Yes. Yes, if he stayed out of trouble, as Captain Franklin had often told him, he could be the most famous guitar player in the world.

Franklin finally arrived, and as he walked slowly to his desk and quietly sat down, his face revealed the news. "They turned us down, Leadbelly. I'm sorry. They refused the pardon."

Leadbelly didn't believe him. "Why? They been lookin' at it for a month." His voice cracked.

Franklin shook his head. "I don't know why. They just plain wouldn't accept it." He handed him the folder. Huddie opened it and looked at the first page, his hands trembling as he read the terse, rubber-stamped message: DENIED.

"Can't we do it again?" Leadbelly asked. "Can't we ask them to look at it some more?"

"Sit down," Franklin said. "Read the next page, too."

Leadbelly didn't sit, but turned the request over and saw the next page. He couldn't read the long words, but it was a transfer.

"What's this mean?"

"I guess it means the two of us are too much for them. And since they can't do anything with me, they're sending you to another farm."

Leadbelly looked at the page again. The name caused a sour sickness to rise in his throat.

Sugar Land.

###

Chapter Eleven

Fanklin tendered his resignation at Huntsville, and a week later, on his way to a teaching job in Austin, he escorted Leadbelly and nineteen other prisoners as far as Houston. It was a long, dark trip and it rained heavily the whole time. In Houston, as the prisoners were being transferred to the Sugar Land spur, Franklin said goodbye to the man he'd tried to help. All his words of encouragement dried up in his throat, and he turned silently away.

The Southern Pacific spur paralleled the Old Spanish Trail from Houston to Central Unit No. 1, the notorious Sugar Land, twenty miles to the southwest. The locomotive pulled in at midnight, and the wind whipped the rain across the searchlight beams like a shower of needles. There were men in slickers, shouting and waving red flares. The car, unhitched from the engine with a jolt, rolled slowly through a tall barbed-wire fence and into the yard. The prisoners, still shackled together, strained to peer out in the flashing lights and darkness. At last, with a grinding of brakes, the car stopped. A voice yelled for them to climb down fast.

The mud in some places was two feet deep, and the prisoners lined up two-by-two in the raw glare of the searchlights. A bell rang in the distance. Twenty minutes later the men were marched past the cannery and locked up for the night in an empty wooden barrack, with little shelter from the rain. They slept as best they could on triple bunks and damp, straw-filled mattresses.

The following morning the men were given weak coffee and bread and marched out to the canefields for their daily misery. The conditions at Sugar Land were no better than those at Huntsville. Day after day, six days a week and sometimes seven, teams of men were marched to the outcamps, which were nothing but wooden barracks heated by single pot-bellied stoves. There were no sanitary facilities except for a line of trenches filled with lime in the rear of the camp. A barbed-wire fence was strung around each building. The menu was the same every day: bread, molasses, beans, rice and cold coffee. If the men were lucky enough to catch a squirrel, or even an armadillo, they were allowed to cook it themselves. Other than that, meat was absent from their diet.

Leadbelly worked as hard at Sugar Land as he had at Huntsville, perhaps harder, for Franklin had engraved the idea of parole on his mind. He helped those who couldn't roll as fast. He was tireless and kept up a swift, grueling dawn-to-dusk pace, and the months dragged on.

Captain Foster, who ran the farm, was another fair man, a good friend of Franklin's, and also without the universal stripe of brutality. Only on a few occasions would he reluctantly order a prisoner whipped. Best of all though, for Leadbelly, Billy Foster liked music as much as Franklin. So much so, that he let Leadbelly have Sunday to himself, to play his guitar for the other inmates who were lucky enough to have Sunday off.

One night, in the top cell of the main housing unit, Huddie was talking with three other prisoners. They had been trading stories for an hour or so, talking about women and music, about their hometowns and the tragedies of their lives. The other three were in for murder. The oldest one, a lifer, was called Ironhead. He was a stocky man, very black, with a fringe of white hair circling his bald head, and he'd been singing for as long as he could remember. His partner, a man named Clear Rock, also sang in a coarse, rambling style. The third man, Yellow Joe, was a quadroon from New Orleans, and he sang stories about the Cajuns in a lilting, semi-French *patois*.

A distant whistle wafted through the iron grillwork of the cement openings. "It's the Midnight Special," Ironhead said. "May as well git to sleep now."

"That's the train what brought me here, I guess," Leadbelly said wistfully.

Ironhead grinned at him. "Man, you come here on the Midnight Special? You should of jumped like a jack-rabbit to get you face in that beam!"

The men laughed, but Leadbelly looked perplexed.

"They's a story here 'bout that train what's been hangin' in the air for a long time," Ironhead said. "If you is lucky enough to get hit from the beam of the locomotive's light, that mean you gonna be set free."

They talked on into the night, swapping stories of Sugar Land. Ironhead told of a girl named Rosie who lived there a long time ago and who was married to one of the prisoners. "Every week she'd get her master to write her a note, nice and educated like, to take to the warden askin' to set her man free."

"Yeah?"

"That's right. They said she was right pretty. And every week, in the rain even, she would show up regular like the hands of a clock."

"Mighty interestin'." Huddie was silent for a long time. At last he said, "Does that locomotive light really come in here?"

"Ain't nothin' comin' in here but the bugs," Ironhead said. He laughed. "Jus' a story, that's all."

The whistle was louder. The Midnight Special was coming into Sugar Land, its bright yellow beam illuminating the tracks before it. White steam poured from the engine and the brakes squealed and scraped it harshly to a gritty stop. Huddie could see there was no chance for a prisoner to be hit by the light from the locomotive.

For the rest of the week, as he worked in the fields, he thought about the legend of the Midnight Special. And the following Sunday, when many of the trustees had the day off, Leadbelly sought out Ironhead, Clear Rock and Yellow Joe. He had them sit under an old oak tree, and he stood in front of them holding his guitar. "Listen to this here," he said. "I been thinking 'bout that train, and this here's a song about it."

> *Yonder come Miss Rosie,*
> *How in the worl' do you know?*
> *Well, I knows her by the apron,*
> *An' the dress she wore.*
> *Umbureller on her shoulder,*
> *Piece o'paper in her hand.*
> *Well, she's gonna tell the gov'nor,*
> *Please, turn a-loose my man.*
>
> *Let the midnight special*
> *Shine its light on me;*
> *Let the midnight special*
> *Shine a ever-lovin' light on me.*

When you wake up in the mornin'
When the ding-dong ring,
Go marchin' to the table,
Meet the same ol' thing.
Knife an' fork on the table,
Nothin' in my pan;
Ever say a thing about it,
Have's trouble with the man.

If you ever go to Houston,
Boy, you better walk right,
Well, you better not squabble,
An' you better not fight.
Mason an' Brock will arres' you,
Payton an' Boone'll take you down;
The judge gonna sentence you,
An' you Sugar Land bound.

Well, jumpin' li'l Judy
Was a mighty fine girl,
Well, Judy brought jumpin'
To the whole roun' worl'.
Well, she brought it in the mornin'
Jus' a while 'fore day,
An' she brought me the news
That my wife was dead.

That started me to grievin',
Hoppin', holl'in' an' a-cryin',
Then I begin to worry
'Bout my great long time,

Let the midnight special
Shine its light on me;
Let the midnight special
Shine a ever-lovin' light on me.

###

Chapter Twelve

The old man stood there pathetically, almost in tears, his fist clutching wads of ten-dollar bills. He was in tattered workclothes, thin and wan, his white hair in tight tufts hiding his wrinkled ears. His eyes were downcast, his shoulders stooped.

At last he threw the money on the desk and said, "It's all I've got, suh. I even sold mos' of my land to get it. But I don't care how much money it cost me. Huddie's the onliest one who can help me on my farm."

Captain Foster got up from the table and clasped his hands behind his back. He wondered how he could make the old man understand. "Mr. Ledbetter," he said politely, "I know you went to a lot of trouble to come all the way down here from Shreveport, and I'm terribly sorry you had to sell your land. But what you're doing is what we call 'bribery,' and it's illegal. We're simply not allowed to release prisoners in return for money."

The old man didn't understand, and continued to plead with Foster. He had never heard the word "bribery." "Captain, suh, it cost you lots of money to keep my son here. All I'se doin' is offerin' to take him back, save you that money, and I promise you, suh, I see he don't get in no more trouble. I promise you that, sure thing."

"I've no doubt at all that you'd look after Huddie. But it simply can't be done, sir. I know you don't realize it, but it's actually a crime for you to even be here offering me money. You're not supposed to do it."

Wes shifted his feet. He'd never been called "sir" by a white man, and wasn't sure how to act.

"A crime to want my boy back? No, suh, I didn't know that. All I want is my boy. His mama cryin' and weepin' all night long and prayin' to the Lawd he come back and be a good boy. And he…" Wes couldn't hold it in any longer and began to cry.

Foster turned to Wes helplessly. "He _is_ a good boy, sir. He's one of the best workers we have, and everyone thinks he's the best guitar player they've ever heard. We treat him well, and…"

Foster stopped as he saw old Wes put his hands to his face and slowly turn toward the door. He started to leave, clutching his bills and stuffing them into his pants.

"Wait a minute," Foster said as he came around his desk. He put his hand on Wes's shoulder. "Wait here and I'll go check with the warden. Maybe you can at least see your son after coming all that way. It's against the rules, but I'll check."

He sat Wes down in a cane chair and trotted across the courtyard to the warden's office.

"Of course not," the warden said to him. "You know the rules. No visiting except on Sunday."

"But he's a very old man, sir, and he came all the way from Shreveport. He even thought he could give me some money that he got from selling his farm. He's a very gentle person. I thought as long as he's here…"

The warden shook his head again. "Sorry, Foster." The words hung icily in the air. "It's out of the question."

"It wouldn't be any trouble to send out for Ledbetter, sir. Just for a few minutes break."

The warden was adamant. "If we let that happen we'll have the goddam family of every eight-ball in this camp on our asses with wagonloads of money. Probably stolen, at that."

Foster just looked at him, then averted his eyes, trying not to look disgusted. As he shut the door to the warden's office a few seconds later, he heard the warden muttering, "Stupid niggers..."

Four months later, Wes Ledbetter was dead.

$$* \quad * \quad * \quad * \quad *$$

Huddie was grief-stricken and bitter. The summer was long and hot, but he kept his mind busy by composing new songs. From time to time he saw his friend Franklin, who was now teaching at the University of Texas in Austin, and they discussed the possibility of a pardon. Franklin, through Foster, sent a couple of requests through, but they were all denied.

Sunday afternoons at Sugar Land were special occasions for the inmates. Besides affording welcome leisure time, there were the visitors. Wives, children and girl friends spoke in hushed tones through a wire-mesh screen. Leadbelly could not keep his eyes off the women, and his sexual frustration was agonizing. He welcomed the chance to work in Foster's garden on Sundays.

The niece of Captain Foster's black housekeeper, a girl named Mary from Houston, began to accompany her aunt on Sunday visits to Sugar Land, and Leadbelly managed to talk with her as she strolled through the garden waiting for her aunt. The first Sunday he only chatted with her when they met, playing her a few songs and asking her questions about life in Houston. The second Sunday he showed her around the main courtyard, with Foster's approval, and the third Sunday Foster invited them both inside for tea and cookies.

On the fourth Sunday, Leadbelly made his move. He turned on all his charm and enticed the girl for a longer walk, this time out toward the barn in back of Foster's house, skirting the edge of the cornfields where most of the less fortunate inmates were sweating among the tall rows of cornstalks. As they leaned against a fence, looking out toward the fields, Leadbelly blurted out that he had to have her. He had to find a way to get her off unseen somewhere on her next visit. He pleaded for her cooperation.

Her softspoken "uh-huh" almost sent him reeling, and the following week was a long one as he plotted and planned each night in his bunk, almost on fire with his need.

When Sunday came, the rear door of the barn just happened to be unlocked, and inside there just happened to be a horse blanket spread neatly over the hay and dirt. She was down in a second, giggling impishly, and he was on her pounding heavily and grunting, and she finally had to clap both her hands over his mouth as he began groaning loudly. He never wanted to stop, but she pleaded that they had run out of time. The promise of next Sunday and the threat of discovery made him stop, and she returned through the garden while he doubled back across the cornfield.

On occasional Sundays afterward, until for an unknown reason she stopped accompanying her aunt to Captain Foster's, Mary from Houston was the weekly outlet for Leadbelly's voracious lust.

*   *   *   *   *

Patrick Morris Neff was fifty-three years old, of slight frame, with a full crop of sandy hair. A successful lawyer and member of the House of Representatives, he ran a strenuous and heated campaign for the governorship of Texas and was successful in beating the famous orator, Joseph Weldon Bailey. Neff was inaugurated on January 18,1921.

Governor Neff ran a quiet, dignified administration. He never vetoed a bill for education, and he worked hard at preaching economic responsibility and the wise use of the natural resources of the state of Texas. A highly religious man, he held God and the law above all things. A good cigar was his only vice.

Now, dressed as always in a suit of dark blue and a matching vest decorated with a watch chain, he looked up and frowned at his visitor. "Professor Franklin," he said quietly, "I've been planning on touring the entire Texas prison system for a long time, and I'm aware that some say it's one of the worst in the world."

The statement pleased Franklin. In the five years since he had taken his post at the university, he'd been in correspondence with Neff, bombarding him with a series of reports and requests for restructuring the Texas prison system. He'd also written, on behalf of Leadbelly, two formal requests for a pardon. But so far it had all been in vain.

Neff fingered his wide gold wedding band and ran his finger under his wing collar, wilting in the 112-degree heat. The problems of Texas had been overwhelming in the past six months, and Neff had put in many 16-hour days. But prison reform was not one of the most pressing problems for him at the moment. "However, Professor, I'm afraid that I will not be able to get to it for quite some time. Other things have come up. The oil people are at it again. I haven't seen so many lobbyists in Austin in thirty years."

Franklin pulled out a cigarette but didn't light it. "I know, Governor. But Houston is not that far away. It would only take a day or so."

Neff sighed. "All right. I'll be going to Houston next month, anyway. Perhaps I can find the time to inspect the Central Unit. It'll only discourage me, however; I hate to be reminded of the conditions there and have my hands tied by the legislature. Believe me, if there were something I could do, I'd do it. But education comes first, and it consumes a sizable portion of the budget."

"May I join you, sir?" Franklin asked.

Governor Neff stood up as a gesture that the interview was being terminated. "I think not, Professor. I'll have Mrs. Neff with me, and I think it best that we make this a casual visit, not a formal inspection. You understand."

"Yes, sir. I just wanted an excuse to accompany you. Assistant Warden Foster is a personal friend of mine. And I do want you to meet my favorite musician."

A smile creased Neff's face. "We'll see, Mr. Franklin. We'll see."

It took Neff longer than he thought to make the visit to Sugar Land. On two occasions other business took precedence, and Houston was a small town he seldom had to visit. But on March 13, 1924, Governor and Mrs. Neff sat in the living room of the Foster home and sipped from frosty glasses of iced tea.

Billy Foster himself was now the warden, his predecessor having been transferred to Corpus Christi to help organize a new penal farm in that area. Foster hadn't liked the idea of another bigoted hand in a new operation, but he had accepted the promotion with enthusiasm, eager to do what he could at Sugar Land. The excited telephone call from Franklin had taken him completely by surprise, and when Neff formally notified Foster of his planned visit, Leadbelly was the first prisoner Foster told.

Mrs. Foster entertained Mrs. Neff while Foster and his two captains toured the governor around the unit, pointing out its deficiencies and explaining the work routine. Foster talked continuously about the poor health and hygiene conditions, and dropped blatant hints at what an increase in his budget could do to ease the problem. Neff nodded, but remained noncommittal, and he made copious notes on a little pad of paper he carried with him. When the tour was over, they returned to Foster's house.

Through it all, Leadbelly had sat in his hot cell, choosing not to roam the grounds with the other prisoners this Sunday. He was busy concocting another of his plans. Foster had promised to let him play for the governor, and he was nervous. He thought about his friend Franklin and the hastily written note he had sent three days before, explaining why he wouldn't be there for the meeting but wishing Leadbelly luck. He reminded Huddie of the long years of trying to conjure up exactly such an audience and urged him to play the guitar better than he had ever played before.

Leadbelly had been practicing for more than six hours straight by the time the guard showed up. He polished the guitar with his sleeve and walked timidly across the recreation field to Foster's house.

They were all seated around a coffee table at one end of the room. Foster stood and greeted Leadbelly. Mrs. Foster sat next to Mrs. Neff, on the davenport, while the governor, impeccably dressed in his suit and vest, sat erect on a plush velvet chair, puffing slowly on a cigar. Leadbelly suddenly felt embarrassed by his shabby prison stripes.

"Your Honor," Foster said as he ushered Leadbelly into the room, "may I present Huddie Ledbetter. Huddie, Governor and Mrs. Patrick Neff."

Leadbelly held the neck of his guitar in one hand and made a stiff half-bow toward the visitors. The governor stood and acknowledged the greeting, and Mrs. Neff smiled uncomfortably from the sofa. "How do you do, Mr. Ledbetter," Neff said. "We've been hearing quite a bit about you." His smile was warm, pleasant and reassuring.

"As you've probably heard many times from my friend Jack Franklin, your honor, Huddie is an accomplished musician and a model prisoner," Foster said. "I whole-heartedly reaffirm Huddie's good conduct during his confinement here at Sugar Land."

Neff nodded and sat down again, resting his hands on the top of his walking stick and looking at Leadbelly. "We're looking forward to hearing your music," he said kindly. "Please be seated."

Leadbelly felt awkward at first, but he quickly warmed to the two ladies and slipped into his characteristically rapid-fire conversation. He told the governor a few stories about some of his musical escapades, and he fascinated Mrs. Neff in particular with various legendary origins of the blues and work songs sung on the prison farms throughout the south. Finally, perched on a stool in the middle of the room, Leadbelly began to sing his songs. He started slowly, softly, going through "Mister Tom Hughes' Town" and gave a comical narrative of what life was like in Shreveport. Then he sang "Green Corn," and Mrs. Neff tapped her foot lightly on the carpet. "The Midnight Special," together with the story of Leadbelly's first few evenings at Sugar Land and the legend Ironhead had related to him, was especially well received by the governor. "Get On Board," a moving spiritual urging close union with Jesus, which Leadbelly sang with his eyes shut tight as if he were alone in the room, visibly moved the governor.

After several more songs and colorful tales, Leadbelly activated his ploy. Now fully warmed to the occasion and as relaxed as he'd ever be under the circumstances, he knew he had the governor and his wife enthralled.

"Now I'd like to sing the song I jus' made up for the Gov'nor," he announced with a broad grin. "I sittin' in my cell this mornin' thinkin' 'bout what to sing for you, an' I said, 'Huddie, why don't you jus' make up a brand new one for this here distinguish gentleman and lady.' So I think of the words and find the right music for it, and here it is. I calls it 'Gov'nor Pat Neff.'"

He sang it at precisely the right psychological moment, and it was a carefully calculated appeal to let Leadbelly go home to his wife, Mary, in Houston. The lie was an important ingredient in his appeal. Leadbelly had caught the looks of affection that the governor gave his wife from time to time and, at the last minute, decided to use his invented marriage to elicit as much sympathy from Neff as possible. Mary from Houston would help set him free.

He began the song, in 2/4 time, the voice reverberating in the small room.

> *Nineteen Hundred and Twenty-Three,*
> *The judge took my liberty away from me,*
> *Nineteen Hundred and Twenty-Three,*
> *The judge took my liberty away from me,*

The notes of the song progressed in a major key up the scale.

> *Left my wife wringin ' her hands an' cryin',*
> *"Lawd have mercy on the man of mine,"*
> *Left my wife wringin' her hands an' cryin',*
> *"Lawd have mercy on the man of mine."*

And then, strumming the chords, he looked at Neff and said, "Bud Russell had me goin' on down. I couldn't do nothin' but look back at her. He had chains all around my neck and I couldn't do nothin' but wave my hands. I look back at her an' here's what I tol' her,"

> *Tol' my wife 'fore I lef' the lan',*
> *Never no more see her, do the bes' she can,*
> *Tol' my wife 'fore I lef' the lan',*
> *Never no more see her, do the bes' she can.*

He spoke again. "Her name was Mary. I look back at Mary."

> *Goodbye, Mary,*
> *Oh, Mary,*
> *Oh, Mary.*

Leadbelly's voice cracked plaintively.

> *I'se your servant compose this song.*
> *Please Gov'nor Neff lemme go back home.*
> *I'se your servant compose this song.*
> *Please Gov'nor Neff lemme go back home.*

Aside and tilting his head upward he said softly, "Had thirty-five years," then repeated the stanza again for good measure.

> *I know my wife will jump and shout.*
> *Train rolls up I come steppin' out.*

Leadbelly's eyes widened. "I know she be pretty glad. I know I be glad, myself." He repeated this stanza also, then continued as if he had already been pardoned. "I look 'round and begin to thank Gov'nor Pat Neff," he said, still strumming the notes. "I wanted him to have a little mercy on me 'cause I had thirty-five years."

> *Please Honorable Gov'nor be good and kind,*
> *Have mercy on my great long time.*
> *Please Gov'nor Neff be good and kind,*
> *Have mercy on my great long time.*

"They turn loose some on pardon, some on parole. Some they's cuttin' they time."

> *I don't see to save my soul.*
> *Don' get a pardon, try me on parole,*
> *I don't see to save my soul.*
> *Don' get a pardon, try me on parole.*

He imagined what the governor would say. "He ask me where did you want to go an' here is what I tol' him." Then, breaking the melody:

> *Goin' back to Mary.*
> *Oh, Mary,*
> *Lawdy, Mary.*
> *Um, um, um.*
> *Some folks say it's a sin.*
> *Got too many womens an' too many men.*

"In the pen," he said aside.

> *Some folks say it's a sin,*
> *Got too many womens an' too many men.*

"I want to talk to him 'bout my time again, If he didn't cut it, he might pardon it."

> *Please Honorable Gov'nor be good an' kind,*
> *If you don' get a pardon,*
> *will you cut my time?*

"Give me a pardon," he entreated.

> *Please Honorable Gov'nor be good an' kind,*
> *If don' get a pardon, will you cut my time?*

And then he launched into an adroit climax.

> *Had you Gov'nor Neff like you got me,*
> *Wake up in the mornin' and I'd set you free,*
> *Wake up in the mornin' and I'd set you free.*

The last notes of the plea died away. There was a momentary, uncomfortable silence as Leadbelly opened his eyes and looked at the governor. Neff was obviously moved and puffed thoughtfully on his cigar. His wife was shaken and covered her eyes. Foster gave Leadbelly a quick wink and started clapping. Governor Neff stood and applauded loudly, then he walked over and took Leadbelly's hand and pumped it vigorously. In a quiet voice he said, "Young man, I'll see what I can do." He placed a five-dollar gold piece in Leadbelly's palm.

Neff turned to Foster. "Warden, would you forward an official summary of this man's record to me? Now, I think it's time we left."

The next day Leadbelly was gloomy and sullen. He thought he'd be paroled on the spot and Foster told him not to get his hopes up. Since he'd been governor, Pat Neff had pardoned only five prisoners. What's more, the inmates told him that Neff "wouldn't turn loose his own mammy, and you ain't gonna hear anythin' for a year and most likely never."

Ten months later, a polished black Whippet Model 96 ground its way to a noisy stop in front of Warden Foster's house and Jack Franklin bounded from behind the wheel, forgetting to shut off the ignition and leaving the door of the roadster ajar. He ran up the stairs, rang the bell and opened the door himself.

Ten minutes later, Leadbelly stood in the middle of the room and with quivering hands read the full pardon from the office of the governor:

> *TO ALL TO WHOM THESE PRESENTS COME:*
> *WHEREAS on 21 day of February A.D. 1925 of the District Court of Bowie County, whereas,*
>
> > *WALTER BOYD*
>
> *was convicted of a felony, to wit: Assault to murder, and his punishment assessed at thirty-five (35) years confinement in the State Penitentiary; and*
> *WHEREAS, applicant has now served a part of his sentence with a clear prison record and executive clemency is granted for the reason that it is believed applicant has been sufficiently*

*punished for the offense committed, and that he will make a good
law-abiding citizen after his release.*

*NOW, THEREFORE, I, PAT M. NEFF, Governor of
Texas, do, by the virtue of the authority vested in me by the
Constitution and laws of the State of Texas, hereby grant the
said WALTER BOYD, a full pardon, hereby restoring him to
full citizenship, giving him the full...*

The words, those he could read, fell away from him. It was hard to
believe. Foster shoved a glass of whiskey at him and he remembered
blurting out his thanks and Foster shaking his hand. With his
talent and wits, Leadbelly had managed to sing his way out of a
thirty-five-year prison sentence after only six years, seven months
and twenty-seven days. He had one hundred and fifteen dollars in
his pocket, made from prison singing and working. He was strong
and confident, and his features were still sharply cut. He had a right
to feel proud.

It was January 21, 1925. He was thirty-eight years old. Invisibly,
The Midnight Special had shone her ever-lovin' light on Huddie
Ledbetter, and that very week there had been another eclipse of the
sun in the Texas skies.

###

Chapter Thirteen

Although Jack Franklin had arranged a job for him as a janitor in a Buick agency in Houston, Leadbelly, after just two weeks, decided the work wasn't for him. He knew the big city would eventually overwhelm him and that trouble would inevitably track him down. He considered applying for an I.W.W. membership card and becoming a lumberjack or a longshoreman. Without the temptations of liquor and women he could save his money and cast his lot with Blind Lemon in Chicago. After all, there were much younger musicians making records up north. Determined as ever, he made yet another resolution: to return home, work for the Gulf and save his money.

He set Chicago as his long-range goal; there was no Jim Crow in Chicago.

*   *   *   *   *

Sally, now fifty-nine years old, had gained weight and lost much of her vitality. She had gray streaks in her hair, and Leadbelly noticed her memory often faltered.

On the other hand, Edmond was strong and active. He had twin sons and three daughters, the prettiest of whom was Florida, now nine years old. Leadbelly found it difficult to suppress his envy. How different their lives had been. Huddie had never thought much about raising a family -- another missing chunk of his life.

He met and took up with a woman named Era, who spent most of her time at the Ledbetter farm. For the first year he spent his free time attending to the whims of his mother. He would even refuse to report for work at the Gulf if she was ailing. Anything his mother wanted, he made sure she received. At night he sang her the old songs she had taught him as a boy, watching her drift to sleep in the chair. He then lifted her gently and put her to bed.

On Saturday nights, Leadbelly and Era went to dances across the lake in Oil City. Era sang along with Leadbelly, and they earned extra money and lived well. Even his occasional infidelities went unnoticed. People knew of his Texas pardon and crowded to hear about it again and again. Young boys sought him out and shook his hand. After all, Mooringsport had never spawned a celebrity. Leadbelly relished it and characteristically embellished and filigreed his grim prison memories and invented whole new anecdotes for his own amusement. In the middle of singing a lyric, he'd get a better idea and change it to suit his audience. "Yes, suh, " he said, "I sure did get hit right smack in the middle of my head from that ol' lamp in the front of the Midnight Special. Jus' as bright as mornin' even though it was in the middle of the night. An' the very next day, ol' Pat Neff come right to the farm with my pardon and he also give me twenty dollars 'cause I sung for him."

When the audience was exclusively male, he told about his women. "Yes, suh," he bragged, "I used to be terrible with the wimmins, terrible rough. I'd treat them every whichaway. An' I'se had trainloads of them, trainloads, sometimes eight or ten at a dance. Used to be when I'd take a woman in my car, I'd put her right out if she wouldn't ride with me, put her out no matter how far she was from home an' make her walk. I'd tell her, say, 'Well, you can step right on out my car, then, 'lowin' me to take you where you want to go in a five or seven hundred dollar automobile an' then you won't 'commodate me a little! Well, you can jus' walk! Get out, you nappy-haired bitch! Get out! An' I'd shove her out no matter what she said to me an' be gone down the road an' leave her hollerin' after me."

Then he played a song. He called it "Shorty George."

Running parallel to the Southern Pacific tracks outside of Sugar Land, Leadbelly explained, were narrow-gauge rails. Every Sunday afternoon at exactly one o'clock, the train they called "Shorty George" would bring the men their wives and girl friends. And Leadbelly sang about it.

> *Shorty George ain't no friend of mine,*
> *He keeps a-takin' all the women,*
> *leavin' the men behind.*

Leadbelly explained what he meant. "Ol' Shorty George, why he was a li'l ol' train what come to the penitenshuh every Sunday after dinner. Why all the gals and wives and friends of the prisoners would jus' wait all week for that train to arrive. Gals of all sorts, fat and skinny, tall and li'l tiny things. Why, the prison would let all these gals just go away with their men."

> *Laid down last night, dreamin' in my sleep,*
> *That I saw my baby, makin' a four-day creep.*

"Yessuh, I seen the women jus' comin' back from the surprise party and I gets awful lonesome. But then Sunday come and everybody

169

screamin' at each other. Man! You never seen such a sight! Why, they even bring in some gals from Mexico!"

Some got six months, some got two an' three years.
But they's so many good men got lifetime here.

"Some afternoons I jus' go with any gal what ain't got no man, or maybe they put him in confinement for doin' bad. But then Shorty George would call the women back and they would all go home. He take the women away."

Shorty George done been here an' gone.
He keeps takin' all the women,
leavin' the men alone.

"Oh, yeah! Ol' Shorty George was some 'sweet black.' Jus' as heartless and jus' as mean. Take all the women from the men. Men who had to spend a lifetime in jail."

Shorty George ain't no friend of mine.
He keeps takin' all the women,
leavin' the men behind.

He began secretly to see the daughter of Big Ted Promise. Her name was Martha. He also ran into a tall woman named Mary Elizabeth Pugh, a distant relative of Sally's from somewhere along the tertiary branches of that particular Caddo Indian family tree, and had a brief affair with her. The result of this was a daughter named Jessie Mae, born down in Port Arthur. Leadbelly went to see her briefly, and tried to keep track of her welfare. He worked and sang and saved his money.

For the next few years he continued to live with Era in what had now become a stormy relationship, and seeing Martha on the side. Martha was taking more and more of his time, and he believed he'd fallen in love with her. She was a perfect counterbalance for him: soft-spoken, demure, forgiving, slow to wrath and an eager recipient for his boundless stamina.

There were several fights, a few knifings, one of which in Oil City almost killed him. With the summer, Era left him and the last he heard she had taken up with a man in Baton Rouge.

He began to think about asking Martha to marry him and move to New York. He was impressed when Fiorello LaGuardia, then a candidate for mayor, spoke out strongly against Jim Crow judges. Perhaps there would be a place for him in the United Colored Socialists of America, down in Harlem. He asked Martha what she thought about it. As always, she went along with anything he wanted. They talked about getting married, but a date was not set.

It went that way until October, when the stock market crash forced the Gulf to lay off many workers, mostly blacks. Leadbelly was among the first to go. In the ensuing local strife, brought on by the inability of the Mooringsport community to understand fully the reasons for their sudden relapse into deeper unemployment, fifteen blacks were found slaughtered in the Oil City trainyards, and the Klan lit a cross in the field in front of the Shiloh Baptist Church. It distressed Leadbelly so badly that he began to leave the Mooringsport area whenever possible, going down to Shreveport where he could earn a few dollars playing music in Saint Paul's Bottom. He occasionally took Martha, especially after their relationship became known in Mooringsport and ill feelings ran high among the younger men and women. At one point, in broad daylight, Leadbelly was ambushed by four men who waited for him outside a roadside beer joint on the way to Leigh, where the road makes a right-angle turn from Mooringsport toward the Texas border.

The men confronted him with a gun, but Leadbelly's speed was too much for them. He had his own pistol in his hand in less than a second and fired a shot at the ringleader, shredding his left ear. At the sight of blood and the sound of screams, the other three took to their heels, and one of them caught another bullet in the arm as he fled. Leadbelly hastily jumped in his car and sped home. News of the event traveled fast, and Leadbelly became a target for every young black who thought he could beat him. Sally prayed and Martha returned to her mother.

Leadbelly went to Shreveport again and rambled. He came home for Christmas and brought his mother a bolt of cotton cloth and a bottle of expensive perfume. He brought a present for each of Edmond's children as well as for Martha. Martha was gone, however, spending the holidays in Biloxi, Mississippi, with her mother's family.

Leadbelly returned to Shreveport, still trying to avoid trouble. But a black man maintaining the pace Leadbelly set for himself, without the aid of an influential white man, was doomed.

*   *   *   *   *

It was early evening as he was coming home from a temporary job in the fields, swinging his lunch pail nonchalantly. He thought of the evening ahead, when he planned to go into Bossier City for a night's fun. Suddenly six figures blocked the path before him and he saw the glint of a knife flash in the hand of the tallest one.

"Ledbetter," he said, "give us you whiskey!"

Leadbelly stopped short. He had only seen one of them before, and they obviously had been drinking heavily. "Who's you guys?" he asked. "'Sides, I ain't got none with me."

"No use lyin' 'bout it," another man said. "You always got whiskey and we all know it."

"Now, hold on. I been workin' all day and I'se gonna have my whiskey tonight. I'm tellin' you I ain't got none now. You better get on back home before you start any trouble." Leadbelly spoke pleasantly, almost soothingly. He didn't want to have to run through their blockade.

"Then if you ain't got none in that lunch bucket, you better have some money for us to buy some. Which is it, Ledbetter?" The other five men leered behind him.

"Ain't I tol' you I ain't got no whiskey? An' I ain't got no money, either. Now stop foolin' with me. I'se tired and I don't feel like no foolishness."

One of the men came around the ringleader, flashed his own knife, and stepped up to Leadbelly. The others came over and crowded around him. "Lemme see what's in that bucket, then," be said, and held out his hand.

Leadbelly accommodated him, handing over the pail. The man looked into it and threw it to the side of the road like the discarded windjammer of long ago. "Okay, then," the man said. "You give us you money and we leave you alone."

"Now, I ain't givin you niggas a fuckin' penny, you bastids. An' you better know how to use that knife o' yours, because I'se comin' right through you and goin' home." He looked over at the pail, covered now with dust. The men didn't move.

Leadbelly stepped slowly to one side, and reached down to pick up his lunch pail. He wished he had his gun with him but he never brought it to work. Then one of the men leaped toward him, swearing. He stood up quickly and turned to meet the attack. He squeezed the man's hand as if it were a lemon and felt bones cracking as the man shrieked. The knife dropped in the dust. Shoving the man away and bending down to pick up the knife in one motion, Leadbelly jabbed his elbow up hard into the solar plexus of the next attacker, and as the man started to double over he stabbed him in the chest. The first two men were screaming. Behind him, he heard a scramble and saw the other men run into the field. His right hand felt the slippery handle of the knife almost slide from his fingers as he twisted it out of the man, who shrieked and fell to his knees. Leadbelly kicked him in the groin, hard, and heard the man curse and choke as he fell backward.

He stood over the man, then closed his eyes and dropped the knife. He staggered into the fields, falling at first to one knee, breaking his fall with his hand, a mixture of blood and dust clinging to it like syrup. The next thing he knew they had taken him in custody. He awoke in the Shreveport jail.

The city hall of Shreveport was only five years old. It dominated a square block of lawns and shrubs facing Texas Avenue at the corner of Marshall. The jail blocks, Leadbelly found out later, were situated on the seventh and eighth floors of the building's tower. The next morning he was led, handcuffed, into the sheriff's office on the first floor, then transferred by an elevator to the seventh floor and booked on a charge of suspicion of assault to murder.

To the right of the booking desk was a double iron-barred door, flanked on each side by wooden benches. It led to a cell block consisting of six cells, each thirty feet square and secured by a solid steel door with a single peephole covered by a metal disc. The floors were rough cement, and everything was painted a dull shade of yellow. The plaster ceilings were already cracked and chipped.

Leadbelly was locked in a cell with twenty-four other black men waiting arraignment. The bunks were inadequate, and the prisoners sprawled in various stages of undress on the floor. A commode stood in one corner caked with vomit and excrement; someone was sitting on it, bent over, holding his chin in his palms and staring at the new arrival with detachment.

Some of the men greeted Leadbelly with a mixture of guffaws and obscenities. Others just looked at him vacantly, with no interest at all, as if he were a fly. Leadbelly stepped to a vacant spot on the floor and slumped against the wall. A few more sharp comments and jibes were thrown at him, but he merely scowled at the others and remained impassive and forlorn. He spent the day and night there, never moving from his spot, never speaking a word.

At ten o'clock the next morning, Leadbelly was escorted from the cell to the outer office by a guard in an open-collar khaki shirt. Another man, behind the counter, shuffled a pile of papers officiously. "Ledbetter," he said without looking up, "I don't suppose you have anybody to represent you, either."

Leadbelly shook his head. "No, suh. I ain't."

"Well, with a record like yours, you bet your black ass you're gonna need somebody. Can't you stay out of trouble?"

"They started the fight."

"Listen, you better wise up. All your records are here, and you're not in Texas now. We don't put up with that shit here. In Lousiana you're guilty until proven otherwise."

Leadbelly looked at him blankly. The very word "guilty" caused a rising panic. "I don't know," he said finally. "I jus' didn't do nuthin'."

"You call cuttin' up another nigger nuthin'?"

"No, suh."

175

"Well, Ledbetter, counsel will be assigned to you. Now take him back and lock him up, Bobby Joe."

"Can I see my woman?"

"Counsel will take care of that. Okay, Bobby, open the door."

###

Chapter Fourteen

Leadbelly waited on the sixth floor in a small paneled room down from the coroner's office. It was bare except for two straight-back mahogany chairs and a yellow pine desk. On one wall was a picture of Governor Huey P. Long, and next to it a photograph of President Hoover. A yellowing American flag hung incorrectly with the Union on the upper right. Next to it was the flag of Louisiana.

He'd heard about the Louisiana prison system. A man in Sugar Land had told him, "Jus' thank the Lawd you wasn't in Loosiana, Huddie. Man, youse treated like a king now compared to what they got waiting for you in ol' Angola."

Guilty until proven innocent! He couldn't shake the words off. He'd heard them before. "In Loosiana you gotta prove yourself, man. It ain't like here where they got to prove you done it."

For the black and for the poor in Louisiana this evidentiary presumption had a stark meaning unique in the nation: summary punishment, inquisition, being hustled in and out of court, and tried by the biased intuition of community leaders. It was only in 1928, just two years before, that a new code of criminal procedure replaced the Napoleonic Code and changed the state law; a man was now presumed innocent. But among the indigent the old law stuck. And given the realities of drawn-out criminal procedure, not without good reason.

Leadbelly was afraid. He couldn't stand another term in prison. The horrorible memories of the Harrison County chain gang and Sugar Land churned within him. He remembered how his mother had explained away the curse of being black. With pain and indignation she had intoned from the Bible's Song of Songs: "Look not at me so because I am black for the sun hath burned me, the children of my father were angry with me and they made me watchman of their vineyard, but my own vineyard I have not kept."

He shook the thought from his mind.

E. B. Herndon, Esq., opened the door and hobbled into the room. Leadbelly turned and looked nervously at him. He was a frail, skinny man, a victim of polio, who stood shakily on two steel canes. The handles were the pearl grips of two Colt revolvers, sawed off and welded to the cane tops where the barrels should have been. When Herndon talked or pondered a thought, he nervously cocked the hammer of the pistols and clicked imaginary rounds. The click of the hammer punctuated his sentences. He had found it was an effective device for distracting juries when the prosecution was summing up its case.

Herndon had the sharp face of a woodchuck. He was barely five-feet-five and his frail body, when he stood next to Leadbelly, made him look like a sapling beside a sequoia. He wore a peach-colored suit and a black string tie.

Of the fifteen lawyers used in the defense pool for Shreveport's District Court, Herndon was the wealthiest and most controversial. He actively sought poor Negroes in need of defense, and was one of the most vocal spokesmen for their plight. Consequently, the citizenry barely tolerated the "nigga lovin' lawyer."

With a brusque gesture of his cane, Herndon clapped on the back of a chair. "Sit down," he said crankily. "We don't have much time."

Leadbelly obeyed instantly. He sat straight in his chair, palms on his knees. Herndon remained on his feet, pacing awkwardly as he spoke.

"All right, Mr. Ledbetter. I want to hear your own version of the whole incident. Right from the beginning and don't leave out anything. Names, times, conversation -- all of it."

Herndon listened to the story of the fight, interrupted frequently to clear up a point, and when it was over he asked Leadbelly for the names and addresses, as near as he could recall, of anyone who might be a character witness. "They're going to drag up everyone on the face of the earth who has something against you, Mr. Ledbetter, and the more people we have to offset that tactic, the better off we'll be. Your record isn't exactly a passage from Leviticus."

Leadbelly gave him all the names he could remember.

Herndon finally sat down, aimed his cane at the pelican on the state flag, and mock-shot it through the head. "You know, Mr. Ledbetter," he said pensively, "I got the handles for these canes from one of the first defendants I ever represented. He was a man who was framed for shooting a couple of men down in N'Orleans. He was black and he was mean. But he was also innocent, and every goddam lawyer in N'Orleans was itching to get him lynched regardless of his innocence. When he was acquitted he gave me his revolvers and promised never to use a gun again. Today, that man is a history professor at Southern University in Baton Rouge. He writes to me at least once a month. I had his pistol handles welded onto my canes so I'd never forget the value of a human life, or what a terrible crime it is to take one, regardless of motivation."

He eyed Leadbelly narrowly. "Now, you've got a bad record, but from what you say -- and I believe you -- you reacted in self-defense to a deliberate provocation. They say you're a fine musician. If I bring in an acquittal, my fee to you will be your promise to start getting serious about your music and to stop fighting with everyone who looks cross-eyed at you. Do you understand me?"

"Oh, yessuh," Leadbelly said shaking his head. "I surely do. Yessuh, I do."

"Then cut out that 'yessuh' crap!"

Leadbelly looked at him, amazed. What was he saying? All his life he'd been taught that white men liked to be talked to like that.

"That's jus' the way us niggas talk."

"No it's not!" snapped Herndon. "It's just what you *think* white men want to hear, so you talk that way to get a better deal from them. Christ, you sound like a goddam *slave*! And you're not a nigger. You're a Negro. A black man. Haven't you learned any better?"

"What's the difference?" Leadbelly said. He was still confused but he instinctively liked Herndon. "If a white man like to hear it, then---"

"What I mean, Mr. Ledbetter, is that it's about time you stopped acting like someone's pet. We're not here to make people like us. We're here to make the jury respect us, but if you sound like a stupid lackey they'll treat you like one!"

Leadbelly eyed Herndon closely. The lawyer was hobbling around the room, and he hadn't looked directly at Leadbelly as he spoke. But maybe Herndon was right. After all, if he really started being honest with himself, he had to admit that playing the role of the poor servant had been his standard behavior whenever he was around white folks. What's more, he hadn't even stopped to consider whether in fact it did get results -- he just acted that way out of habit. He shrugged.

"Just remember what I said," Herndon grumbled as he left the room. "Talk like the person you want to be treated like."

A week later, after Herndon waived the arraignment, Leadbelly, dressed in a dark suit, a bow tie and black-and-tan perforated oxfords, was led into the courtroom. Although clean, it looked dingy from the dim orange of the filtered sunlight. During the past week, he had renewed his confidence. Herndon had been able to give him a new perspective on himself, and Leadbelly was positive he would soon be set free.

The five jurors were drawn from the regular criminal <u>voir</u> <u>dire</u>. The judge, whose name would mysteriously go unrecorded, was a portly, benign-looking man with a florid red face and two chins. The prosecutor, named Pyburn, was a short but well-built man about sixty years old. He had spent his entire life in Louisiana.

Leadbelly sat next to Herndon. Six huge wooden fans whooshed the air, making the tassel-edged flags tremble. The court was called to order, and the prosecution and the defense made their opening remarks. Herndon took the opportunity to inform the jury that the plea would be self-defense.

After Herndon concluded, Pyburn rose. "Your Honor, at this time I should like to introduce into evidence a deposition. It was taken on February sixth of this year from Jim Harris. Pursuant to Article 155 of the Code of Criminal Procedure the deposition has been certified by a committing magistrate, the Honorable Thomas E. Burbidge, Judge of the City Court of the City of Shreveport, and by one Billy L. Campbell, a stenographer appointed and sworn for the purpose of this deposition. The deposition was given at the clinic where Mr. Harris is now in a coma. If it pleases the court to receive said deposition, I---"

"No! No! No!" Herndon banged his fist on the table and shouted loudly. The courtroom was stunned into silence. With the support of his canes he rose to his feet. "That deposition is inadmissible!"

The judge stiffened in his seat. "Mr. Herndon!"

"I knew Pyburn would take Tom Burbridge down to see Harris and not notify me. He knew I could make a liar out of Harris. Well, the only way I can upset this cozy little arrangement is to cite the law. I won't let those lies go into the record by default!"

Pyburn screamed an objection.

"Just a minute," Herndon shouted back. " I want that deposition excluded."

"Objection!" Pyburn said, outraged.

"Overruled. Proceed, Mr. Herndon."

"The constitution of our state, which is only nine years old, remember, says a man has a right to be confronted by the witnesses against him. Article One, Section Nine, makes no exceptions. A man has an absolute right to be confronted by the witnesses against him. A deposition cannot be introduced unless the defense can cross-examine the deposed, when it is given, or when it is offered into evidence."

"May I be heard, your honor?" Pyburn walked toward the bench. Recognized, he turned in the direction of Herndon and launched into a complex analysis of various articles of the Louisiana constitution concerning the validity of depositions.

The arguments about the deposition took all morning, with Herndon objecting noisily and often about its evidentiary validity, until finally the exasperated judge ruled against the irate Herndon and allowed the Harris deposition.

"Your honor. My client is being denied a right under the constitution."

"The court has ruled, Mr. Herndon. Now sit down, *please!*"

Herndon clicked at his pistol-canes. He was livid, but turned to the jury and shrugged his shoulders eloquently.

The deposition was read by Pyburn. It told how Harris and his five friends were walking through the field on their way home when Leadbelly accosted them and demanded whiskey. They had none, the deposition explained, but Leadbelly insisted that out of the five surely one had a bottle of something. When they again demurred, Leadbelly threatened them with a knife and grabbed one of the men to search him. Leadbelly appeared to have been drinking heavily. The other five men tried to assist Harris, but Leadbelly held them at bay with the knife. When Harris tried to struggle free, Leadbelly stabbed him. The others approached again, but seeing Leadbelly crazed with alcohol, they fled while Harris lay crumpled on the ground. The next thing Harris recalled was being taken to the "Shreveport Negro Clinic."

The deposition shocked Leadbelly, but Herndon admonished him not to whisper. What did he expect? That Harris would agree with his story? Herndon patiently explained to the court the importance of being able to cross-examine Harris and moved to strike. But the judge was adamant and overruled him.

Pyburn now called his first witness, one of the five men with Harris. He told the same story: the demand for whiskey, the knife threat and the ensuing stabbing.

Herndon approached the witness and rocked precariously on his canes. "Are you normally the sort of man who runs from a fight in which one drunken man is attacking five strong, sober men in a desolate field?"

The witness explained they were afraid of Leadbelly's reputation for being a wild, no-holds-barred street fighter. Herndon then attempted to question the witness as to his special knowledge of

Leadbelly's reputation, but Pyburn broke in to object that the actual reputation was immaterial and heresay.

Herndon retorted sharply. "When a character witness testifies about someone's reputation, he is first qualified. I want to see whether this man is qualified."

"This man is not a character witness," the judge said. "The court sustains the prosecution's objection. Have you any further questions, counsel?"

"Yes, your Honor. Mr. Witness, did the district attorney tell you what to say here today?"

"Objection! No foundation!"

"Sustained."

The witness was excused and the following four witnesses corroborated the story. Herndon asked them the only question he had previously been able to ask the first witness. "Are you the type of man...?" From each, he received the same answer.

Finally the judge called a lunch recess.

*   *   *   *   *

The morning had gone badly and Leadbelly knew it. His confidence was waning rapidly, and dread began to descend upon him. He had difficulty following the constitutional and procedural arguments: the men talked fast and used unfamiliar words. His mouth was so dry it felt like sandpaper. It couldn't be happening again! Oh Lawd, it just couldn't be happening again!

Herndon also knew he was in trouble, but he blamed no one but himself. He should never have taken on the judge over the deposition. From that point on, he was in serious disfavor. Moreover, he had not cross-examined Riggs well. A shift in his proposed order of questions would have possibly allowed him to get the testimony of Harris's bad character. He faced the afternoon behind and injured.

He had to soften his client's image. He looked over at Leadbelly, who sat with his head bowed hard against his chest. He was sweating profusely and his white shirt was soaked around the collar. The sight distressed Herndon. The poor sonofabitch, he thought.

A character witness could be put on, but it would not be easy to get testimony unless the witness would give evidence of Leadbelly's specific traits relevant to the crime for which he was charged. Pyburn would object and the judge would sustain. So he would carefully prod over the sensitive rules of evidence.

It was hot and humid when the court came to order that afternoon at two o'clock. Herndon appeared unruffled but was sweating. Pyburn was calm, and the judge was on the verge of irritation. The jury stared blankly.

"Your Honor," Herndon began, "my first witness is Professor John Franklin."

When Leadbelly heard the name of his old friend his hopes leaped. Franklin looked at him warmly on his way to the stand.

"Professor Franklin, hold old are you?"

"Forty-three."

"And what is your present occupation?"

"I'm with the department of sociology at the University of Texas in Austin."

"A new department, is it not?"

"Yes sir."

"What was your occupation before going to Austin?"

"I was captain of the guard at Huntsville."

"And now you are doing work at the university. Isn't that a bit peculiar?"

"Well, perhaps. I didn't agree with the disciplinary procedures throughout the Texas prison system. I thought the treatment of the inmates was brutal and despicable. Now I'm trying to correct things from the outside, which I wasn't able to do from inside Huntsville."

"I see. Do you know the defendant, Huddie Ledbetter?"

"I do."

"How long have you known him?"

"Well, I knew him first in 1919 when he entered Huntsville. I was acquainted with him until 1925 when he was pardoned. I haven't seen him in five years."

"Do you know others in the prison administration during that time who knew him?"

"Yes."

"Do you know of the reputation of the defendant among such persons?"

"Yes, I do."

"Did the defendant have a reputation for the truth -- honesty and veracity?"

"Most assuredly."

"And a reputation for moral conduct?"

"Yes."

"It would be fair to say that the reputation in no way suggests a trait for violence or robbery?"

"That's correct."

"Now, Mr. Franklin, can you tell us why the reputation was as you say it was?"

"Yes. Huddie was a model prisoner. He was well liked by the guards and the administration. He was also well liked by the prison population. Everyone knew he worked harder than most and would willingly take up the slack for weaker prisoners."

"Can you tell us what, from your personal observation, justified Mr. Ledbetter's good reputation?"

"Huddie wouldn't do an unjust thing to anyone. For instance, when he wanted something to drink or when he was broke or needed the rent, he could get it by simply playing his music and he knew it. He never intentionally committed a crime. As far as I've ever known, every time he got in trouble it was instigated by someone else. He's fundamentally a peaceful man."

"Finally, Professor. Wasn't Huddie fully pardoned?"

"Yes, he was. Warden Foster at Sugar Land recognized that Huddie was sorry for his crime and that the sentence in New Boston was quite extreme. Since he'd already served seven years, we did what we could to have Governor Pat Neff review the case. When Neff met Huddie and heard his music, he agreed with us that he'd been punished enough."

"You had no misgivings about letting a convicted murderer loose again?"

"None whatsoever. To us, he never was a convicted murderer. We also thought the sentence was extreme. We knew he was the type of man who always bore the brunt of provocations, and we never really thought he actually murdered anyone."

"Thank you, Professor."

Pyburn glared at the witness before he began his cross-examination. He held a piece of paper in one hand. "Mr. Franklin," he began. "Did the defendant ever escape from prison?"

"Yes sir," Franklin said evenly.

"And was he punished?"

"No sir."

"He wasn't disciplined at all for escaping, or trying to escape?"

"I had a long talk with---"

"I just want to know whether he was disciplined, Mr. Franklin. Yes or no."

"No."

"And was the escape ever recorded in his file?"

"No." Franklin's voice was low.

"Was he given extra work duty or other chores?"

"No."

"Wasn't he, in fact, given a better job? Made leadman on the Number One Hoe Squad, I believe it's called?"

Herndon jumped up. "Objection your Honor! Leading the witness!"

"Overruled. The validity of the testimony is in question. Continue, Mr. Pyburn."

"May I have your answer, sir?"

"Yes," Franklin said. "That's what it's called."

"Doesn't that sound like more of a reward than a punishment?"

"It's one of the better jobs, yes sir."

Pyburn turned and walked to the jury box. He wheezed in exasperation and waved the piece of paper. "This is the testimony of a former inmate at Huntsville who corroborates the escape of Huddie Ledbetter, the defendant. Now, gentlemen, doesn't it seem to you that a man who desires to change the Texas penitentiary system would not -- would not -- attempt to do so by rewarding a prisoner for escaping? In fact, not even entering the escape into the records? I'm sure we all understand this man's motives."

And Pyburn sat down, smiling, as Herndon yelled at the bench to instruct the jury to disregard Pyburn's last remarks as being vindictive and convoluted, as well as addressed directly to the jury. Herndon requested a re-direct.

"One last thing, Professor Franklin. Why didn't you discipline Huddie when he came back?"

"Because he came back of his own accord, sir. In fact, he was crying at the time."

Herndon called another character witness to the stand. Captain Billy Foster had been the warden at Sugar Land when Leadbelly was there. He gave much the same story as Franklin. Pyburn asked a few pointed questions and then excused him.

The judge leaned forward, then turned to the jury. "Gentlemen of the jury, I should like to make a comment on the testimony of Mr. Franklin and Mr. Foster. Both were called as character witnesses for the accused. Under the laws of this state a character witness is supposed to attest to the reputation of the defendant among his neighbors. What these two character witnesses have testified to is a reputation among what might, by some stretch of the imagination, be called his neighbors -- his prisoner friends, his guards or even his wardens. But that was *five years ago.*

"The code does not say the defendant's neighbors must be his present neighbors, although I'm sure it means that. But I'm allowing their testimony, to give the accused the benefit of the doubt. I'm construing the code very, very liberally. You should keep these considerations in mind when weighing their testimony."

Herndon was on his feet, flabbergasted. "Your honor, the Court cannot comment on the testimony. Article 384 makes it the sole province of the jury to determine the weight of the testimony."

"Mr. Herndon. Shall I tell the jury to disregard it?"

"You have already. I move for a mistrial."

"Your motion is denied. Please remember that I'm doing this to protect the inherent dignity of the Court."

Herndon sat down in disgust. He had to call Leadbelly to the stand. There was simply no other choice and he hated to do it. But no one else could tell his side of the case.

"Your honor," Herndon began, "the defense calls the defendant, Huddie Ledbetter."

In response to a few questions, Leadbelly nervously narrated his story. Occasionally he appeared uncertain, unable to overcome the handicap of his dialect, but Herndon nodded to him reassuringly. Hunched in the chair, he told of being surrounded by Harris and the five others, of being pushed and threatened and of finally being attacked. He used force to protect himself. He denied wanting liquor that night. He had no grudge at the time against Harris or any of the others.

It was Pyburn's turn. He walked over to the witness stand, leaned against it and began loudly. "Mister Ledbetter, how old did you say you were?"

" 'bout forty-three."

"About! Don't you know?"

Leadbelly nodded. "Yessuh, yessuh. I know, but I don't know exactly. I'se 'bout forty-three."

"And where were you born? Do you know *about* where you were born?"

"Yessuh. I'se born over in Leigh, Texas."

"On a farm?"

"My papa was rentin' a farm, but then he move over to Mooringspo't."

"You got in some trouble there, didn't you?"

"Objection!"

"Sustained."

"You fathered an illegitimate child when you were fourteen?"

"Objection!" Herndon's face was flushed.

"I'm showing unsavory character, your honor," Pyburn said patiently.

"Overruled."

"Your honor," Herndon pleaded. "The district attorney can go into past conduct to show bad character only if the conduct has some pertinence to the crime he is charged with. Or if it bears on credibility."

"I think it has pertinence," the judge said.

"How?" Herndon asked.

"Objection overruled, I said. You needn't question the Court, Mr. Herndon."

"So you fathered an illegitimate child when you were fourteen?"

"Yessuh." The questions were coming fast for him.

"You carried a knife with you the night of February 5, when Harris was stabbed, didn't you?"

"Yessuh."

"Do you always carry a knife?"

"Almost always."

"Yes or no, boy?"

"Yessuh."

"You like whiskey, don't you?"

"Yessuh."

"You like it a lot?"

"I guess."

"Sometimes you can't get it, can you? Prohibition?"

"No, suh."

"What? Can you always get it? Yes or no?"

"No."

"But sometimes you really want it."

"Yessuh."

"But you get it anyway, don't you?"

"Yessuh."

"The law doesn't stop *you*, does it?"

"No, suh."

"It didn't stop you in Mooringsport, did it?"

"No, suh."

"Or Dallas?"

"No, suh."

"Or when you stabbed Jim Harris?"

"I didn't stab nobody on purpose."

"Why? Because it was against the law?"

"I dunno."

"If Jim Harris had whiskey that night and you wanted it, what was

there to stop you? The law?"

"Yessuh."

"But you said you broke the law to get whiskey."

"Not that way."

"Not that way? *What* way?"

"I dunno."

"Jim Harris with four others didn't scare you, did they?"

"No, suh."

"Of course they didn't, boy. If they had whiskey you wouldn't be afraid to take it, would you?"

"I didn't take no whiskey."

"Sure you didn't. No more questions, boy."

As Pyburn walked back to his seat, Herndon whispered to the bailiff loud enough for everyone to hear. "That sonofabitch'll use every cheap trick to mix up a poor, wretched Negro."

Herndon, from his seat, turned toward Leadbelly. "I have one question on re-direct. Mr. Ledbetter, have you ever been attacked in the vicinity where Mr. Harris was stabbed?"

"Yes, twice."

"That's why you carry a knife?"

"Yes."

Pyburn then proceeded to put on several rebuttal witnesses attesting to Leadbelly's unsavory character, including Sheriff Tom Hughes and some antagonistic neighbors from Mooringsport. He brought out that Leadbelly had escaped from the Harrison County chain gang and thus was a fugitive from justice. He did everything he could to show how Leadbelly's past pointed to the fact that he was capable of premeditated acts of violence, that his thirst for women and whiskey ignited this violence, and that this current case was simply another episode in a violent, lawless career.

When the parade of witnesses ended, it was six o'clock. No one had noticed the time creeping up. After dinner there would be final arguments. Leadbelly, totally confused, was certain Franklin's testimony had been the turning point. And the jury looked like nice folks.

The prosecution's summation was vicious. Pyburn, in a terse, matter-of-fact manner, ticked off the evidence against Leadbelly, laying heavy stress on the fact that the pattern of the man's life had gone beyond the realm of rehabilitation. He charged Leadbelly with being a walking menace to society, an arrogant, knife-wielding, gun-toting, irresponsible Negro. A man whose life was warped beyond restoration.

"Gentlemen of the jury," he said finally, pointing to Leadbelly. "I want you to look at this man. Look at the scar around his neck, the scar on his face. Disregard, *if you can*, his color. Look at his features.

Look at his forehead, his flattened nose, his fuzzy hair. I've never been known as a bigot, gentlemen, but there are differences. I ask you now, is this the type of sub-humanoid creature that God created to fill the earth? Is this killing, brawling, lying Negro the man you want to walk down the streets of Shreveport next to your women and children? That man is one who would deliberately kill in cold blood and stop at nothing else. I want every member of the jury to raise his hand if he would invite this man to a family picnic. A man who would dare to cross the color line!"

The five jurors looked at each other uncomfortably, avoiding Leadbelly's and Herndon's astonished stares.

In a lower voice, Pyburn pleaded menacingly. "I direct you men, who think of yourselves as God-fearing, law-abiding citizens of the great state of Louisiana and the great city of Shreveport, and who owe it to yourselves to do your one small part to protect the women and children of this city. I direct you to bring back a verdict of guilty as charged, so that we may put this man away for the rest of his life!"

The sudden low murmur throughout the courtroom was cut off by Sally Ledbetter's shrill scream. She had to be taken from the room, sobbing as she went. Leadbelly turned briefly, his own eyes moist, and saw them take her out. He looked at Herndon, paralyzed.

Herndon's face was stone. "That sonofabitch!" he whispered. Turning to Leadbelly, he said, "That filthy bastard has been doing this his whole career. Just hang on, Ledbetter. I'm not sure it worked this time."

Herndon rose. The courtroom fell silent once again, and the only sound was the clicking of the hammers on his pistol canes as he walked to the jury box. He stared at the men for two full minutes in silence, probing deeply into their eyes. He twirled the chambers on his cane handles and cocked the hammers again.

"Now, gentlemen." Herndon's voice was soft and incredulous. "Now, I have seen and heard everything. I'm not sure I believe it, actually. Did I actually hear, with my own ears, a man of the law, a man who has sworn to uphold the law, with liberty and justice for all -- did I actually hear what this official of the city of Shreveport said? Tell me. Just nod your heads -- did I actually hear a man condemned, not because of a crime, but because he was 'sub-human'? Nod your heads, gentlemen. Did I hear that?"

Herndon fell silent again, and glared at the jury. To a man, no one moved. Self-consciously, they adjusted their suspenders, crossed their legs, scratched their ears. Herndon walked back to his table, and called across the room to them.

"And what about our eyes?" he asked. "Can there be something wrong with our sight? Surely the same God Mr. Pyburn mentions gave us each a similar set of eyes. Yet, I don't see what he sees. Tell me now, gentlemen, if you agree.

"I see a man whose hands have been given an extraordinary talent by Mr. Pyburn's God. I see a man who can do with a guitar what I'll wager none of you can do. And I've heard his music, maybe many of us have without knowing it. I've heard the tenderness in his voice. I've seen him caress his guitar more tenderly and more respectfully than any of you gentlemen have caressed your wives and babies.

"But even more than that. I see a man who never had a chance at a decent education, and who, as a small boy, was forced to pick cotton alongside his mother and father. Have any of you gentlemen been raised similarly? I'll wager not. I see a man whose environment has been a violent one, true -- but a man who has proven time and time again that he didn't look for trouble, but merely wanted to play his music in peace. To be left alone, in his own town, with his own people. Is that too much to ask? Don't you think Mr. Pyburn's God would grant him that one, single request, in the light of all He has denied this man? Gentlemen, I know *my* God would!"

Herndon ceased his regard of Leadbelly, and walked back to the jury box, waving one of his canes as he stopped. The jurymen looked with interest at the pearl handles.

"Gentlemen of the jury, the seed of life right now grows within each of you, and you're free to create life at will, according to God's command in the Bible. 'Increase and multiply and fill the earth,' He said. And yet, did He mean to create life that would be unbearable? Did He mean to raise a child to be whipped and beaten and tortured by other men created by God? Or did He mean to create a world where we all live in peace and harmony, to enjoy the fruits of God's creation? Can you, as men of God, send this man to hard labor in a terrible, devilish prison just because five other known criminals *say* he attacked them? Can you weigh, as I personally think and as the Bible tells us, as only God can, the word of one man against another, without concrete evidence, and sentence one to hell and the other to heaven?

"I quote Proverbs, Chapter 15, Verse 33: 'The fear of the Lord is the lesson of wisdom; and humility goeth before glory.' Now, isn't that what a court of law is all about? Isn't it the fear of the Lord that tells us to strive for wisdom? To find the truth, lest the loss of that truth bring the Lord's wrath down upon us? Isn't our humility, in the quest for the Lord's truth, more urgent than our own personal glory?

"And as true, God-fearing men, can we sit back, satisfied, and send this poor, uneducated man whose only desire is to play his music in peace… can we send him to a hell on earth because we're afraid to humble ourselves and admit we don't know the truth?"

Herndon slowly turned and limped back to the table in absolute silence. His words had visibly moved the hard-line Baptists he knew were sitting on the jury. The judge sat stoically, watching Herndon closely, as the latter turned once more.

"And I will not even insult this court of law by mentioning again the pitiful lack of concrete evidence on which you are asked to render your decision. Each of you knows, deep in your soul, the real meaning of what has transpired in this room today. Each of you knows, in your life-giving heart, what real justice is being questioned here. Do you know the word 'empathy,' gentlemen? 'Empathy' means putting yourself in the other man's place, to project yourself into the mind of another man. If you were to practice that right now, right here, then I should be prouder than ever before in my career of the justice you will have wrought. I shall be supremely happy, if you will, just this once, imagine yourselves in this poor man's place. What would you have yourselves, then, say to the charge as you have heard it here today?

"If this man were you, or your son, or your mother, could you say 'Guilty'?"

And that evening, a withered old man, a clerk in the Shreveport County Courthouse working evenings during his retirement, made the following entry in the log of the day's proceedings:

28640 State of Louisiana

V.

Huddie Ledbetter

Assault to Murder

This case having been regularly fixed for trial, the accused being in open Court, accompanied by his Counsel, E. N. Herndon, Esq., now comes Aubrey M. Pyburn, Assistant District Attorney, who prosecutes on behalf of the State, the State and defense announcing ready, when in came the following jurors, drawn from the regular criminal venire, to wit: A. S. Farr, R. A. Querves, L. V. Rogers, Ben Haywood, Jr., and Paul Slattery, making five (5) good and lawful men, all of the Parish of Caddo, who were duly empaneled and sworn, and after hearing the evidence, the argument of Counsel and the charge of the Court, retired to their room, in charge of the Sheriff, to consider their verdict, and returning to open Court, through their Foreman, upon their oaths do say:

"We The Jury, find the defendant guilty as charged. (Signed) R. A. Querves, Foreman." Whereupon, the court ordered the verdict recorded, the jury discharged and the prisoner remanded for sentence.

And on the evening of February 25, 1930, the same old man wrote again in the leather-bound ledger:

28640 State of Louisiana

V.

Huddie Ledbetter

Assault to Murder

The accused being in open Court, now comes for sentence. Being asked by the court if he has anything to say why the sentence of

the law should not be pronounced upon him and having replied,
was sentenced as follows: "It is the judgement of the Court that
you, Huddie Ledbetter, be confined in the state penitentiary
at Baton Rouge, Louisiana, at hard labor, for a period of not
less than six (6) nor more than ten (10) years, subject to the
commutation provided by law, and that the Sheriff conduct you
hence and deliver you to the Keeper thereof.

Once again, the "King o' the Twelve-String Guitar" was going
to jail.

###

Chapter Fifteen

Leadbelly was taken from Shreveport to an institution known as "The Wall" on the corner of Sixth and Laurel Streets in Baton Rouge. Designed from the floor plan of the Connecticut State Prison, it had been in operation for a century. The lease system, whereby prisoners were rented to farmers and factories, had been abandoned, and the control board arbitrarily decided which prisoners would remain in "The Wall" and which would be herded up to work the farms at the dreaded Angola. The control board transferred Huddie Ledbetter to Angola.

He arrived on a bitterly cold, rainy March 12, along with sixty-three other convicts. The trip took longer than usual; a minor flood had occurred ten miles from Bains, and it took eight hours to repair a trestle. By the time the engine finally steamed its way into the Louisiana State Farm, it was late at night. None of the prisoners had eaten.

In 1930, Angola was just a place where criminals were sent to be forgotten.

Where the Mississippi River twisted at Tunica and curved sharply back on itself to cut the state line on its way from Fort Adams, there sprawled 18,000 acres of West Feliciana Parish. Bordered on three sides by impenetrable woods and marsh and on the fourth by the brackish water of the river, it contained seven outcamps scattered like flyspecks over the fields of cane and cotton.

The decrepit outcamps were nothing more than overcrowded pens. They were made of brick and cinder block, covered with dome-shaped roofs of corrugated metal. The buildings were two stories, heated in winter by a single wood-burning stove, and each housed as many as 200 inmates, even though they measured only 30 by 70 feet. The wooden floors were filled with rickety triple bunks covered with straw-filled mattresses. The lights burned all night long. There were no bars on the windows, but each camp was secured by a fence strung tautly with twenty-four strands of rusty barbed wire. At times, during the summer months, the temperature inside these camps could reach as high as 130 degrees.

Although the prison was only thirty years old, it had already fallen into shambles through misuse and neglect.

The entrance to Angola was secured by a barbed-wire fence, inside of which was a tiny, cube-like guardhouse. In this shack two gigantic safes housed a small arsenal. Across from the guardhouse loomed a light gray structure, its windows barred and its entrance sculptured in angular configurations. This served as the medical clinic and administration building. There was no hospital. In cases of emergency the victim was taken sixty miles south to Baton Rouge.

The first thing that caught Leadbelly's attention at Angola was that the guards, though they walked around carrying shotguns and rifles, were dressed in prison fatigues. At Angola, he learned, the prisoners guarded each other.

The convicts were marched into a dimly lit hall on the first floor of the administration building and there, seated on wooden benches, were given coffee and bread. The door was locked for the night, and sixty-four prisoners, still shackled together by leg irons, were left to their own devices to find a way to sleep on the damp floor. When Leadbelly awoke the next morning, he was soaked through and shivering.

They were given weak coffee and were casually inspected by a medical officer, and then assigned to the fields for work. Leadbelly and three other men were marched two miles out to Camp A, which was to be his home for the next ten years. Sometime later he heard that there were a hundred women at Angola, living in Camp F, another two miles to the north. Camp F was in his mind often, but the two miles might as well have been two hundred.

Each day at Angola was a duplicate of the preceding one. The prisoners went to work at six in the morning, marched out by men on horseback who were careful to stay just to the right of the work squadron. The backbreaking day was spent knee-deep in mud during the rainy season, planting, hoeing, chopping and cultivating the crops. When summer came, the roads and fields turned to dust and the finely powdered dirt was everywhere. The men were in tatters. One man boasted that his fatigues were eleven years old. From daylight to dark the prisoners worked. There was no recreation, no Sundays off, no iced tea at the warden's house, no visitors -- nothing but endless work.

There were attempted escapes, but none succeeded. It was fifty miles through the woods to the nearest crossroads, and if a man were lucky enough to survive the bloodhounds, he could never survive the canebrakes. Inmate murders were a day-to-day occurrence, and most went unsolved. The food was little better than swill, delivered to the outcamps and shoved through the wire fence in metal containers. It was always the same: rice or beans, bread and fat, sometimes coffee -- never meat.

Leadbelly believed he'd been wronged, and the prospect of spending another decade of his life in prison made him bitter and angry. It was this attitude that led to his first brush with discipline, Angola style.

On his fourth day there, a guard prodded him unusually painfully in the back with the sharp handle of a hoe. Leadbelly turned and cursed at the man -- a fellow prisoner -- and the guard immediately separated him from the rest of the team and took him to a small, box-like building near Camp E. The building was known at Angola as the Red Cap.

With the help of three other guards, Leadbelly was stripped naked and staked spread-eagle on his back near the entrance to the red-roofed building. Amid taunts and jeers he was flogged with a Black Betty from his nipples to his knees.

When he passed out, they untied him and threw him into the small Red Cap room, where he cooked in solitary for a week, and where it consistently measured a hundred and thirty degrees.

From then on the worst form of torture for Leadbelly was suppressing his anger. He lived for the day he would be free again. In his occasional letter to Martha he pleaded with her to find someone -- anyone -- who could possibly arrange for a parole hearing. He even wrote to his old friend Professor Franklin, asking for help. Franklin promised to try. He also wrote that Blind Lemon Jefferson had been found frozen to death on the streets of Chicago. Leadbelly worked on in sullen silence, waiting.

The harsh winter of the following year caused the Mississippi River to break over its banks, and a thousand men at Angola were cordoned off into teams for emergency work around the clock.

Leadbelly picked his moment precisely, one day near sundown. He was carrying sandbags near Shreve's Cutoff. The far edge of the river was a half-mile away, and the black forests behind it were silhouetted behind a sky flared with crimson-edged storm clouds. When the last bag was unloaded from the cart, the guard turned his attention to a group of convicts assigned to take the cart back and fill it with more sand. Leadbelly edged closer to the water, slipping carefully on his belly, and worked his way down a furrow toward the east bank of the river. Sludge filled his work boots as he neared the edge, and he felt the icy Mississippi soaking into him.

Fifty feet away, a guard momentarily relaxed his vigilance while he struggled to light a cigarette against the wind. Leadbelly was on his feet and headed toward the river. As he plunged in, the frigid current knocked the breath out of him and twisted him backward. He struggled against it and began to swim.

He didn't know that no one had ever made the far bank.

His disappearance was noticed immediately, and a launch was dispatched to retrieve him. They spotted Leadbelly unusually close to the far bank at Torras Landing. "Christ Almighty," someone yelled. "The sonofabitch almost made it!"

When the searchlight picked him out, Leadbelly knew he was doomed. For the first time in his life he wanted to die. To just let go and drown. He began to shake with despair. Someone in the boat fired at him. "Hey you, you stupid coon! You wanna drown or be shot?"

Leadbelly gave up. They dragged him aboard and one man battered the rifle into his stomach. Someone else hit him on the head.

He awoke when a pail of water was thrown in his face. He was strapped to two trees along the west bank. The place was deserted except for the two men. One of them, a beady-eyed, rodent-nosed man with a toothbrush mustache, was shining a flashlight in his face.

"Well, well," he said casually. "I hope you had a nice rest, 'cause you sure gonna need it."

Leadbelly shivered. The wind was stronger now, and it turned his wet clothing into strands of ice. His head throbbed. He could taste the salt of his own blood. "I'se sorry. Please don't whip me."

"A regular Jack Johnson, eh? Well, black-ass, I'm the Great White Hope and I'm gonna beat your ass right into the ground. Or maybe…"

He flashed the light in the direction of a weather-beaten log. "Y'know, when I was workin' down river with a bunch of cons not too long ago, one of 'em took a hankering to take off, just like you. You know what they did to that nigger? Well, they wedged open a log just like that one yonder, and they took his nuts and jammed 'em in the crack. An' what you think they did next? They just pulled the wedge from the log and handed him a knife."

Leadbelly gaped at him in horror. The other man cackled.

"Lucky for you we ain't got no wedge." They laughed again.

The light flashed. The man was waving a Black Betty at him. "Well, Jack Johnson, I'm gonna go twenty-six rounds with you. Let's see how much gumption that'll take out of you."

Leadbelly set himself and grunted as the thick black strap seared into his shoulders. He heard one of them shout, "Round One!"

*   *   *   *   *

He woke up inside the Red Cap room, hungry and thirsty. He had no idea how long he'd been there. The scabs were itching. He rolled his head on the brick floor and opened his eyes. The walls were cement block, and a trench, teeming with flies, bordered one side.

The only ventilation was from a pipe jutting like an elbow above his head and disappearing into the roof. He could tell by the heat and the slits of light threading through the cracks in the roof that it was day. But which one?

He lay quiet, blinking his eyes. His back and shoulders ached and he tried not to move. He drifted into a hazy stupor, reliving a time in his childhood. He was five, or maybe six, and his mama had sent him on an important errand. All the way from the farm into Mooringsport. She had carefully combed his hair and given him money to buy meat. "Get some center-cut pork chops, Huddie. Tell the man you want 'em center cut."

There were two white women ahead of him, so Huddie waited. When they had finished, he gave the butcher his order. But three other white women came in, and the butcher turned from him. He guessed grown-ups got served first.

When butcher finished with the women, Huddie held up his money and his order. "Please, could I have the chops now?" he asked.

The man grabbed a handful of meat and wrapped it up. "Boy, you got to learn that white people get served first." He slammed down the package.

Huddie took it and ran home crying. He told his mama what had happened. She opened the package. It was all fat.

When Leadbelly awoke again the slits of light were gone. His tongue was thick in his mouth. He felt along his bare shoulders and reckoned by the scabs that he had been there several days. When he tried to get up, the gashes on his back tore open and began to bleed again.

The next day an iron door at the bottom of the wall opened abruptly, and a surge of light blinded him. A square tin plate, the size of a book, was thrust inside. The door clanged shut. He crawled to the plate and probed at the food, shoving whatever it was into his mouth. Then he threw up and staggered back to the corner.

He lived like that for a month.

He used the time to think, because there was nothing else to do. He examined his life as if he were inspecting a mosaic. He was positive now that he would have nine more years in Angola, and that meant he would be in his mid-fifties when he got out. The days of rambling and fighting would be gone. He'd rotted away most of his adult years in prisons, and his dream of becoming a great singer and musician was rapidly vanishing.

The only way to get out of Angola was for them to let him out. And the only way anyone would let him out was if he acted like a "good nigger." He thought about writing Franklin again -- maybe the governor of Louisiana would be visiting. And he would write to Martha again at his first opportunity. He would tell them how he planned to tote for everyone, become "the best white man's nigga on the farm" and perhaps even get his guitar back. Of course it would be at least a couple of years before he could request a parole for good behavior. After two beatings, not many people would listen to him.

Then despair crowded into the room, the sheer depression, the feeling of being totally lost. As he resigned himself to life as a slave, he knew the next years would be the worst in his life. Each day would be a heavy granite block to be hauled away and piled into a week, and then more until a month was formed, and then he would look back at that enormous pyramid of time and know there were still a hundred more pyramids to be built.

sept 6 1932

dear huddie,

*the sherif in shrevport tell me there no womens allowed to visit
you so i cant see you like i want to, so i am very glad you is being
good and hope you will be getin a parden in the nex few years.
i am glad to here you say you love me and i love you too. i aint
seen no other man.*

*you mama is fine but ailin lately and she say that she try to rite
you a letter soon. edmond is also fine and i get to see him now
and then. i sure wish i cud here you sing to me again. your honey
martha.*

Leadbelly read the letter twice and then carefully folded it and stashed it under his straw mattress with the others. As he did after reading each preceding letter, he sprawled face down on his wooden bunk and buried his face in his shirt and pressed his abdomen hard against the mattress.

It was Sunday, but before he was marched to the field he was summoned by a guard and taken to the main administration building and into the office of Captain Andrew Reaux.

Reaux was nothing but a snuff-dipping politician from Florida who had bounced around the prison system a long time. He was a hard worker, and during his career he had been in high places and low. He had always coveted the opportunity to run his own prison, and now he was actually running Angola, because the real warden, a cousin of Huey Long, was an incompetent lush.

Reaux ran a stubby hand through his black curly hair and wiped the pomade on his shirt. "Says here you're a musician, Ledbetter. Is that true?"

"Yessuh."

"Guitar?"

"Yessuh, guitar. Some piano. Windjammer and fiddle. But I'se mostly good on the guitar."

"I have a letter here from a man named Franklin. Some professor at Austin who knew you when you were serving a sentence in Texas. Rather impressive, in view of your record."

Leadbelly caught his breath. To him, Franklin meant pardon.

"The state's been asking a lot of experts like this Franklin to come up with some sort of answer to the discipline problem here. There's been too many escapes and fights and murders. Hell, even over in the women's camp they're beatin' the crotches out of each other. Franklin seems to think one of the answers is to give the prisoners something to do with their spare time. I personally think eliminating spare time completely would solve it better." Reaux laughed.

He dropped the letter and looked up at Leadbelly. "It looks like you've made up your mind to be a good nigger and wait out your time."

"Oh, yessuh. I know now there ain't no sense in bein' whipped. Just make the days ache even more."

"Good. How do you think the inmates would go for some kind of entertainment on Sundays? Like in Texas?"

He was disappointed that it was not a pardon, but at the same time he thought he could get some better treatment if he had his guitar. "It sure was fine at Sugar Land. You give the men some music and it sort of make their meanness go away. Sometimes when they hear the blues it sort of make their troubles seem littler for a while. Don' know why, that's jus' the way it is."

"I've never been much for that music. But what do you think about gettin' up some kind of band?"

"I'd sure like that, yessuh. 'Ceptin' we ain't got nothin' to play."

"Well, don't worry about that. I'll get us something out of Baton Rouge. I haven't made up my mind yet, though. Might be a good idea, but I don't want them to think I'm gettin' soft. They're still gonna have to earn some free time to listen."

"That would be right fine, Cap'n. Please ask Cap'n Franklin to get my guitar from my wife in Shrevepo't. I can't write too good and sure would appreciate it, Cap'n. I be the bes' damn nigga at Angola."

"Never mind that shit. What I want is a thousand best damn niggers. And if letting them sing will do it, maybe that's the way to go."

Leadbelly was dismissed. And that evening back at Outcamp A he exuberantly canvassed everyone he knew. Everyone eagerly agreed that some music on Sundays would be a good thing. It would have been funny if everyone hadn't been so bitter.

A month later it was announced that prisoners with relatively good records for any given week would be allowed to listen to others entertain the white visitors on Sunday afternoons. A few dozen men played solo or formed small groups, and none was happier than Leadbelly. For he, more than anyone else, now had a shred of his prior existence returned to him.

###

Chapter Sixteen

In the summer of 1933 a black Ford sedan appeared at the main gate of Angola. It was covered with dust, having chugged its way from Austin, and the back seat was loaded with a large metal machine, coiled wires and unidentifiable gadgetry. The driver, a young man in his late teens named Alan Lomax, was handsome and neatly dressed. Beside him was his father John, a heavy, double-chinned man dressed in a dark suit and clenching a long unlit cigar between his teeth.

They were collecting folk music under a commission from the Library of Congress, and for the past several weeks they'd been recording prison songs throughout the southern states. The Lomaxes had permission to record whatever music they could coax from Angola's inmates, and many of the two thousand men and women were eager to play. They were startled when they heard their own voices played back to them, and there were some excellent singers. But among them all, Leadbelly stood out. He fascinated both father and son with his virtuosity and his seemingly endless repertoire. His resonant voice rocked through the recording room each night.

Frequently, when Captain Reaux wasn't about, Leadbelly would punctuate his songs with pleas for the elder Lomax to help him get a pardon. "I ain't a bad nigga, Mastah Lomax, no suh. I sometimes got into a lot of trouble from drinkin' whiskey, but that's all. I'se up for parole, and maybe you ask the Gov'nor to turn me over to you. I'll go to work and do anythin' you want."

Lomax told Leadbelly he couldn't do much, since he had other prisons to visit and everyone wanted the same favor.

"But I'se the bes' guiter player in the field. I'll make you a lot o' money jus' pickin' at this twelve-string box. An' you don't got to give me nothin' but a few nickels when you feel like it."

"I appreciate the offer, but I just don't think I can." Lomax struck a match and lit his cigar. "Have you ever been in jail before?"

"Oh, no. I ain't never been in this penitenshuh. I'se always been never botherin' nobody. Jus' a peaceful ol' nigga what minds his own business. I never did nothin' before in my life."

Lomax went over and put his hand on Leadbelly's shoulder. "Leadbelly, I believe you. I'll see what I can do. I don't know when or if I'll ever get back here again, though."

"Oh, Mastah Lomax, I hope you do. I ain't never been punished like I been gettin' punished here. Please help me get out!"

Leadbelly sang songs and entreated Lomax to help him up to the very last day. He sang almost every song he ever knew, and made up new ones. He told stories about him and Blind Lemon Jefferson and his days and nights in Saint Paul's Bottom and in Dallas. He bragged that he could introduce Lomax to every decent musician in the south. He promised he would be Lomax's personal chauffeur and Man Friday, and pointed out that with his immense strength he could haul Lomax's heavy equipment anywhere it needed to be. Lomax was intrigued with the idea.

John and Alan Lomax drove to Baton Rouge. In the back of the sedan were a dozen acetate discs in whose grooves were etched the first recorded voice of Huddie Ledbetter.

*   *   *   *   *

In Baton Rouge, Lomax learned more about Leadbelly's record. He was not eligible for parole, and he'd often been in jail. He'd been whipped for misconduct at Angola and served time for murder at Sugar Land. Lomax wrote Leadbelly that he'd looked at his record and had discovered certain facts that Leadbelly neglected to mention. Leadbelly replied with another plea that he was not guilty and had been framed. He begged Lomax to let him come with him on his tour.

At first Lomax and his son discussed the possibility of doing what they could to obtain his freedom. The prospect of having a personal valet and chauffeur for his tour through the South was attractive, and Lomax saw that a free Leadbelly could contribute a wealth of folk singing to America. But after discovering the truth about Leadbelly's past, he had misgivings about traveling on lonely roads with his son and a convicted murderer.

Leadbelly heard no more from the Lomaxes during the following months, and he plunged back into despair. Then, in December, he received a letter from Edmond informing him of his mother's death. He was not permitted to attend the funeral at Shiloh Baptist Church, even under guard, and he grieved for months. His father had died when he was a prisoner at Sugar Land, and now his mother passed away while he was at Angola.

He lay awake at night under the glare of the outcamp floodlights, and thought of Sally, and of Martha.

> *Gonna tell my baby when I get back home*
> *Gonna tell my baby when I get back home*
> *Lawd, I been down yonder where the lights*
> *burn all night long.*

213

In July of 1934, John and Alan Lomax returned to Angola with a more technologically modern recording machine. Once again Leadbelly sat on the four-legged wooden stool, the microphone carefully placed in front of him like an enormous ear. A few feet away Alan worked the machine and placed a new aluminum disc on the turntable.

Leadbelly was wearing prison stripes and his high-pitched voice was still resonant and strong. It was Sunday and it had been raining all day. When Leadbelly was brought into the makeshift recording studio he was dripping wet, and drops of water clung to his face and mingled with sweat as he sang.

Time after time, Leadbelly pleaded with Lomax to ask the governor for a pardon. "Please help me get out. I do anythin' for you. If somebody tries to shoot you even, why I'll jus' jump in the way and catch the bullet myself. I shine you shoes and that old black car o' yours and I jus' do anythin' you wish."

Lomax was finding Leadbelly's entreaties hard to resist. He knew Leadbelly could be of considerable aid in breaking down the wall of suspicion that often shielded a northern white researcher from the black convicts. When Leadbelly told him again of his success with Pat Neff, Lomax cautioned him that such events were infrequent, and that Louisiana Governor 0. K. Allen would probably not be as benevolent as Neff. But Leadbelly remained positive and steadfast in his claim that if the two men would take a recording and play it for Allen, a pardon would come.

Leadbelly soon abandoned the subservient "Mastah" when addressing Lomax, substituting what he thought was the more dignified "Boss." As in, "Boss, help me get out o' this place. I'se in a livin' hell every day!"

Lomax thought a bit and consulted again with his son. "Leadbelly," he said almost casually, "sing that pardon song again. We'll make a record of it. Then on the other side of the disc we'll record your favorite song -- one that you select -- and tonight Alan and I will drive back to Baton Rouge. Tomorrow I'll call on Governor Allen and, if possible, play him the entire record."

Leadbelly dropped the old tired guitar, which was now heavily taped, and jumped up. He profusely thanked the Lomaxes and danced about, praising their generosity and already thanking the Lord for his pardon.

Leadbelly had intended to simply modify the words that he sang to Governor Neff, but he finally decided to throw out the old Sugar Land melody and replace it with the tune from "Shreveport Jail." It was a much simpler tune, a black modification of a white melody -- the kind of music he knew white people liked to hear. He even changed dates to fit the rhyme.

> *In nineteen hundred and thirty-two,*
> *Gov'nor O.K. Allen, I'm appealin' to you.*
> *An' Mister Hymes looked over the pen,*
> *Told Gov'nor O.K. Allen, "You got too many men."*

> *Gov'nor O.K. Allen began to turn about,*
> *"Got to make some 'rangements*
> *to turn some of them out."*

> *I know my wife gonna jump and shout,*
> *When the train rolls up and I come steppin' out.*
> *Had you, Gov'nor O.K. Allen, like you got me,*
> *I'd wake up in the mornin', let you out on reprieve.*

And on the other side of the disc he recorded a seldom requested song he wrote years ago, called "Goodnight Irene."

The next morning Baton Rouge was clear and hot -- 102 degrees, with humidity in the high 90s. Lomax parked his car along the row of tourist vehicles, and the father and son walked toward the state capitol. The air smelled of refineries and cement factories along the nearby Mississippi.

The two-year-old building rose four hundred and fifty feet above the great valley like a yellow granite finger. Forty-eight granite steps, each bearing the name of a state, led to the entrance. Alan paused and touched his father's arm, and the two men read the inscription chiseled at the right of the embellished brass doors:

THE INSTRVMENTS WHICH WE HAVE
JVST SIGNED WILL CAVSE NO TEARS
TO BE SHED. THEY PREPARE AGES
OF HAPPINESS FOR INNVMERABLE
GENERATIONS OF HVMAN CREATVRES.

Governor Allen's office was on the first floor, in a corridor behind the elevators. Allen was known as a rubber-stamp man for Senator Huey Long, and in fact even now the two were in conference.

Lomax was undaunted, however. He knew the capitol had possession of a new RCA Victrola and left Leadbelly's recording with Allen's secretary, a helpful and cheery man who promised he would encourage the governor to play the record and to read Lomax's accompanying note at his earliest convenience.

On Wednesday, July 25, 1934, Governor O. K. Allen of Louisiana granted a commutation of sentence for Huddie Ledbetter. It may have been the song or it may have been Allen's awareness of the fact that the warden of Angola State Penitentiary was Huey Long's first cousin. If the warden had allowed the recording to be made and to be sent to him in Baton Rouge, it might be safer to grant the pardon. Whatever the reason, the paper was signed and sent to Angola and miraculously, Huddie Ledbetter, imprisoned for murder, had sung his way to a pardon a second time -- and in two different states!

But Leadbelly, of course, was certain his song had done it again. The next day, when he held in his hand the paper that told him he was free again, he danced and shouted all over the administration building. "I'se free again! I'se goin' home to Marthy! Great Lawd, I'se free! Goodbye, Cap'n Reaux! Goodbye, ol' Angola! I ain't gonna see you no more!"

Holding his guitar and a paper bag with the carefully folded pardon inside, and with a new ten-dollar bill in his pocket, he headed across the river at Baton Rouge and aimed himself for Shreveport.

###

Chapter Seventeen

Martha Promise lived in a neat, rented cottage set off from the road and surrounded by mimosas. Not far away, on the road from Shreveport to Mooringsport, was a Gulf station and a cluttered roadside market. He stopped at the bottom of the porch and peered curiously at the front door. Lace curtains blocked his view of the inside. He climbed the steps and tried to peer in again. Finally he knocked firmly on the door.

There was no answer. He knocked again, and called her name. Still nothing.

The door was unlocked and he went in. The house was still and quiet; only the birds and an occasional passing automobile could be heard. He tiptoed to the middle of the front room and looked around. There were antimacassars on the furniture and fresh flowers in small jars. Although the chairs and parts of the sofa were threadbare, the room was clean.

"Marthy?"

He walked lightly to the kitchen and looked around. In the cooler there were two bottles of soda pop, some eggs and a loaf of bread. No whiskey or beer. A small wooden table and a single chair seemed to serve as an eating area, and each of the windows had flowered curtains tied neatly back. He went back to the front room, laid his guitar on the sofa and walked to the only other room, the bedroom.

The bed was neatly made, and five pretty print dresses hung on a makeshift clothes rack in one corner. He walked to a dresser and inspected the top of it. There was a cross and a prayerbook, a small ornate bottle of Sachet of Lavender and a folded hankie. He opened the top drawer and found a pile of his old letters, tied in a red ribbon. He read some of them and smiled to himself, hearing his own words again in his mind.

He also found an unfinished letter she had been writing:

dear honey huddie
im sorry i havnt writ in so long time. i workin now in a landri
and go to work early in the mornin and come home late in the
evenin. im happy about you playin you music again in the pen

He went back to the front room and sat down. He could go try to find the laundry and just take her out of it for the afternoon, or he could wait here for her. He decided to wait, and finally went to the bedroom to lie down. He was asleep within minutes, for the first time since he had left Angola two days ago.

Martha Promise came home at eight-thirty that evening, when the mimosa leaves were curling closed. She went directly into the kitchen, where she put down a sack of groceries and began making coffee. She then came back into the front room and took off her white uniform, folding it neatly and placing it on a straight-backed chair in a corner. She would wear it again tomorrow.

Martha, at thirty-two, was a stunning woman. Her long black hair was slightly waved, parted on the right side, and a brass barrette held it from falling over her left eye. She wore two tiny gold earrings. Ever since her mother's death she had lived alone in this cottage, working six days a week, ten hours a day, saving money and waiting for Huddie's return. She never doubted that he would return to her. In recent months his letters had been optimistic. He was certain this man, Mr. Lomax, would get him out. She also knew God, in all His mercy, would return her man. She seldom saw anyone else and spent what little spare time she had in the garden.

She stood in the front room now in only her underclothes and looked around. Then she saw it. Her eyes widened and she stood rigid, her arms tight and stiff at her sides. Against the deep brown of the sofa, the battered old green guitar rested with the neck propped over the armrest.

She stopped humming and her eyes darted about the room. "Huddie?" She went to the bedroom door and, shaking, opened it.

He lay on the bed, sprawled out and breathing slowly but deeply, his muscular right arm arched over his head as if to ward off a blow.

"Huddie," she whispered to herself as tears came to her eyes. She silently moved to the bed and reached down, touching his fingers delicately. "Huddie," she said again, and then she went back to the front room, closing the door gently behind her. She cried. Oh Lord, she thought, thank you for sending me my man. And please, Sweet Jesus, keep him here this time.

*   *   *   *   *

They sat on the front porch in rocking chairs, watching the cars chug by on the dusty road, and Leadbelly strummed his guitar. They had just finished dinner, and both were drowsy. He'd been with Martha two weeks now, doing odd jobs wherever he could find them and coming home every evening before Martha did, waiting for her when she came through the door.

At last, Leadbelly was content. He often looked at Martha and smiled, saying nothing, as she worked on her mending.

He began to play "Careless Love," softly, humming the tune to himself. Martha stopped and looked over at him. "At least that song's better than the wicked ones you always singin'," she said.

"What you mean, wicked?"

"Oh, all those ones about loose women and the fights you had."

"They ain't wicked, Marthy. They's just the way life is down in them parts. They's the blues songs. The happy songs ain't the blues, and I gotta play all kinds, you know."

"Well, anyways, none of those songs ain't my favorites. I like the happy ones and the spirituals, not the ones about the killins."

Leadbelly put the guitar down and rocked back in his chair, folding his hands in front of him. He looked up at the trees. "Did you ever think we'd ever be sittin' here like this?"

"I always hoped we would, Huddie, but I never really thought it would be."

"Well, it's the new Huddie now, Marthy. Ain't gonna be no mo' penitenshuh for me, no suh. No more fightin'."

"When you gonna start playin' you music regular at a job? Can't spend all the time down at the fillin' station lookin' to fix cars or somethin'."

"That's what I been thinkin' about. You know, I been with all kinds of wimmins, and the bes' kind to get is the one what loves you and you can trust. An' they ain't many 'round like that. None like you, anyhow."

Martha smiled at him and rocked slowly. She idly wondered why he ignored her question.

"You ever think of leavin' Shrevepo't?" he asked.

"No, why?"

"Out at Angola, I talked to a lot of the niggas what been up north. They say they's a lot of people makin' records of their music up in Chicago. Jus' like the record I made for that Mr. Lomax. Only the ones up north get paid money for their singin'. They even say ol' Blind Lemon made a lot of money 'fore he died. That's a good way to stay out of trouble, too, havin' enough money so you don't have to go to the saloons to play."

"They's mostly white folks up in Chicago," she said.

"Yeah, but they's the ones what's payin' all the money. They like the nigga music and the blues. Even lots of white singers copyin' it now, and I hear on the radio the bands been playin' lots of blues, like that man, Ellington. Lawd, don' know how many men he got in that band. but he playin' it right off."

"I heard him too. Even saw his picture in the magazine. He a mighty fine lookin' nigga."

"He a colored man? With all that big band and playin' on the radio all the time?"

"That's right. An' he sure good-lookin'. I just---" Martha's voice broke. Oh Lawd, she thought, don't tell me he's thinking of leaving.

"What's the matter, honey?" A vision of the Ellington band stirred in his mind.

"Nuthin'."

"Now, don' you say nuthin'. What you thinkin'?"

"It's not what I thinkin', Huddie. It's what youse thinkin'. You plannin' on leavin' here?"

"Oh now, Marthy," Huddie reached over and brushed her hair. "I ain't goin' nowhere."

"In you letters you mentioned 'bout goin' to New Yawk with Mr. Lomax."

"Never mind. He didn't want me. 'Spect he was 'fraid of havin' a mean ol' nigga like me along," he chuckled. "He sure look rich, though."

"All white folk look rich to us."

"An l'il Alan, he nice, too. They got gov'nor Allen to hear my song and get me pardoned. Then I ain't heard no more from 'em."

Martha turned sadly and looked at him in the falling darkness. "Ain't you never gonna learn, Huddie? Ain't you never gonna learn that they's people what do nuthin' but take? Don't bother to give you nuthin' back for what you got? What did Mr. Lomax pay you for you music?"

"Nuthin', but he helped get me out of Angola. That's enough pay for me. Don't worry, Marthy, I ain't goin' nowhere. 'Sides, Mr. Lomax ain't like most white folks. I ain't never gonna see him again, anyway." He brushed the subject away with a flip of his hand.

They talked well into darkness, and for the next three weeks he continued to work at the filling station. Then, like an unexpected thunderclap, the telegram arrived.

PLEASE MEET ME AS SOON AS YOU CAN AT
MARSHALL HOTEL, MARSHALL TEXAS STOP WE
WANT YOU TO ASSIST US IN GATHERING
MORE MUSIC STOP

JOHN LOMAX

*   *   *   *   *

The Marshall Hotel was the tallest building in town. Located on Houston Avenue, it was a seven-story cube with a sculptured portico around the uppermost floor of suites. The lobby was musty, small, dark and cluttered with mildewy overstuffed chairs. Three large, cut-glass chandeliers, spider-webby and crusted with dust, hung from the pale green ceiling. The windows were covered by faded jalousies, which were kept closed during the day.

It was Sunday, September 16, when Leadbelly reached the hotel. He had hitched a ride from Shreveport, fifty miles to the east. He carried his battered guitar and a brown paper sugar bag. He wore an old felt hat, a remnant from a barroom brawl, a patched pair of overalls and a blue denim workshirt. On his feet were a pair of yellow shoes.

He'd been jubilant ever since the telegram arrived. "Lawd, Marthy," he said, "I tol' you they wasn't like most white folks! They want me. Me! To help 'em. They got a new car and they be goin' everywhere! Maybe even Chicago or New Yawk!"

Martha had taken the news quietly, as always. The past three weeks had given her a new confidence in Huddie. He seemed sure of himself -- resolute but less demanding. When the telegram arrived, he promised her he would write her that very night and would return soon. His pockets would be bursting with money -- enough to get married and have a chance at turning out a family. Martha Promise nodded sadly, smiled, kissed him softly and waved from the porch as her man trotted toward town.

It was with some trepidation that Leadbelly walked into the Marshall Hotel. The sign in the window said "Whites Only." What if Mister Lomax was not there? Where would he go?

He pushed himself tentatively through the revolving door, banging his guitar as he did. He stood inside and took off his hat. His heart was thumping so hard it made him short of breath. Then, to his genuine delight, he saw a puff of cigar smoke bloom from behind a newspaper in the lobby.

He eagerly strode toward it and peered over the paper. "Boss," he said almost apologetically, "here I is." He shrugged, for lack of anything else to do.

Lomax crumpled the newspaper into his lap and looked up at him. Surprise creased his forehead. "Leadbelly! So soon?"

"Huh?"

"Why, I just didn't expect you so soon."

Leadbelly gave him a broad grin. "I'se come to be you man, Boss. To drive you car and wait on you. You telegram is here in this sack."

Lomax heavily lifted himself from the overstuffed wingback chair and tossed the paper onto a nearby table. "Come upstairs to my room, Leadbelly. Let's talk about it."

Leadbelly followed him, opening the creaky elevator door, reiterating how glad he was to see him. "Yessuh, Mr. Lomax. You sure did help me get out of Angola. I sure didn't like it there. They leave the lights on all night long, and I never did get much sleep. No suh, now me and my gal, Marthy, is gonna get ourselves married."

In the room Leadbelly paced the floor, and only after Lomax insisted did he finally sit down. Even then, he was tense and fidgety, scraping the side of the chair with his paper bag. "Leadbelly," Lomax began after relighting his cigar. "I do need a driver and someone to help me lug the recording machine around. Alan is sick and can't come with me. But before we talk, I have to ask you some direct questions. Do you mind?"

"No suh, Mr. Lomax."

"First of all, I'd like to know whether you're carrying a gun."

Leadbelly controlled a momentary twinge of panic. He shook his head and then looked in the paper sack. "No suh, Boss. But I got a knife."

Lomax frowned. "Let me see it."

Leadbelly timidly handed him the switchblade knife. Lomax opened it carefully and ran his thumb over the edge. He then clicked it closed and looked gravely at Leadbelly.

"Leadbelly," he began, clasping his fingers together, "down in Austin I have a home and a lovely lady for my wife. Also a very dear daughter, Bess Brown. I hope to live a long while, for their sakes. Now, if you sometime, when we're driving along a lonely road, decide that you're going to take my money and my car, you need not stick that knife into me. Just tell me and I'll hand you the money, get out of the car and let you drive on."

Leadbelly made a great show of being shocked. "Oh, Boss," he said, "don't think you oughta talk to me that way. Boss, this here's the way I feel about you. You the man what got me out of Angola. I protect you from anyone what tries to fight you an' I drive real careful so's you don't come to no harm on the road. I keep you car sparklin' clean and wait on you day an' night, and you don't even have to tie you shoes if you don't want to." He babbled on for five more minutes, promising Lomax favors and swearing to carry out his promises to the letter.

Finally Lomax interrupted. "Do you know much about handling cars? You used to own a car, didn't you?"

"Yes, Boss," Leadbelly said eagerly. "I used to own a great big Packard car, and I even once drove around in a big Buick down in Houston, when I get out from Sugar Land and went down to live with Mary. I even worked at a Buick store down there for a while. Yeah, Boss, I made lots of money demonstratin' the cars and fixin' them real good," Leadbelly paused, trying to think of something else to add, but he saw that Lomax already looked like he believed him.

"Well, I'll tell you," Lomax said finally. "We'll try it for a while and see how you do. I'll---"

Leadbelly lept up, shouting. "Oh, that's fine, Boss! That make me very happy! Yeah!" He grabbed up a whisk broom from the dresser and began dusting off Lomax's clothes, to the latter's consternation. "Yeah, Boss, you gonna be the cleanest and bes' kept white man ever," he said, grinning.

"You know," Lomax said as he went to his suitcase. "If all goes well, we'll probably end up in New York. Did you ever see a picture of New York?"

"Oh, yeah, Boss! New Yawk's the greatest city in the world. It's the capital of the world and I surely want to see it." Leadbelly raised his eyes to heaven and called to the ceiling. "Oh, Lawd, I'se gonna go to New Yawk with my new boss-man! Oh, thank you, Lawd, thank you!"

Lomax cast him a quizzical glance, as if to say, "Oh, come on, now!" and started packing his suitcase.

Thirty minutes later they checked out of the hotel and were on their way northeast, toward Lomax's first stop on his hunt for what he called "Negro work songs." Little Rock, Arkansas. They were a strange pair, the portly white man and the black, ex-convict with his paper sack and his battered green guitar.

They were quiet at first, with Lomax giving directions and explaining where their first stop would be. In the back seat of the car was a huge, five-hundred-pound electric recording machine Lomax had acquired from the Carnegie Foundation to cut permanent records of folk music for the Library of Congress. Lomax made arrangements to meet with the governors of the states he intended to visit, to get permission to enter the prisons and record the inmates' music. He also arranged for a suit of clothes to be sent from his home in Austin to the home of his oldest son, John Junior, in Little Rock. He told Leadbelly this, and the musician was further elated. "Lawd, I ain't never had no real suit to wear," he said.

The trip was two hundred miles, and Leadbelly drove skillfully and carefully, telling stories and humming tunes and singing a capella lyrics all the way.

"Boss, you should see it down in N'Orleans," he said at one point. "They's things goin' on down there you don't know ever could happen at all. They's fightin' and cuttin' all the time, and men beatin' up other men jus' the same as eat their lunch. Boss, I even heard a story 'bout one o' the wop-men what got strung up from the lamppost by his neck right there on Canal Street. They jus' hang 'im dead, and everybody what ride by they take out their pistols and plug the poor bastid full o' holes. They jus' ride by, shootin' at the man hangin' right there from the lamppost. One man tell me the wop-man, he weigh on'y ninety pounds when they string 'im up, and when they cuts him down he weigh more'n three hundred, he so full o' lead. And that's the truth!"

Lomax enjoyed the stories, but he had a difficult time deciding which ones were true and which ones were fabricated. Leadbelly went into lurid detail about his numerous escapades with women, all with explicit description that made the proper Lomax wince. Overall, Leadbelly preferred color to accuracy. He often contradicted himself, and when the discrepancy was pointed out he either retraced his steps or brushed off the contradiction by simply not saying anything at all. The trip remained cheery and pleasant, and Lomax began to relax.

In Little Rock, Lomax saw the governor and received permission to make an appointment with the superintendent of the Arkansas penitentiary system southeast of Little Rock. He and Leadbelly spent three days exploring the black ghettoes of the town and recording songs.

The superintendent of the prison was the only white man among the population of some two hundred inmates. The guards were long-term convicts who were housed separately.

"I'm not going to tell anyone about your prison record, Leadbelly," Lomax cautioned. "Not the guards nor the superintendent. I think it's best that way."

"Okay, Boss," Leadbelly agreed. "I won't say nothin'." Leadbelly peered from the windshield of the car and watched the prison loom closer, and as he steered the car through the high wire fence and up to the guard shack, the still-fresh tortured memories of Angola swarmed back to him.

A heavy black guard approached the vehicle on Leadbelly's side and brandished a sawed-off shotgun. He sneered at Leadbelly's neat new suit and looked at Lomax with suspicion. Lomax smiled. Leadbelly, feeling superior to a guard for once in his life, returned the guard's sneer.

A few minutes later they were in the superintendent's office. The man explained that Lomax would be housed in his own guest cottage while Leadbelly would have to stay with the black trustees in their dormitory. Leadbelly started to protest at the prospect of being locked up for another night in a prison, but Lomax nodded at him reassuringly, winking to remind him of their decision not to mention his previous record.

"It's best, Leadbelly. With your own people. You can ask who are the best musicians and warm them up to play for us tomorrow morning. Explain to them what we're after."

"I jus' naturally don't like it, Boss," he said. Why, he thought, didn't Lomax insist on something better than a cell for him? After all, he was a free man and not a convict. He decided to protest but immediately had second thoughts. He would be Lomax's man -- at least for the time being.

The superintendent agreed, and Leadbelly had no choice. The first night of his new job was spent in a confinement cell. The irony wasn't lost on him -- at least, he thought, he would walk out free the next morning.

The following morning, Leadbelly was charged with warming up the prisoners. He made a few friends among the trustees, and, inevitably, word swept quickly through the camp that Leadbelly had served two sentences for murder in two states and had sung his way to a pardon each time. This had the opposite effect from what Lomax had feared; he was suddenly overwhelmed. Every convict who could sing a note, blow a harmonica, strum a guitar, squeeze a windjammer or make any kind of sound whatever come out of any kind of contraption, swarmed to be recorded.

They collected music at night and on Sunday, setting up their equipment in cell blocks, in the hospital and even in the execution chamber. By the time they were finished Lomax was weak with exhaustion.

Monday morning they left Little Rock and drove to the larger prison farm to the southwest. Leadbelly had risen at four o'clock with the field hands and had spent half an hour meticulously polishing the car. When they were on the road he said, "Boss, you won't have to worry about no gas today. I tipped one of the nigga guards, and he filled her plumb full from the state of Arkansas's tank. Best quality gas, too."

Lomax had difficulty suppressing a laugh. "You know, Leadbelly," he said, "that's stealing. And they put people in jail for stealing. Do you want to go back to jail?"

"Shit, Boss. White folks always has plenty o' everthin'. They won't miss a little gas."

A high point for Leadbelly came when the two entered Birmingham a week later and were granted permission to visit two women's camps. The women made a great fuss, coaxing song after song from him, hanging on each word. Leadbelly loved it and exaggeratedly told his old stories. It was, however, somewhat less than a fruitful trip for Lomax. He was only able to record a half-dozen songs by three young black girls. He had Leadbelly drive them back to town.

Leadbelly had a room by himself in Birmingham, and as he lay awake on the second night he studied a photograph of Martha. The women in the prison camps they visited that day preyed on his mind. How long had it been? One of them in particular had shot him a provocative glance that still had him throbbing alone in the dingy room. He lingered over the photograph, mentally enlarging it to fill out her whole body, naked, walking into the room and pressing against him. He closed his eyes. Lawd! I'se sick, sick, of these damn prisons! If I see another nigga looking out from behind them bars I'll tear this fat white man apart with my own hands! 'Leadbelly, turn right here.' 'Leadbelly, not so fast.' 'Do you want to go back to jail, Leadbelly?' What am I doin' here driving that bastid around when my Marthy's back in Shreveport waitin' for me? Two weeks, it's been.

A moment later he burst into Lomax's room. "We gotta go back to Shrevepo't, Boss. We gotta do somethin' else. I jus' ain't no good without my Marthy. I don't know how you can do it, Boss, but I gotta have a woman!"

Lomax was alarmed at the intensity of Leadbelly's voice, still not completely awake. "But we're not through with the tour yet, Leadbelly," he muttered. "I've made appointments at a few more prisons."

"The hell wit' you appointments!" Leadbelly exploded. "Maybe you can jus' keep smokin' that shittin' cigar, but I'se gettin' on the bus in the mornin' and goin' back to my Marthy. It ain't right for a man like me to be playin' with hisself, Boss!"

Lomax's original fear returned and he decided to be cautious. "I'll tell you what," he said finally. "I'll shorten the prison tour in the morning and we'll go back to Shreveport for a few days' rest. Then we'll make plans to head north to New York."

Leadbelly was pacified, and meekly returned to his own room.

When they arrived in Shreveport the next evening, Leadbelly joyously bounded from the car, quickly introduced Lomax to Martha, and promised to be ready two days later when Lomax planned to pick him up again.

Lomax took a room downtown at the Captain Shreve Hotel and busied himself with his notes.

In Martha's house that night, Leadbelly, only slightly relieved, explained his plans. "The boss-man sayin' we goin' to New Yawk after a few more prisons," he said. "An' I figger if I keep bein' a good driver maybe that might be my free ride. Didn't like goin' 'round to all the penitenshuhs, but he sure love the way I take care of the car an' his clothes. I wake him up ever' mornin' with a cup of coffee and makes sure everythin' all ready to go."

Martha turned and propped herself up on one elbow. "Huddie, you ain't seein' any other womens, is you?" she asked playfully.

"Now, Marthy. I told you, youse my only woman from now on. I don't get no chance for any foolin' 'round anyways. 'Sides, I know none o' them is gonna do me like you do. And that's the truth."

The next day Martha didn't go to work, and they spent the time playing like children. Leadbelly told her more of his plan to stay with Lomax as long as things didn't get any worse. He promised that if he ever did make it to New York, the first thing he would do would be to send down for her to join him and become his wife.

*　　*　　*　　*　　*

Lomax was at the door promptly at eight o'clock the next morning and was duly surprised that Leadbelly was packed and ready to go. With a flutter of kisses and promises Leadbelly left Martha, and the car roared off toward Birmingham, Alabama. Leadbelly was jabbering cheerfully behind the wheel.

"Yessuh, Boss. I'se a new man. Marthy gonna marry me some day and I'se gonna get us a bunch of kids. My ramblin' days is over, Boss. I'se jus' gonna stick with you and do whatever you need. I'm you man for jus' as long as you want me. But I jus' don't know how you does it without no wimmins. No suh, got a constitution of iron, Boss. You sure does." Lomax dismissed the subject with an accommodating shrug.

After the visit to Birmingham, they headed toward Tuscaloosa and the University of Alabama. Even having been confined in the confidentiality of Lomax's prison tour, the rumors had raced before them. The crowd in Alabama gave him a standing ovation. Leadbelly was at first bewildered when they all stood up, but as the applause rose and thundered against his eardrums he realized they wanted more. Lomax beamed proudly from the side of the stage. Now he was certain that this man's music and his sheer personal magnetism were unique.

From Tuscaloosa they headed toward Montgomery, and Leadbelly became depressed again. At Killby Prison, Leadbelly's depression intensified when he learned that nine teenage boys were waiting in the death house. They were known as the Scottsboro Boys, and they'd been condemned by a hastily assembled all-white jury for the alleged rape of two white women hoboes. Leadbelly implored Lomax to intercede with what Leadbelly now considered to be a magic personage, the governor, but Lomax demurred. Leadbelly grew even more despondent. "They is Jim Crow, that's all, Boss. They ain't even had no fair trial, jus' like me."

And that night, housed again with the black convicts, he composed a song for the doomed youngsters.

> *Go to Alabama and you better watch out,*
> *the landlord will get you,*
> *Gonna jump and shout.*
> *Scottsboro, Scottsboro, Scottsboro Boys,*
> *They can tell you what it's all about,*
> *They can tell you what it's all about.*

After Killby, Leadbelly began to sneak out of his room at night and venture into the black districts to drink. Lomax urged him to leave his guitar with him at night, hoping that would remove the temptation to ramble, but Leadbelly would have none of it. The more Lomax tried to keep him in tow, the more Leadbelly rebelled, finally disappearing for three days. He returned repentant and promised there would be no more drinking and rambling.

"Boss," he said, "I'se nothin' but a rambler. There never was a nigga what would keep his word -- leastwise, I never seen none. I thought you knew that, I'll never do this way no more."

They left Montgomery in strained silence and drove to the prison farm at Atmore, by the state line. There the recording machine broke down, and Leadbelly was asked to replace the recording sessions with a concert-like show for all the convicts on the farm. He repeated his performance seven times and was a colossal success. His program of songs, punctuated by his ribald stories and jokes, rivaled the most successful vaudeville acts of the era. The prisoners whooped and hollered and almost rioted with disapproval when he finally was almost dragged off the stage. Before he left, the prisoners gave him three dollars and fifteen cents in pennies and nickels, contributed from their tobacco money.

The tour was soon over, but the popularity of Leadbelly wherever he appeared wasn't lost on Lomax. They came home through New Orleans and Baton Rouge, where they ferried across the river. They reached Shreveport late at night.

Lomax wearily thanked Leadbelly for his help throughout the trip and apologized for his shortness of temper during the more strenuous moments. Leadbelly, too, was contrite and assured Lomax that even with his momentary lapses of self-discipline, he was still a "good nigga." If ever Lomax should want him to be his chauffeur again, Leadbelly promised, he'd report immediately.

Leadbelly disappeared into the darkness of Martha's cottage. Lomax headed home to Austin, but the memory of all those pennies and nickels stayed with him.

###

Chapter Eighteen

"Honey, somethin' eatin' at you? You ain't said two words all day."

He shifted his weight on the sofa and looked at her. She stood barefoot in the kitchen, leaning over the sink washing sweet potatoes. A wisp of ebony hair concealed her eyes.

"No, nuthin'," he said. "Is there any beer?"

"Some outside in the cooler."

He started to get up, but she motioned to him. "I get it for you, honey."

He heard the screen door slam and Martha walk to the cooler. He had to tell her. After all, it had been almost a week since the letter came. But if he left again, Martha would leave him for sure. Their life these past weeks had been slow, simple and peaceful. He was happy with her, but restless.

Martha came back in and handed him a beer. She sat down and put her hand on his leg. "It's that man, Mr. Lomax, ain't it?"

He twisted. "What?"

"Oh, I ain't seen no letter. I don't <u>need</u> no letter. I can see it all over you face."

He felt blood rush to his face. "Marthy, I---"

"Drink you beer."

He took a couple of long swallows, which drained the entire bottle, and got up from the sofa. He paced the room. "Marthy, I didn't tell you 'cause I don't want you to go away. Mr. Lomax want me to go up north with him and show off. He wrote me and told me so. This is our big chance, Marthy! When them city folks hears me, why they just throw money at me! Just like Blind Lemon! Then we can get married."

Martha watched him, his toned hulk pacing back and forth, his arms gesticulating wildly. He's still a boy, she thought. A boy-man who refused to believe in anything except fame and fortune, who never recognized trouble 'til it had him down too late. She felt sorry for him at that moment, but she couldn't allow herself to tell him so. She listened, and nodded, and smiled, and told him she would wait for him to send for her. Then she returned to the kitchen and finished preparing dinner. She heard him rustling in the bedroom packing his clothes. Lord, she thought, he couldn't even wait until tomorrow.

The Ford, its rear seat jammed with rattling recording equipment, arrived in Shreveport early in the morning of December 6. Leadbelly left Martha by the Excelsior Laundry and promised he would write her every day and send for her as soon as he reached New York.

Spirits were high, and Leadbelly insisted on driving while Lomax sat in the front seat. His son, Alan, rode in the back and asked excited questions about Leadbelly's guitar. Their rapport was immediate, and by the time they crossed the Georgia state line, Leadbelly and young Alan Lomax had become fast friends.

In Atlanta, the prison board had misgivings about letting them record inside the penitentiary. Lomax reassured them that he was only after music, not an expose of Georgia prison conditions, but they were still delayed for four days. After finally being granted entry, Leadbelly found a few banjo players and a decrepit old burglar from

Valdosta who thought he could sing. They collected songs for two evenings, none memorable, and went on their way.

At their next stop, in Milledgeville southeast of Atlanta, Alan became ill again. Huddie asked why he was sick so often, but Alan explained that the doctors didn't know. He called it "vulnerable immunity," but Leadbelly didn't understand it. While Alan rested, Huddie manipulated the recording machine expertly. He enticed the prisoners to play by warming them up with his own music and then issuing a challenge for them to better him. "Can any you guys play better than the 'king o' the twelve-string guitar'?" he would shout. "If you can, my boss-man Mr. Lomax wants you to step up here and sing into the mikaphone." He pointed to the audience. "You there! Ain't you got no songs?"

Then, grinning broadly, he would offer his guitar, or Alan's, to the next challenger.

A minor crisis developed in Columbia, South Carolina, a few days later. Leadbelly knocked on Lomax's door one morning and sat down morosely.

'Mornin', Boss."

"What's the matter, Leadbelly? Don't you feel well?"

"No Boss. I hurt in the mouth."

Lomax noticed a swelling on the left jaw. "Your tooth?"

"Yeah, Boss. Last night my tooth hurt awful and I couldn't get no sleep. Jus' pain right through the whole mouth."

Alan went into the bathroom and brought out some aspirin. He gave three of them to Leadbelly. But the pain continued throughout the morning. Lomax finally said, "We have an appointment to visit Warden Brown this afternoon, Leadbelly, so you'll have to drive me out and when we get back to town we'll find a dentist."

Leadbelly was still miserable when Lomax left him in the car outside the prison and went into the warden's office. He sat behind the wheel, trying to get his mind off the pain in his jaw. During the past week he had become quite fond of Alan Lomax. The boy was intensely interested in learning the guitar and music, and he usually smiled when Leadbelly came in late from a brief ramble in the black district. Lomax Senior, on the other hand, disapproved of his drinking and even began giving him money only just before meal time, so that Leadbelly wouldn't squander it on whiskey.

That's another thing, he thought now as his jaw ached. If I'm so good for them and such an important part of the team, how come I still have to eat with the niggas? He hated it when, after a particularly long drive or tedious recording session, the car would pull up to some roadside diner and the two Lomaxes would enter one door while Leadbelly was given two dollars and sent off to eat by himself in the section marked "Colored." Jesus, he thought, I can't even pee in the same room. What's so different between black pee and white pee? It all goes down the same hole in the ground, don't it?

His aching tooth was doing nothing for his mood, he realized, and he didn't want to get cranky again. He decided the only thing to do was to pull it out himself. He got out of the car, cursing, and took the new tool kit from the trunk. He removed a pair of shiny new pliers, still oily with rust preventative, and sat down on the running board. Holding the pliers with two hands, he gripped the offending tooth and tried to wiggle it out of his gum. The tooth twisted and pained even more, but the bloody jaws of the pliers kept slipping off it. He cursed and tried it again. He couldn't do it, though, and finally gave up and slammed the pliers back into the tool kit.

Lomax noticed a bloodstain on Leadbelly's shirt immediately on his return. "What's the blood from?"

"I tried to pull it out but I couldn't get a good hold on it. I don't want nobody jabbin' at it."

Lomax was amazed. "You *what?*"

"I tried to pull it out myself, it hurt so bad."

When they returned to the hotel, Alan, who still wasn't feeling well himself, had located a black dentist by telephone. He drove Leadbelly there, waited while the dentist extracted the tooth, and graciously paid the bill.

From Milledgeville they went to Raleigh, North Carolina, where they spent three more days. Here, though, there was an accoustical problem in the dining hall, and they had to make their recordings in the chamber that housed the electric chair. Many prisoners were reluctant to go inside, fearing some hideous plot to get them to sit down. But Leadbelly reassured them, and before long the ominous white sheet covering the chair went unnoticed as they sang and hollered long into the evenings.

The Ford moved on again, this time headed for Washington, D. C. Leadbelly sang as he drove, and Alan played guitar next to him. The elder Lomax sat in the rear seat.

"I sure gettin' tired again o' seein' all them poor niggas in the penitinshuh, Boss," Leadbelly said eventually. "That's terrible, bein' locked up without no wimmins, sure is. Gets downright depressin'. I want to get to New Yawk."

"We've been through the last one, I think," Lomax said. "We're just going to see some friends in Washington now, and I'll deliver my address in Philadelphia and then we'll go on to New York."

*   *   *   *   *

It was snowing on Christmas Eve when they crossed the Potomac River from Virginia and headed into Washington, D.C. The nation's capital was jacketed in snow, and here and there the wind kicked up flurries. Leadbelly gaped at the dome of the Capitol, illuminated like a white crown against the clear dark sky. As he carefully drove the car along Pennsylvania Avenue past the White House, Leadbelly bombarded Lomax with questions. By the time they reached their destination, Leadbelly had received a short course on United States history and civics.

They were to stay at the fashionable Georgetown residence of Major Isaac Spalding, a retired Army officer and an old friend of John Lomax. Leadbelly sang a few songs for Spalding and his guests that evening, then Lomax suggested he get some sleep. But he couldn't sleep. Washington, D.C.! Tomorrow, they would be in New York! New York on Christmas Day! The excitement was too much for him, and he decided he wanted to see more of the town tonight. Fifteen minutes later, he was driving the car back to the center of town.

He found a bar, and then another. In each, a guitar player had volunteered his instrument to the eager and inebriated stranger. Leadbelly thrilled them with his virtuosity, even though he couldn't find a twelve-string and had to impress them with a six. They roared and laughed and stomped and hypnotized him again with their fervor. By two in the morning he was drunk and lurching up the dingy stairs of a transients' flop-house with a prostitute. He woke up at six to discover the girl had taken his wallet and vanished. Struggling to his feet, he sneaked down the back stairs and out into the morning.

At first the car wouldn't start, but in a few minutes the motor turned over and he headed back toward Georgetown, barely missing a collision as he erratically wove his way around DuPont Circle. Minutes later he had managed to get into bed unnoticed and was soon asleep.

The next day, Christmas, instead of going to New York, he was asked to perform for some newspaper people. His voice was husky and off-key from too much drinking, and he gave a bad performance. Lomax scowled and Alan was silent, but the reporters were fascinated with Leadbelly's history and quickly ran to their typewriters.

By the time the party reached Philadelphia, Leadbelly's name had hit the newspapers and he was being mentioned around the intellectual cocktail circuit. Lomax was invited to bring Leadbelly to the smoker following his address to the Modern Language Association on December 30. The phones rang all day long, Lomax receiving the calls in his room while he kept Leadbelly out of sight in the bedroom. He told everyone who called that they would have a chance to see and hear this incredible personality for themselves.

At the smoker, Leadbelly sat on a tabletop and sang many of his bawdy songs. The prim and proper audience applauded wildly and threw money at his feet. By the time he was finished he had thirty-two dollars.

The next day Leadbelly enchanted another audience, a group of students at a popular literature seminar. He was also scheduled to perform at Bryn Mawr that evening. An hour before departing for the auditorium, Lomax handed Leadbelly a brown parcel. "I want you to wear these tonight," he said.

Leadbelly thought immediately of a new suit -- possibly even a black tuxedo with a bright red cummerbund -- and excitedly tore open the package. There, folded neatly, was a set of convict stripes.

He looked up, baffled, "What's these, Boss?"

"I want you to wear them, Leadbelly. For the concert tonight."

"Oh no, Boss. I swore I'd never be wearing these here ol' prison stripes again," he almost whispered. "They jus' smell too much like blood and hard times."

"Don't worry," Lomax said. "I had them cleaned. They'll add some flavor to your performance."

"But I thought I was gonna sing at the famous women's school tonight."

"That's right. Bryn Mawr."

"But Boss, I don' want to get out in front of the wimmins dressed in prison clothes," he pleaded. "I ought to look like the bes' 'cause they is gonna hear the bes' nigga guitar player ever."

Lomax fumbled for a cigar. "Leadbelly, there are certain things you don't understand yet about performing for the public. The more you can bring the flavor of your life to the stage, the greater your welcome will be."

"But they don't want to look at me. They jus' wanna hear my singin'. What difference it make what I look like? I'se jus' an ol' nigga. I'se forty-seven, Boss."

"Now, Leadbelly." The words came carefully paced. "Just listen to my advice and you can't go wrong. I know more about these performances than you do. They're a different audience, and most of them have never heard songs like you sing, Huddie. We have to approach a new audience with care, particularly if they've been shielded from the realities of prisons and jails."

"Don't make no difference. I jus' don't wanna put on them prison clothes for the gals tonight. I jus' never wanna wear them again. Please, Boss, don't make me do it."

Lomax insisted and grew stern. Leadbelly had to wear his special costume or they wouldn't go to New York. He was embarrassed, and as he dressed that evening for his performance he cursed to himself. He was still just a driver, a performing monkey just like the one he'd once seen chained to a wop-man's music box on the sidewalk in downtown Philadelphia. He did what he was told, and he toadied and he bowed and he "Yessuh'd" and he polished the car and he turned right and he turned left and he stopped here and he got gas there and no, he didn't want to go back to prison and yessuh, he'd sure appreciate another dollar for dinner tonight and yessuh, he'd wear these shittin' prison clothes for the white gals who would hear the bes' goddam music they's ever heared before.

He'd get his revenge in New York. Didn't Lomax himself keep telling him how famous he'd be? Wasn't it this fat white man who kept the dream alive for him, who was planning a great publicity campaign, who insisted that Leadbelly was going to have all the money he wanted? Yeah, he'd get even in New York, he thought again as he finished buttoning the striped prison workshirt and picked up the guitar.

Before a jammed auditorium filled with students, debutantes and matrons, he sang his alien music that evening. Hushed comments floated back and forth. What was the man singing? "Dicklicker's Holler?" Well, I never! "Whoa Buck!" Amazing. "Dicklicker's Holler!" A few girls tittered, several more blushed and one girl swooned. Leadbelly loved it all. Near the end of his performance the normally staid audience began applauding wildly, and calls of "Just one more!" and "Play it again, Leadbelly!" filled the small hall. When he was finished a collection was taken up, and Leadbelly made even more money than the previous day in Washington. One man, a faculty member, gave five dollars, Leadbelly was flabbergasted. He looked at the bill again and again, never having seen one before, and examined Lincoln's picture where Washington's should be, faintly suspecting it was counterfeit. He twitched with excitement. New York would be his!

Later, Lomax decided to drive that very evening, New Year's Eve, to New York. "Anyone who could be such a hit in as tough a testing ground as Philadelphia will be a natural entertainer in New York. What do you say?"

"Oh, Boss, that's jus' great! New Yawk at last!"

"And besides," Lomax added, "your behavior has been generally good on this trip, and I believe you when you say you're going to remain in control of yourself. Just you listen to Alan, and everything will work out fine. I've noticed you two are becoming quite good friends."

"Oh yeah, Boss, the li'l boss-man's a good man. He gonna be a good music man someday, too. I'se showin' him all I know on the guitar, and he pickin' up the tricks real good."

They packed quickly, and in the icy chill of evening they set out once again. On the way they discussed the city, and Leadbelly listened intently to Lomax's descriptions. He couldn't wait. They dipped into the Holland Tunnel, and when they emerged, six thousand miles were behind them. A hundred prison walls were either bad dreams or deep grooves on acetate discs. For better or for worse, Leadbelly was in New York.

###

Chapter Nineteen

"New Yawk!" Leadbelly shouted. Capital of all the worl'! Run under a mile o' water to get to it! Subways up in the air, on the groun' and under the groun' through solid rock! Fifth Avenoo! New Yawk! New Yawk!"

He could scarcely believe it. Finally he had reached his Mecca -- a city teeming with people and life. His thoughts were a blur of images from his past. If only mama could be here, or Clear Rock, or Edmond. They would be so proud. I'se the best there is, he thought to himself.

But New York was a white man's city, and it wasted no time in telling Leadbelly so. The Lomaxes had difficulty finding a place for him to stay. Hotel after hotel refused to admit him. Although apprehensive, Leadbelly tried to remain calm and to suppress his growing anger and frustration.

The Lomaxes didn't know what to do. They were reluctant to leave him alone in the city, but they had no choice. They decided the Harlem branch of the Y.M.C.A. on West 135th Street would be safest. It was only three years old, but despite its newness it was a gloomy structure, the red brick already dirty and the windows broken and cracked. It was eleven stories high, cantilevered, with two white flagpoles jabbing into the night sky.

Alan went in with Leadbelly while Lomax stayed to watch the car. A large painting of a black minister and children sitting with a dog adorned the rear wall of the lobby. It reminded Leadbelly of the simple services held at Shiloh Baptist Church, and the forgotten clarity of his mother's voice. It depressed him and he tried to blot out the images. In the rear, four youths were arguing boisterously over the pool tables. He glanced at the painting again and let his shoulders slump. He was tired, and yet it was New Year's Eve and he wanted to explore the city. He thought of his age. He was almost fifty. Funny -- he always thought of himself as a young man.

They registered and went to the fourth floor in a rickety elevator, walked down the hallway and stopped. Alan opened the door to the room and flipped on the light. It smelled strongly of pine oil, and wasn't much bigger than a cell.

Leadbelly stood out in the hallway. "Huddie," Alan called to him. "Come in. It's okay."

Leadbelly took a tentative step and stopped on the doorsill. "Li'l Boss, I don't guess I like it here." His face was a mask of depression. "This here ain't like I thought it would be in New Yawk. No suh. I had me a better place to sleep down at Angola."

Alan sighed. "I know, Huddie. There's a lot of discrimination up here, too. It's not as bad as where you've been, but there're still stupid people around New York who won't let black men stay where white men stay. I'm sorry, Huddie, but we'll figure something out tomorrow. It's late and it's New Year's Eve, so just for tonight..."

He cut himself off, because he saw Leadbelly's eyes remain unchanged. "Why don't I jus' sleep in the car outside where youse stayin'?

Alan shrugged. "Huddie, it's too cold out. Suppose it snowed or something and you caught a bad cold? You couldn't sing."

"I won't get cold, li'l Boss. I once slept in the field in prison when it snowed and me an' a whole lot o' other convicts got under a tin shed an'---"

"Huddie, won't you do me this one favor? Won't you please stay here just for tonight, and the first thing in the morning we can all get together and find another place. Father and I will be staying at that first hotel we went to near Washington Square, and we'll pick you up very early. It's not far, really."

Leadbelly slumped even more, but he stepped into the room. Outside horns blared and a siren went off. He sat on the bed with his hands between his knees and looked up at Alan.

The boy squeezed his hefty shoulder and said, "Don't worry, Huddie. I promise I'll be back to pick you up first thing in the morning."

When Alan had left, Leadbelly turned off the light and lay on the bed listening to the sounds of the city below. Already confused, he tried as best he could to determine if he were doing the right thing. He was sure of his talent, but this was a big, cold city. He'd better just continue to play the "good nigga" and wear the prison stripes and do what the white men wanted.

At six-thirty the next morning, a sleepy Alan Lomax was startled awake when he saw Leadbelly's face in the doorway of the "White's Only" hotel. Leadbelly had cleverly talked his way past the lobby desk, and now stepped inside Lomax's room. He explained in elaborate detail how he couldn't sleep much and how he had left the hotel at sunrise and had made his way from Harlem to the other end of Manhattan alone.

That afternoon Lomax received several phone calls and learned that the local music community and literati had planned a party that evening. Leadbelly was to meet New York. The news of a party cheered him up, but he was nervous. Alan took him sightseeing and up to the top of the Empire State Building. It was a cloudless clear day, and Leadbelly was thunderstruck at what he saw. He believed he was seeing the entire rest of the United States and was speechless for the first time in his life. There was no comparing it to Shreveport. It was another planet. He thought of Martha, who seemed so far away.

The party was held in a penthouse apartment in Greenwich Village. News of Leadbelly had spread, and by eight o'clock the apartment was filled with writers, publishers, newspapermen, street musicians and some faculty members from Columbia and New York University.

Lomax mingled with the guests, telling them about his discovery of Leadbelly at Angola. Leadbelly, hidden in a back bedroom, was as nervous as he'd ever been. He paced the room, sat down, got up, went to the bathroom for water, looked out the window, paced some more. This was the most important moment in his life, he thought, more important even than the concert for Governor Neff.

Alan found him sitting on the edge of the bed, nervously twiddling his fingers. "Okay, Huddie," Alan said. "They're ready for you. Now, just relax. They'll love you, I promise."

He took Leadbelly back to the parlor and, as they entered, every eye turned to the doorway. Alan entered first, then stood aside and waved Leadbelly in. He wore a gray pinstriped suit, white shirt and a black bow tie. He carried his guitar stiffly in front of him. His face was rigid, and it was obvious he was nervous and frightened. The sea of white faces dotting the room smiled at him, and there was a trickle of polite applause.

"Leadbelly, these are my friends," Lomax said. "I've told them about you and they're anxious to hear you play and sing."

Leadbelly just nodded, still uncertain whether he should say anything.

"Welcome to New York, Mr. Ledbetter," one girl said, and a few more in the room echoed her. They nodded courteously and smiled. Leadbelly jerkily returned their greetings. He looked at their neat suits and dresses, their glittering jewelry and elegant manners. It was so different from a bawdy-house lobby or a dingy bar on Deep Elm in Dallas. Here there were soft chairs and paintings on the tapestried walls, and everyone spoke softly. It seemed to Leadbelly that they should all be on a movie screen and he, in turn, should be back down in Shreveport.

"Have a drink," someone called, but Alan was next to him immediately with a glass of orange soda. Leadbelly tasted it and tried to hide his disappointment. It was only soda. He smiled again and Lomax resumed talking.

"Leadbelly has one of the greatest repertoires of folk songs I've ever run across, as I've said before. He says he knows more than five hundred songs by heart, ranging from work songs and hollers to ballads and spirituals. I'd wager he's composed several hundred different selections alone."

Leadbelly clutched at his guitar, hoping his fingers would work and wishing it was over.

By midnight he was a resounding hit and he knew it. He was surer than ever that the "king o' the twelve-string guitar" would be on every front page of every paper in the city. He had loosened up considerably after his first number and had sung his way through fifteen songs, steadily relaxing. And when he sang "Mister Tom Hughes' Town," his cockiness crept back into his style. At last all of his doubts and fears were gone.

Newspaper reporters interviewed him, with Alan as a buffer for the rapid-fire questions. There was even a publisher who discussed the possibility of a book. Another man wanted him to record some songs the very next day for his fledgling recording company. One man with a flashy silver chain strung across his vest tried to talk to Leadbelly in highly technical terms. Idiom? Glissando? Portamento? Grace notes? Leadbelly let Alan answer the questions.

It seemed as if the people at the party had as much difficulty understanding him as he did them. His backcountry Louisiana patois was almost a different language. But it didn't matter. He was able to interest the men and charm the women, and for the first time he felt at ease with this audience.

When the last guest left, Lomax cautioned him to get a good night's sleep. Tomorrow they had an appointment to see a publisher. "Come right to our rooms at eight o'clock sharp, Huddie. It could be a very important day for you. And tomorrow for sure we'll get a place for you to stay. That's a promise."

Leadbelly's thoughts swept back to the tiny room in Harlem. "I sure don't want to go back to that place I'm stayin'. Don't want to take that train again, neither."

"It's all right," Lomax said, putting his arm on Leadbelly's shoulder. "Just go right home and get some sleep."

"Don't like them Harlem niggas neither, Boss. They ain't the same kind o' people as the niggas I'se used to."

"People are people, Leadbelly. Now, go on home."

Leadbelly hefted his guitar over his shoulder and walked out into the cold New York night.

The streets were icy and slick, and Leadbelly almost stumbled when he climbed up the I.R.T. station steps. Harlem loomed before him, the tenements stacked like huge dirty gray bricks. The more he thought about it the angrier he became. Why couldn't I have stayed with them? Here I am by myself here in Harlem. Damn it! This is no better for a nigga than down in Shreveport. They ain't no equals here. It's just like everywhere else.

He crossed the street, pausing to read a poster in the window of a shoeshine parlor:

> FATHER DIVINE
> IS THE SUPPLIER AND THE SATISFIER
> OF EVERY GOOD DESIRE

Another sign read:

> PEACE
> Home Cooked Meals 10¢ & 15¢

He found himself standing in front of the Harlem Y.M.C.A., but he simply did not want to go back to his room. Further, there was something about those white faces that still bothered him. They seemed eager to hear his music and quick to applaud him, but their smiles seemed frozen on their faces and they talked to him as if he were a child. Hell, he thought, I was more relaxed with my friends down on Saint Paul's Bottom than in New York. He decided he wanted a drink with his own color.

Two couples were coming out of Godfrey's Beer Garden, laughing loudly, the boys wrapping their arms about their girls. Next door, another couple were making love blatantly in the doorway, the woman sitting on the man's lap. Leadbelly watched them for a moment, then turned and went into Godfrey's.

No one gave him a second look. He sat down at a table and ordered whiskey, throwing it down in one gulp. The place was almost empty; a few men in one corner were huddled together making book. He had another drink, and then another.

An hour later he was drunk and talking to a pretty girl with a strange New York accent whose name was Aretha. He had motioned her over to the table, and she had sat down expecting a drink. But he made no such offer. "Baby, you got a husband?"

The girl thought a moment. "Yeah," she said, "but he's mad."

"Then there ain't no chance for me, huh?"

"No, man! Ain't no chance at all!"

He feigned amazement. "You mad at me?"

"No. I ain't mad."

"You ain't got no husband. You jus' teasin', ain't you?"

"Buy me a drink?"

"Naw."

Aretha started to leave, but Leadbelly reached over and stroked her hand. "Listen, sweet baby. I was jus' jivin' with you. Ain't you gonna be nice to me tonight?"

"If you stay here awhile."

"Okay, now. What you want to drink?"

"Whiskey."

Aretha Ryan worked as a housekeeper for a family on Park Avenue. She usually stayed there, but a sister of hers lived over on 131st Street and tonight she was supposed to celebrate with them. But at the last moment, they drove over to New Jersey and left her a note and the key to their apartment. After an hour, Leadbelly, dragging Aretha behind him, lurched out onto the street in search of action. "Usually, I only givs the wimmins a few nickels, but youse special, baby."

West 125th Street was a mad, harsh jumble of electric signs, pawn shops, ten-cent stores, haberdasheries, theaters and saloons. Buck and Bubbles were starring in "Brown Skin Models" at the Harlem Opera House and Lee Tracy was featured in "I'll Tell the World." Cab Calloway was everybody's idol, and his thirteen-piece band played in front of a garish backdrop of spikes of angular lightning while Calloway himself, dressed in white tails, jived to the music and wiggled his head.

Harlem's hopes were riding on a young boxer named Joe Louis and on a baseball team called the New York Black Yankees. Harlem was old men huddled in dark overcoats playing checkers on Lenox Avenue and children hitching a ride on the Third Avenue trolley, or playing at the fire hydrants in sweltering summers or begging for food from the nuns. Harlem was sucking on flavored ice, meeting at the Monarch Lodge No. 45, registering for unemployment, posing for the Alpha Kappa Alpha; it was the Daily Worker, the Abyssinian Baptist Church, Father Divine's Dusenberg, Paul Robeson or Bill Robinson or Rex Ingram or Ethel Waters or Langston Hughes or Fletcher Henderson. Harlem was Lindy-hopping at the Savoy.

Even the language was unique: a white person was called a "kelt," a dark person was a "blue," a high-class person was a "dicty" and a "passer" was a black who could pass for white. "Birds-eye maple" was a mulatto girl, and a "honey man" was kept by his woman; cars were "buzz carts," suckers were "spruces," West Indians were "monkey huggers," liquor was "lap," a dance was a "scronch," showing some pep during a dance was "walking the broad" and a woman getting divorced was "unsheiking."

Leadbelly reveled in the Harlem night, now that he had whiskey and a woman. He and Aretha tried to do everything, and it was after four when they stumbled into the apartment. The contrast with the apartment where he'd sung for the white people was shattering. There were no thick carpets or lush tapestries in this pathetic, dirty room with peeling linoleum and a 60-watt bulb dangling dimly from the ceiling. Against the window was a skinny Christmas tree; under it, presents. One of the gifts was a bottle of whiskey.

Leadbelly took little time in helping himself to the gift, pouring a tumbler to overflowing and dragging Aretha to the couch. "I ain't had no wimmins for a spell, baby." His hand fell to her breast and he squeezed it. She giggled and snuggled against him.

"You sure you ain't had too much whiskey?"

"What you you mean, baby? Takes more than a bottle of whiskey to get ol' Leadbelly tired, I could drink gallons of it without noticin'."

Aretha took the glass and sipped at it. "Willie -- that's my sister's husband -- he gonna be fit to be tied when he see you drinkin' up his whiskey."

"Don't matter. I jus' go out and buy another bottle. Better brand, too."

Aretha rubbed her palm against his chest. "Man, you're strong as an ox."

"Worked like one, too. You sweat like hell down there in Loosiana. Ain't like here in New Yawk. You folks got it easy."

"Shit," she said. "You don't know what you're talkin' about. Easy! Why, the only thing easy here is makin' babies."

"You got a good job," he said.

"If you think working for board and ten dollars a week is a good job, then you take it!"

"Not me," he said. "I'se here to make it big, jus' like Cab Calloway."

"Well, I tell you, you gonna be workin' in a lot of piss-holes before Harlem gets finished with you. Ain't nuthin' come easy here."

Leadbelly shook his head and sipped again. "It's different for me. My boss takes care of me."

Aretha smirked. "You keep believin' that shit and New York's gonna kill you. Ain't no easy green. Just a bunch of white bastards fuckin' you. I been in New York all my life and I'm tellin' you that you were better off down South where you come from. At least down there you know where you're supposed to be. Up here, just a bunch of pimps and guys with greasy conks talkin' big and actin' smart. Haven't you smelled it, already? Shit, your boss, if that's what you call him, couldn't even find you a regular room! You think I'm pretty?"

"Youse beautiful, baby. You got the nicest, longest legs I ever seen."

Aretha stood up and weaved to the window. "Mama worked hard so I could be a dancer. Worked down in the bakery. Every mornin' she got up at four and not come home 'til it was dark. Never did have no papa. Anyway, I danced good and tried out for the follies. Then one of the big money men in the show knocked me up and I had to quit."

"Where's the kid?"

"He was born dead. Choked on the cord. It was all wrapped around his neck." She sat down again and lit a cigarette. "Now, listen, I don't know who you are, but if you got any brains you'll get out. You jus' get as much money as you can from your boss and you beat it out of this shit-hole. City folks are much different from your kind. And, man, I can tell you're country!"

Leadbelly took another sip of whiskey. She was wrong, of course. Oh, maybe she was right for most singers, but most singers didn't have record companies and book publishers wanting them. After only a day, New York was opening up for him.

"Well, you jus' go on talkin' like that, 'Retha. I know what I'm doin'."

"You'll see," she said. Then she touched him again and he pulled her close.

His hand raced up her skirt, and she was panting into his ear within seconds. He played with her and whispered to her, and she tore at his pants, murmuring, "Oh, come on, country boy! Come on to your big city gal! Give it here, now, you hear me?" Her other hand felt for his chest and pressed him hard, moving swiftly to his biceps and forearms. With each squeeze she whimpered again, as if his muscles themselves provided her orgasms. Leadbelly knew there was one thing that never changed, from Shreveport to Harlem. They were all the same.

At daylight the apartment was a shambles. Clothes were everywhere and the bottle was empty.

By seven o'clock Leadbelly and his guitar were out on the wintry street again. He headed toward West 125th. He went into a place called Little Larry's, but there was no one there except a mustached bartender. At the Green Lantern he had three more whiskeys and stayed almost an hour. He played the guitar at Wheetstraw's, and people bought him more to drink, and the time for his meeting with Lomax passed.

Finally, at eleven o'clock, he wove his way back to the Lomax apartment in the Village. Lomax was furious. "Where the hell have you been!"

"I'se in my whiskey, boss. I'se in my whiskey. Cab Calloway offered me a thousand dollars to sing for him! If I wasn't so drunk I could make a million dollars today. But I'se in my whiskey."

Lomax slammed the door behind him and jabbed an unlit cigar in his mouth. He had waited at the publisher's for two hours. Now the telephones were jangling and Alan was preparing a news release, but Leadbelly was too drunk to stand up. He staggered around the apartment explaining the reason for his behavior, "I don't like whiskey. No, gin cuts the gizzum in my throat and helps me sing better! I ain't goin' to drink no more whiskey, but I got to have my gin."

Lomax looked at him in disgust. Leadbelly staggered to the couch and fell down. He put a red bandanna over his face.

The telephone rang again.

###

Chapter Twenty

Through all his misconduct, the New York newspapers were thrilled with Leadbelly's appearance on the local scene and pulled out all the stops on their florid prose. This article appeared in The New York Herald-Tribune, Jan. 3, 1934:

LOMAX ARRIVES WITH LEADBELLY, NEGRO MINSTREL

Sweet Singer of the Swamplands Here
To Do A Few Tunes Between Homicides

Sniffs at Cab Calloway
Why, He Himself Has Sung
Way to Prison Pardons

John A. Lomax, tireless student and compiler of American folksongs, has arrived in New York with his son, dozens of records made by them for the Library of Congress on a year's tour through the prisons and plantations of the South, and a walking, singing, fighting album of Negro ballads: Leadbelly, self-acknowledged king of the 12-string guitar.

Leadbelly, born Huddie Ledbetter, of the Louisiana swamps, is a powerful knife-toting Negro who has killed one man and seriously wounded another, but whose husky tenor and feathery string-plucking fingers ineluctably charm the ears of those who listen. Twice has Leadbelly sung for the governors of Southern states and twice has he been pardoned by them from serving long terms in state penitentiaries.

*   *   *   *   *

The Lomax apartment hummed with activity. *Time* magazine wanted to interview him. The Associated Press put out a national wire story. The American Record Corporation was interested. More publishers were interested. The National Broadcasting Company wanted to put him on the air. Contracts were offered like *hors d'oeuvres*. William Rose Benet wrote a poem for the January 19 issue of *The New Yorker*.

Everything was working according to plan.

*   *   *   *   *

Martha Promise i want you to come on
to New York now when i tell you somthin
means i want you to do it and not wait.
Shut you doors and come on Some other
Shreveport wimmen will come when i say
come i look for you tomorrow Come on
i want to marry you at once as you
are my intended wife

Huddie Ledbetter

With that letter, Leadbelly formally proposed to Martha Promise. The Lomaxes and Leadbelly moved to Wilton, Connecticut, fifty miles northeast of New York. There, in relative isolation, they worked and Leadbelly served as cook, laundryman, chauffeur and snow shoveler. Lomax promised to let Leadbelly bring Martha up, but at first she delayed. She wanted to sell the things in the house. An annoyed Leadbelly replied and insisted that she come immediately. Then the news finally came that Martha was on her way to New York by train. His melancholy instantly changed to ecstasy. Things were going to be all right, after all, he decided. With a woman around things were always better. Alan and Leadbelly were close friends now, and evenings were spent recording the notes of Leadbelly's prison years. A tour was being discussed. He'd soon have everything he'd always wanted.

Another article appeared on Page One of The New York Herald-Tribune:

LEADBELLY GETS A BAD SCARE
AS FIANCEE ROLLS IN

Homicide Harmonizer At
All the Trains from Dixie
But Martha Arrives Early

Red Cap Unites Lovers

Now All Guitar-Strummin'
Champ Needs Is License

A comedy of errors, well wrought in accordance with
Aristotelian unities and infused with all the dramatic elements

of love, hope, fear, despair, and ultimate jubilation, was enacted at Pennsylvania Station yesterday in the 45 minutes between noon and 12:45 P.m.

The hero is the Negro minstrel, Leadbelly, erstwhile slayer, equally adept with knife or guitar, born in Louisiana swamplands, now tasting for the first time the sweets of musical success as they drop from the richly laden branches of radio and stage. He has come to Pennsylvania Station, refulgent in a double-breasted tan suit with red pin stripes, tan shirt with red tie, tan shoes agleam, and a white silk scarf, to meet the heroine, his old sweetheart, Martha Promise of Shreveport, La., who in the past has sheltered him when he was hungry and broke between prison sentences.

Promptly at 12:05 the Washington train, to which Martha has transferred from the Southern Railway, glides into Track 8. The doors open. Passengers step out. Red caps forget Leadbelly and seize the discharged baggage. Leadbelly excitedly leaves Mr. Lomax and dashes down the platform to the rear.

A moment later he returns, worried and makes for the front of the train. The passengers file upstairs. No Martha appears. Leadbelly, wild with alarm, runs in and out of the empty cars. The platform is deserted.

Leadbelly, too heartsick to eat, sits glumly with head bowed above the rising fumes. Mr. Lomax, sympathetic and worried, drinks his coffee and lights a new cigar.

The second train hisses to a halt. The passengers step forth. Leadbelly repeats his frightened dashes in and out of the cars, up and down the platform. But his fiancee is not to be found. Slowly and sorrowfully, he mounts the stairs. Mr. Lomax has to return to Alan. He will leave Leadbelly at the station all night if necessary to meet each southern train as it arrives.

A red cap says a lady in the waiting room had just sent a telegram to Mr. Lomax at Wilton, Conn. "That's my wife, that's my wife," cries Leadbelly. He dashes to the waiting room and meets a tall sweet-faced Negro woman with a brilliant smile and lustrous eyes. She and Leadbelly rush into each other's arms and kiss. Photographers flash their bulbs and they kiss again.

"Where have you been, anyhow?" Leadbelly asks.

Martha Promise laughs. "I just got an early train by accident," she says. "I got here at 20 minutes to 12, so I jus' walked in here to sit down and wait 'til you came."

"She was sitting here waiting when I came in to phone," says Mr. Lomax.

"Was you scared, honey?" asks Leadbelly in joyful solicitude. '

"No, I wasn't scared, I knew you'd find me, all right. I was much more scareder on the train."

*　　*　　*　　*　　*

To Leadbelly's disappointment, a special Connecticut law delayed the wedding ceremony for five days, but finally Reverend Samuel Weldon Overton married the pair in the Wilton mansion at noon the following Sunday. Leadbelly, as excited as ever, was resplendent in a new suit Lomax had bought him. Martha, a slight coyness creeping into her manner, was dressed in a new wool dress.

Once again, reporters and photographers crammed the parlor. Lomax gave the bride away, and young Alan acted as best man. After the ceremony Leadbelly doffed his white gloves and seized his old guitar, playing songs and dancing for his Martha. He held Martha's hand as they greeted more guests and toasted the days and months and years to come.

But Lomax was soon at his shoulder, reminding him of a concert scheduled for that afternoon in Brooklyn. They piled into the Lomax car and drove in. In the home of the editor of the <u>Brooklyn Eagle</u>, Leadbelly was greeted as a celebrity. There had been syndicated stories about him in almost every newspaper across the nation. The Brooklyn concert was a huge success and Martha, for the first time, saw her Huddie received with loud applause. She was genuinely impressed and for many days commented constantly on how wonderful it was. Her rambling boyfriend from Mooringsport had achieved his dream -- to be recognized as the "King o' the Twelve-String Guitar" in the city of New York.

After the concert, new offers began to flow into the Lomax house in Wilton via telephone, letter and telegram. Lomax carefully began to plot out a concert tour through New York State, for college and private groups. While this was going on, Martha and Leadbelly settled easily into life in Wilton. They had divided the chores between them, with Martha assigned as cook, bed-maker, ironer and general housecleaner. Leadbelly took great delight in making her laugh, and occasionally teased her with ribald lyrics, which never failed to send Martha into a stern religious lecture about "sinful songs." Their lovemaking, often at odd times of the day, was frequent and boisterous, to Lomax's chagrin.

One day Martha answered the phone and heard the long distance operator announce a call from Texas for Walter Boyd. "Texas?" she said. "Mr. Boyd?"

Leadbelly froze. Oh, Lord, he thought with a sinking feeling. Another lawman after me. They tracked me down, even way up here in the capital of all the world!

Lomax finally stepped to the telephone and said, "There is no Mr. Boyd here, sir. May I ask who is calling?"

They all waited. Lomax looked at Leadbelly, then turned away. "Yes, I see," he said.

Leadbelly looked at the door, then at Martha. His eyes told her he would run if it was bad news, as fast and as far as possible.

"Yes," he heard Lomax say again. "Well, if that's the case, yes. Yes, there is a Walter Boyd here." Then he turned to Leadbelly. "It's for you."

They watched in silence as Leadbelly reluctantly took the telephone. "Who's this?" he said right off.

"Walter?" the voice asked.

"How you know I'se Walter? Who's this?"

The voice on the other end laughed. "Leadbelly!" it shouted now. "Leadbelly, you old con-man! Now that you're a star you don't want to talk to your old friend Captain Franklin?"

Leadbelly whooped and hollered and danced as he spoke into the mouthpiece, and they talked for half an hour. Franklin was pleased at all the publicity he was reading about his old friend, and he made Leadbelly promise to stay out of trouble, not to drink too much and to do what Lomax told him. He told Leadbelly of Lomax's reputation as a respected folklorist, information which Leadbelly had never really believed. But if it came from Franklin, it had to be true.

Franklin also promised to try to make a trip to New York soon for a visit with the Lomaxes and Ledbetters, and Leadbelly sadly said goodbye when the conversation ended. The captain -- Leadbelly still couldn't quite comprehend the academic status Franklin had attained -- was the only white man he trusted, besides Alan Lomax.

Leadbelly and Martha, during these peaceful days prior to his first concert tour, often went down to the black district in South

Norwalk, a few miles from Wilton, and visited with new friends. Leadbelly played for them, and often returned to Wilton buoyed with new enthusiasm. When he had no heavy work to do, though, Leadbelly sometimes grew sullen, doleful, and groused around the house mumbling to Martha about finding something to do. The day-to-day monotony of life at Wilton, the repetitive questions about a life long past and which Leadbelly would have preferred not to think about, soon bored him.

Lomax planned to leave the first week in March for a tour that would take them to Albany, Rochester, Buffalo, Cambridge and Harvard. On Sunday, March 3, they were ready to depart, but Leadbelly was visibly gloomy about the prospects of spending so much time away from Martha. Lomax had also made him pack his convict clothes, against his protestations, and for Leadbelly that frosty March morning was a cheerless one. "I don't want to leave Marthy," he said as they were preparing to depart. "She says the rats scares her at nights."

"Oh, nonsense, Leadbelly. She said no such thing."

"Oh yes she did," Leadbelly said, and walked out the front door.

Lomax called to Martha and asked her what was wrong, whether she was nervous about staying in the house while he and Leadbelly traveled. "Them rats sure did scare me one or two nights when I first come up," she said. "They sounded as big as horses runnin' up and down in the upstairs. But I'se over that, now. Mr. Alan will stay with me. I don't need to 'spect Huddie to be with me every night when he's out workin'."

Lomax walked to the window and looked out. "I guess he was just grumbling. He's out there working on the car."

Martha looked out with him. "That's right, Mr. Lomax. Jus' had to grumble. That nigga sure is proud of that automobile."

An hour later they were headed west to Albany, where Leadbelly sang for a group of Professor Harold Thompson's friends. From Albany, a quiet Leadbelly drove them to Syracuse and then on to the campus of the University of Rochester. Lomax had made plans to call on the university librarian, an old friend named Donald Gilchrist.

Leadbelly promised to pick him up for lunch, then headed directly toward the ghetto district of Rochester, steering the shiny car confidently.

Dammit, he said to himself. Just can't seem to get out of these blues. Life at their house is just plain boring, and now they take me away from my Marthy again. Boss-man, he takin' all the money anyway, and I'se just the same old monkey again, jumpin' up and down whenever he says to and playin' for these people what don't even know what the blues is all about. How can I get famous in New York when they keep me away from my own people and everyone always starin' at me like I'm a freak or something?

His mood changed immediately when he was in the first saloon. He had little difficulty finding companionship. Within minutes he was in another bar with a group of new friends who were clamoring to hear him play more music and who bought him drinks with each new song. Two women attached themselves to him, and a man named Gasoline Charlie helped him stagger to the car when the bars closed. The four of them got in the front seat, the guitar tucked carefully in the trunk, and went to the girls' apartment, where Leadbelly happily and drunkenly recounted the prison tales everyone loved to hear. He told them he would be a movie star, and he told them how recording companies and publishers were after him.

As Lomax fretted about the outcome of the performance, a four-person orgy was taking place downtown. Leadbelly was doing things to the girls that Gasoline Charlie had never thought possible. Leadbelly vaguely remembered the concert, and that he had left Lomax's car somewhere, but the only thing that bothered him was that his guitar was in the car.

Late in the afternoon, Leadbelly staggered back to the car with Gasoline Charlie. "Let 'em be, Charlie, plenty more gals for us. Right now, I want to eat."

Meanwhile, Lomax was forced to entertain the students himself. When he arrived back at his room in the dormitory, he spotted the car and furiously dashed up the stairs. Leadbelly was in his room. The guitar was flung across the bed, Gasoline Charlie slumped in a chair, and Leadbelly was ravenously tearing shreds of meat off an eight-pound smoked ham. He looked up as Lomax burst into the room. "Hello, Boss," he said, still chewing. "This is the bes' piece o' ham I'se et since I left Loosiana."

"Where the hell have you been?" Lomax shouted, "It's almost time for the concert!"

"I found some of my color and been stayin' with them. That there's Gasoline Charlie."

"Why didn't you telephone? I've been worried sick about you!" Lomax looked with disgust at the bum slumped in the chair. "Come with me," he said. "And bring that guitar."

"Boss, don't you ever worry 'bout me none. When I get in trouble I'll always phone you," he said as he meekly followed.

In his own room, Lomax made Leadbelly prove he could still play. Leadbelly sang "Death Letter Blues" passably, and Lomax reluctantly decided to let him go on.

The concert was a shambles. Leadbelly's voice was cracked and feeble. He missed notes and skipped words. The lyrics he sang were entirely blurred by a sluggish tongue. Even though the novelty of his act was enough to carry him through and the students applauded generously, Lomax was disappointed. After the concert, he led an embarrassed Leadbelly and his still staggering friend back to the dormitory in chilly silence.

In the room, Lomax, chewing on an unlit panetella, lectured him. "Leadbelly, you know I've tried to help you, that everything I've asked you to do has been for your own good. Tomorrow night comes the most important engagement we have on this trip. I expect you to show those Buffalo people how you can sing. I'll drive your friend back to town, but I want you to go to bed and get a good night's rest so you can be in fine form tomorrow."

"Don't worry, Boss." Leadbelly was on his feet and at the door. "But if you don't mind, I promised I'd go back with Charlie."

"I do mind!" Lomax said. "I want you to stay here."

"Don't worry, Boss. I gotta go to a party because I promised someone." Arrogance crept into his voice.

Gasoline Charlie looked at Lomax blankly and then grinned, displaying a decayed set of teeth. "I make sure he gets back by 'leven-thirty," he said.

Lomax had no choice; he was afraid to try and restrain Leadbelly. Against his better judgment, he agreed. "Now, it's a promise, Leadbelly. I'll give you one more chance. You be back here by eleven-thirty!"

"Don't worry, Boss. Jus' please don't worry." And with that he was out the door and down the hallway.

Gasoline Charlie leered at Lomax before following Leadbelly. "That boy found himself a little brown-skin pussy down on Eighth Street, and you jus' can't stop him. Nobody can stop him now."

Lomax slammed the door in his face.

Of course, it was almost daylight when Leadbelly returned.

*   *   *   *   *

They were to spend three nights in Buffalo, give three concerts, and then drive to Cambridge and Harvard. Lomax took Leadbelly to the black Y.M.C.A. and begged him to get some much-needed sleep. But when Lomax left, Leadbelly found another room on Williams Street. Lomax, he decided, did not understand him. He was a man who all through his life had rambled and sucked every ounce of living he could from what life had given him. And how he hated parodying himself in a desperate attempt to over-assure Lomax. With Alan he could be himself, but, unfortunately, Alan was not the boss-man. He would have to be a boot-licker for a while yet. At least until he was a major star, maybe with Cab Calloway's band.

That evening, dressed in the hated convict stripes, he delighted the audience with his tales and songs. Later, he found himself regaling a petite female reporter with his oft-told stories, his fights, his sexual conquests and adventures. The young woman was wide-eyed as he bantered with her, casually tossing off accounts of murder, sex and violence.

"Yeah, missy. You should have seen what happen to me. Now, I want you to know I never bothered nobody unless they fool with me. I jus' don't like to see people get in trouble by mistake. One time, six mean niggas come a-rushin' at me, tryin' to get me to give up some of my whiskey. Well, I wasn't 'bout to let 'em have none so I popped open my knife and began to cut all o' them. Before I know it, all six of them was on the ground and bleedin' like pigs butchered up for sausage. I jus' stick the ol' knife right up to the handle and give it a little twist, like this, and before I knows it, blood gushin' out all over the place."

The girl paled and scribbled notes. "Mr. Leadbelly, you certainly have been a lucky man, gaining your freedom nevertheless."

"No, ma'am. Ain't no luck. Played the music what touched the heart of the wardens and the gov'nors. Ain't nobody ever heard an ol' box like this. No ma'am, wasn't no luck. Jus' my playin' and singin'. And that's the truth."

The evening went well, but afterward Leadbelly was again sullen. It had been their custom for Leadbelly to pass his hat around for donations after each performance, then to turn the proceeds over to Lomax. It seemed like begging to Leadbelly, and it was embarrassing. It seemed to him that someone else should do the money-collecting. So that evening Leadbelly refused to give Lomax the money.

"Jus' seem like if I do all the playin' and then I have to do the collectin', well Boss, it jus' seem like I oughtta be keepin' it."

"But don't I give you enough to live on?" Lomax asked, taken aback. "Don't I give you some to send back to Martha, and aren't the two of you saving for the future?"

"Jus' seem like I'm the onliest one earnin' it, that's all." Leadbelly jammed the bills into his pocket and folded his arms defiantly.

After a few more mild arguments from Lomax, he promised to turn it over the following day, and Lomax, supressing a trickle of fear, reluctantly gave in once again.

The next day Lomax lectured to the students of Buffalo State Teacher's College. Leadbelly still hadn't turned over the proceeds of the previous night. He sang a few songs, got paid by the dean of the school, and left with a pocket crammed full of paper money and jingling coins, refusing again to surrender the money.

Back in the dormitory, Lomax tried again. "Leadbelly, I promised Martha I wouldn't let you squander your money away during this trip. If you turn it over to me we can save it for when we get back to Wilton, and you'll have all the money you need for quite some time. Besides, there's still more coming from our other offers from radio and record company people."

"Boss, I decided I can take care of my money all by myself. I don' need nobody to tell me how to take care of it. An' I don't like the way the niggas is bein' treated here up north. Ain't the same as down in Loosiana. No suh, I'se keepin' my money from now on." He looked evenly at Lomax, and took another swig from a bottle he had hidden in his valise.

"Leadbelly, what's wrong with you? You're not the same. I thought if you met some of your own people you'd relax more. But you're becoming the same man that got thrown into Angola state prison."

Leadbelly scowled. "Boss, I tol' you many times that I wasn't thrown in there for my account. Now, I ain't givin' you this here money, and I ain't gonna play no more for you unless I gets to bring Marthy along. I ain't never got in no trouble with my Marthy beside me. I want to go back to the house in Wilton."

Lomax gave up and went to bed, but he slept fitfully. He decided he'd recruit someone else to collect the donations, and then turn it over directly to him. But he was worried. He had thought that occasionally letting Leadbelly go out by himself would be therapeutic for him, but it seemed that these drunken rambles in the Negro districts did nothing but make him more morose and violent. During the next two weeks of the tour, Lomax slowly realized he and his son had probably failed to prepare Leadbelly adequately for life in the cities of the north. They had taken him from his home, his family and his friends, and had put him on display among strangers. No wonder the poor devil was confused, Lomax thought sadly.

The next day Leadbelly sat in his room while Lomax was working in the college library. He thought about playing his guitar, about practicing and maybe showing off something new tonight. Maybe that would impress Lomax and make him leave him alone. No, he decided. No sense. He took another drink from a small pint bottle he had hidden inside his pillowcase. The bottle was empty now.

Leadbelly got up and paced, trying to figure out what to do. The musician in him wanted to play his music; the man in him wanted to ramble downtown. He thrust his hands into his pockets and counted out only a dollar and seven cents. Someone had sneaked in and stole his money while he was sleeping! Swearing, he threw the change at the wall.

He left the room and weaved down the hall toward the exit on the side of the dormitory that led to the library. On the way, he grew more furious. Through the alcohol haze, he decided the end had come. He would get his money back from that greedy Boss-man and take Martha back to Shreveport. Then they would come back after a while and Leadbelly would manage his own affairs.

Lomax was seated at a long desk in a special room off the college's large library. As soon as he looked up and saw Leadbelly, he knew it was trouble. He noticed Leadbelly was wearing a new overcoat, a flashy green and gray-checked affair, and he had his hands plunged deep into the pockets.

"Gimme the money you stole," Leadbelly said, not bothering to hide his anger. "I need it."

Lomax thought quickly. Don't anger him. Be casual. "I-I don't have any money with me," he said. "What's the matter, Leadbelly?

Are you angry about something? I just didn't want you to squander it before we get back to Wilton."

"But it's *my* money! I want it now and you got it!"

Lomax smelled the whiskey now, and the warnings of all his friends flashed through his mind. "I can't give you any more money," he said evenly, standing up. "When we get on the road again we'll discuss the money problem. Leadbelly, I'm busy transcribing notes right now. Can't you---"

"I want it!" Leadbelly roared, and took a step toward the desk. He brought a large knife from the pocket of the overcoat and snapped the blade open. "I'se goin' to cut you, you don't gimme that money, Boss! I ain't gonna be no more slave for you. I'se getting back to Shrevepo't with Marthy, and I need my money to do it. No more monkey-playin' for you and not gettin' nothin' out of it."

Lomax moved back, not knowing where to turn. He looked frantically at the door, and as if a magical answer, he heard a knock.

Lomax yelled "Come in!" as quickly as he could. By the time his friend, Judge Louis Hart, entered, Leadbelly had quickly stashed the knife and in a flash his face had changed from an angry scowl to a pleasant smile.

"Howdy, Judge," Leadbelly said sweetly. "It's right good to see you again. How you been?"

Judge Hart nodded, looking at Lomax quizzically. Lomax decided not to say anything about the knife. "Leadbelly wants more money, and we've been discussing it."

"All your money gone, Mr. Ledbetter?" the judge asked.

Lomax answered before Leadbelly could. "He's been squandering it downtown during his evenings, and I told him I wasn't willing to give him more. Have to make sure he'll be healthy for the University Club engagement Saturday night. It's an important date."

"I think Mr. Lomax would be a better guardian of your earnings, Mr. Ledbetter," the judge said.

"I bought some presents for my Marthy, Judge," he lied. "Bought her four dresses, and I bought this here new coat, too." Leadbelly kept smiling. "I put the rest in the bank near where I'se stayin' so's I wouldn't lose it. Now I got to pay the cab driver downstairs what took me back here."

"There are no banks where you're staying, Leadbelly," Lomax said.

"The cab driver wants his money, Boss," Leadbelly replied, ignoring the charge. Finally Lomax gave him two dollars, and Leadbelly left the room abruptly.

He bought another bottle of whiskey before returning to his own room. He played songs for himself as he drank well into the night. He sang the songs Martha liked best, and he sang a song his mother taught him. He sang as many old Sycamore Slim songs as he could remember. Then he fell asleep with the lights on.

The concert for the University Club was a complete flop. Leadbelly's voice was dissipated and croaky when he spoke and his husky tenor cracked often when he sang. He didn't care. If he couldn't do it his way, he'd just as soon be sent back to Wilton.

Afterward, Lomax gave Leadbelly his supper and bed money in stony silence. The next morning the two began the drive to Albany. As a guarantee against more bad behavior and carousing, and to ensure no more concerts would go awry, Lomax had arranged for Alan and Martha to meet them there. Like clockwork, the prospect of seeing his woman again brightened Leadbelly's mood considerably.

At a gasoline stop he leaped out and bought Lomax two cigars, but otherwise he made no effort at conversation.

The concert at New York State Teacher's College, by contrast, went exceptionally well. Fifteen hundred students cheered him exuberantly. The Harvard concert was also a success, and Leadbelly's conduct was cheery and ebullient. Martha could scarcely suppress her pride.

Lomax, though, knew he had lost control of his man. Leadbelly had deliberately disobeyed him and had gotten away with it. He would go off whenever he pleased and would get drunk on cheap whiskey at the slightest provocation. In the glitter and glare of New York City, in the newspaper publicity and whooping audience receptions, he had become his own man.

*   *   *   *   *

Leadbelly sat on a three-legged stool in the cream-white kitchen and watched Martha recheck the chicken roasting in the oven. She looked over at Leadbelly and smiled. "You gettin' into one of you moods again, ain't you?" She was glad to have him back in the shelter of the house in Wilton, but his restlessness was unabated.

He looked at her without changing expression. His thick lips were set and his eyes were baleful. His massive shoulders slumped forward, and he held his fingers interlocked in his lap. "Yeah," he said. "I reckon."

"What's the matter this time? You bored again?"

"Marthy, this ain't no place for the kind of niggas we are. I had a better time in Harlem than out here in the woods."

"You makin' some money now, Huddie. We can do whatever you want to do, if you don't like it here none. That what you wanna do, get out of here?"

He shrugged. She had seldom seen him this morose. "That's jus' it. We can't go nowheres. We is slaves to the boss-man, jus' as sure as our gran'daddies was. I always have to ask Boss Lomax for my money. Well, I want to have it to myself an' buy us a big new car, maybe even a great big house somewheres. I can't even say yes to all of them people what want to give me more money for the records and radio an' things, Marthy. That ain't bein' no free man. He makin' all the money! I jus' playin' the music for him. I wish li'l Boss Alan was the big Boss. He's a good man."

Martha got up and went over to him. He didn't extend his hands to her, but she took his and pressed them to her chest. "Mr. Lomax don' mean no harm to you, Huddie. I know it. He jus' want to make sure you don' go 'round ramblin' again and get yourself into all the trouble you did down in Loosiana. 'Sides, young Mr. Alan tell me once that you gotta be careful with all of them money-people grabbin' at you an' tellin' you they gonna make you rich. He say most of them jus' want you to make *them* rich, that's all. An' I agree with you, he's a good man, that Alan. He know what's the bes'."

"But he ain't the boss-man. Marthy, I wanna be my own boss."

She forced a grin at him and poked him in the ribs. "You the boss far as I'm concerned, you ol' King Kong. Now, don't you go worryin' and gettin' things all stirred up again. An' come eat you chicken before I eat it myself."

Leadbelly devoured the entire chicken as Martha watched him and sipped coffee. She let him wash it down with a waterglass full of gin, and she finally opened a bottle of beer for herself. They sat at the table in silence for a long while, until they heard Lomax calling for them. Leadbelly set his jaw stubbornly and didn't answer.

Lomax came into the kitchen, apologizing for bursting in on them, and asked if he could join them. Martha nodded; Leadbelly stared down at his plate.

"I don't want to disappoint you, Leadbelly, but I'm afraid we can't all go on our next trip down South in the one car, as I thought. I have to make some extra stops, and it may become a bit too crowded."

"That's okay, Boss," Leadbelly said evenly. "I don't want to go, anyhow."

"You don't? Why not?"

"I'se tired of singin' for jus' a bunch of white people an only seein' niggas at night when you let me go out. I don't guess I like it here no more. I was jus' tellin' Marthy the same thing. Ask her."

Lomax glanced at Martha, and her nod told him the time had come. "Leadbelly, what do you want to say to me?"

Leadbelly looked up and a glimmer of a smile returned to his lips. "Boss, I want to go back to Shreveport. I'd like to go back there right now!"

Lomax sighed heavily. "I'm sorry about this, Leadbelly. You must remember that you came to see me in that hotel in Texas with just prison clothes on your back, a sugar sack in your hand and a smashed old guitar. Now you've got two leather suitcases full of clothes, an enormous trunk and a brand new guitar. You and Martha used to live on her four dollars a week from the laundry, and here you've paid out nothing for rent, food or laundry, you live free in this beautiful mansion, and yet you've spent three hundred and fifty dollars in two months. I really think you're making yourself miserable, nothing else."

"I still want to go back, Boss."

Lomax got up and looked sympathetically at Martha. "All right, Leadbelly. You start packing right away and Alan and I will drive you to the station. I've still got a lot of drafts for money for you, and you can have it all. Perhaps you can make a new start back in Shreveport."

Leadbelly and Martha were packed in ten minutes and waiting by the car when Lomax and Alan came out. Alan tried briefly to talk him out of his decision, but to no avail. Leadbelly was happy and cheerful throughout the drive to the Greyhound bus station near the Pennsylvania Depot. He joked with Alan and Martha continuously, but said nothing to the elder Lomax.

Halfway to New York it began to rain and Leadbelly, his head resting against the window of the car, dozed. Martha gazed at him. Maybe it won't be the same, she thought. He's older now. She noticed more and more gray hair had been sprouting on his temples, and under his eyes the skin had begun to sag. At the corner of his eyes the crow's-feet wrinkles were etched deeper. He was breathing heavily, and as they pulled to a momentary stop his left hand twitched slightly as if he were groping for a chord. She reached over and gently held his fingers still. They were dry and rough from too much exposure to the winter wind, and the simple wedding band glimmered like a vein of ore around his fourth finger.

Martha thought back to when she was twelve years old, the first time she laid eyes on him. He'd been the handsomest man she had ever seen; he was always laughing and telling jokes, and the minute he walked into any room it was like a bolt of lightning. The room immediately filled with his presence. Even now it was not much different, although she hated to see him moody and overly submissive to the white folks.

She knew he was still at his best with children and young people, but when he chose to he could immediately use the same old charm to sway anyone of any age. She liked him best when he was singing to children on the corner in Greenwich Village with his play-party songs. What the future had in store for them now, only Sweet Jesus knew, she thought. Her man was just a natural born rambler who tried his best to be good. In Shreveport she hoped they would settle down once and for all.

At the station, it was a sad, gray scene as Lomax handed Leadbelly the drafts he'd mentioned. Leadbelly silently stashed them in his overcoat pockets as Martha stood by and watched. Alan helped with the baggage, and when the bus hissed its brakes off and began to roll down the ramp, both Lomaxes waved to the dark faces in the window. As the bus disappeared, it occurred to Alan that Leadbelly and Martha had automatically walked to the back of the bus to look for their seats.

###

Chapter Twenty-One

They settled in a tiny rented cottage in a run-down section of west Shreveport. It was a comfortable life at first, and they lived off the money Leadbelly had earned in New York. But it wasn't enough to last, and soon Martha was commuting to work again at the Excelsior Laundry in Shreveport.

To Leadbelly's delight, word of his moderate success in New York had preceded him. Naturally, Edmond, Florida and the rest of the family knew of his Manhattan escapades, and there had been some gaudy publicity in Shreveport. So in this, the first year, Leadbelly rested on his local laurels. He gave an occasional sing-out for twenty dollars, played for church groups for nothing, and amused himself by singing all day for the children in vacant lots and fields. Every few weeks he and Martha would visit Edmond in Mooringsport, but most of the days were spent walking the boardwalks of Shreveport, sometimes buying food, paying other folks' rent when he was flush with money, handing the youngsters frosty bottles of soda pop.

A year slipped by before they knew it.

*   *   *   *   *

Just before Christmas in 1936, the Macmillan Company published the Lomaxes' book, *Negro Folk Songs as Sung by Lead Belly*. When he received his copy he was momentarily elated, but the photograph of him barefoot, posing with his guitar in front of prop barrels, embarrassed him. When he struggled through the text, he was incensed at the distorted picture he thought it presented. He immediately sent the publisher a telegram threatening a lawsuit. He tried to look up his old attorney, Herndon, but discovered he had died. In his desperation he wrote to John Lomax protesting the book and asking him for money.

A whirlpool of depression engulfed him again. And for a while, Martha put up with it. But soon the income from her long hours in the laundry was being wasted, and he was drinking hard again. She thought about leaving him but had no place to go.

Then, on a visit to Mooringsport, a man by the name of Bill Elliot tried to bar him forcibly from a Salvation Army dance. Leadbelly pulled his gun and shot the man through the jaw, ripping out most of his lower teeth. An hour later a posse found Leadbelly asleep on the front steps of the Shiloh Baptist Church. Because of his new celebrity -- or notoriety -- he received a lenient sentence and spent the next six months back in the Shreveport jail.

It gave him a lot of time to think soberly, and when he was released, he cajoled Martha into trying New York again. Three months later they were living in Harlem. But now, time was passing much more slowly. He needed help. Martha took a job as a maid in an uptown hotel, but he was unable to contribute significantly to their income. In his idleness he began to attract a newer, more insidious group of exploiters -- all of them hanging around his tiny apartment. Lomax was off on another song-collecting tour of southern prisons, and he had no close friends. In desperation they took on a paying boarder, a man by the name of Henry Burgess who worked a shoeshine stand on Fifty-third Street. It was a mistake.

On March 5, 1939, while Martha was working, Burgess and Leadbelly decided to stage a rent party. Whiskey had lifted his spirits. He had some money -- from a brief concert at Columbia University. He read that Artie Shaw had hired a beautiful black singer named Billie Holiday. And it was just last year that a young political tyro named Adam Clayton Powell, Jr. chaired a committee that made the Uptown Chamber of Commerce agree to hire one-third black employees in Harlem. He knew the black man's lot could not help but improve, and he was feeling elated this drunken evening.

The party at the Ledbetter apartment soon got out of control. Two showgirls from the Apollo Theater, high on drugs, made a disheveled appearance, causing tempers to flare among the women. Before long, a lust-crazed Burgess pushed one of the showgirls onto the fire escape and crawled clumsily out with her. The girl, giggling, encouraged him and he grabbed the front of her dress. She made no attempt to rebuff him as he ripped the garment from her. She wore no underclothes. She kissed him and licked him and he guffawed loudly through his drunken stupor. Now she knelt before him and quickly unbuttoned his pants until he finally slid down onto his back and pulled her to a sitting position on top of him.

At that moment a staggering Leadbelly appeared at the window and, seeing Burgess and the girl in their ecstasy, scrambled onto the fire escape. He stood over them, weaving, fumbling at his fly. The girl's glazed eyes hardly seemed to see him as he dropped his pants. Then, suddenly, a searing pain in his testicles made him scream. He fell back, hitting his head on the overhead ladder, and cursed.

"You get outta my action!" Burgess was yelling. The girl fell backward and Burgess started to scramble to his feet. He was trying to kick Leadbelly in the groin again, but he was too drunk. The pain still tore through Leadbelly. He reeled to the kitchen, grabbed a favorite knife, and returned to the fire escape, yelling that he would stab Burgess. The men both screamed, and the knife found its way into Burgess's stomach. People were all around, everyone yelling and screaming. Blood oozed from Burgess and stained his undershirt with ruby patches. There was a siren, and then a screeching of brakes in the street below.

Leadbelly offered no resistance when the paddy wagon arrived and three burly Irish cops manhandled the group of drunken partygoers down the four flights of stairs.

*   *   *   *   *

On May 5, 1939, the case was brought to public attention. Before Judge George L. Donnellan, the jury found Huddie Leadbetter guilty of assault in the third degree, and ten days later he was sentenced to a year and a day in a festering sewer named Riker's Island.

He was taken by boat from Queens. When he took a quick glance backward, the city that jealously guarded its fortune smirked back at him. Sullen, frustrated, defiant, he nevertheless suppressed the urge to thrash out at the hawk-nosed guard beside him. The 600-acre prison in the East River swallowed him up.

It wasn't like Sugar Land or Angola, where the cane and cotton fields loomed every day, sucking sweat and blood from a man but at least leaving him too tired to think about women most of the time. No, the New York prison had no work. The New York prison had nothing but stone walls and "mellow boys," and at fifty-four the still powerfully virile Leadbelly was subjected to the worst imprisonment of his life.

On the first day he was taken to the Remand Shelter and locked in a tiny cell in the old blockhouse. It had two iron bunks, a splintered toilet and a cracked bowl in one corner, and a stool. He tried to tell himself that a year would pass quickly, that it was nothing compared to the years on the canebrakes and chain gangs, but the new admissions screaming with the pains of drug withdrawal kept him awake the whole night.

Then, after brief exercise the next day and a sloppy meal, he was assigned a cell and thrown in with a thin Puerto Rican who looked hardly capable of a criminal act.

"Got any weeds, man?" was the first thing the boy said. His faint smile, an obviously appraising look as he studied Leadbelly, was unsettling.

"No, I don't smoke." Low, curt, leave-me-alone.

"Oh."

Leadbelly frowned at him. The lad grinned wider, amused.

"Ain't you heard, yet?" he asked. "They's only two kinds of money here, man. Cigarettes and assholes. You don't have the weeds, you gotta take the other, you want any favors."

"What? What the shit you talkin'?"

The kid sat up in his bunk and looked down at him. "Man, I said if you ain't got cigarettes, it's your asshole. I been here almost two years, and look at me, man. Look at me! I'm a fuckin' queen!"

The words tore at Leadbelly. The kid leered at him, then jumped from the bunk. "Look at this filthy shit-hole, man. Cockroaches on the walls, piss on the floors, horsemeat for dinner. Yeah, horsemeat, man, I seen the labels. Listen, I don't know why you're in here, but you better be tough. You get hard up. You get lonely. After a while, you take any action you can get. And that's the action, man, whether you want it or not."

"Anybody touch me, I kill him." Leadbelly glared at the youth.

The kid spat in the direction of the toilet, then laughed. "You know, it got so bad they had to put all the booty bandits out in the back quad. Skinny white boys were carved into girls. Man, the guards love it. The cocksuckers! Let me tell you, man, if you want to get along you'd better spread!"

Leadbelly was shaken. The boy couldn't have been more than eighteen. "What are you in for?" he finally asked, more to change the subject than for an answer.

"I fucked up, man, that's all. Got caught pushin' scag. My first month here I almost died. Look." He rolled up the sleeve on his right arm. Leadbelly saw the tiny scars left by dirty needles. "Man, I just kept throwing up. Then the queens in the quad got at me one night and damn near ripped my asshole out. Shit, I bled for a week."

"I never did take no drugs."

"You're lucky, man. I was takin' coke and bennies when I was eight. *Eight*, man!"

The boy told Leadbelly of a past of needles plunged into veins on the roofs of tenements, of brass knuckles with needlesharp spikes, violence permeating the streets and saturating the smelly back rooms like oil-laden rain. At nine years old he was hustling in the city. At fourteen he was sent to the Spofford Detention Home in the Bronx. He lived with his mother and five sisters in a run-down building off Lenox that had no toilet and no hot water. Then, just over a year ago, he was charged with loitering and pimping. When he was booked, they found him carrying drugs, and now here he was.

He sat down beside Leadbelly. His hand slowly crept toward Leadbelly's crotch. Leadbelly whirled and crashed his elbow into the boy's face. "Get you fuckin' hands off me, you goddamn freak!

You touch me again, I'll bash you skull against that wall and crack it open like a watermelon!"

The kid pressed the back of his hand hard against the side of his face. "Man, ain't no reason to hit me. I dig black meat."

"I'll kill you!" Leadbelly roared.

"Man, they'll get you sooner or later. May as well let someone who likes you be the first. Sort of like breakin' it in, you know?" The kid was a pitiful mess, forcing a grin even as he held his hand against the pain in his cheek. "C'mon, man, what's the matter, you scared?"

Leadbelly grabbed the stool and hurled it at him. The kid dodged it, and as the stool splintered against the toilet his expression flared into anger. In a second there was a makeshift knife in his hand and he was lunging at Leadbelly. Leadbelly grabbed his wrist and deftly twisted the pitifully frail boy to the floor, reaching for the knife and plunging it into his face. He felt the blade scrape against bone and settle into pulp. The boy was screaming in agony. Black matter from his right eye was running down his cheek.

Leadbelly spent five weeks in solitary, and the rest of the year dragged on interminably. He survived the beatings and tolerated the abuse. He resisted the gang-bangs with sheer strength and the gay prisoners gave up on him. He was filled with revulsion and pity when he unavoidably witnessed the "initiation" of youngsters newly admitted. Periodically the lights were suddenly switched on in the middle of the night and the inmates were marched naked around the cell blocks. Tough guards with mop handles went down the line punishing the men until blood was drawn. They broke ribs, poked, pushed, inserted, probed. The gay inmates were made to perform various acts before the guards, whose devilish glee went undisguised. They were allowed to stage their own gay review at Christmas time, with drag queens embellishing prison clothes with bits of colored ruffles and crepe ribbons.

Leadbelly sang,

> *Goodnight, Irene, Goodnight, Irene,*
> *I kiss you in my dreams...*

Finally the long year was over and sweet Martha was there to meet him. They were driven by a friend of Lomax's across the Triborough Bridge, but neither one of them said much. It was a bitter and penniless Leadbelly and a confused, frightened Martha who stood before the steps of her apartment watching the children playing in the gutters. He pitied them too, just as much as he had pitied the poor boys who were brought to Riker's Island to be stripped of all dignity. How long would it take New York to strip all the little children the same way? How long did they have to wait before their cheery games and laughter would be turned into crime and tears?

Martha took his arm. "Come on, honey. They's some meat pies and cold beer in the kitchen."

He engulfed her in his arms and carried her up the brownstone steps and inside.

Days thereafter, in that May of 1940, he appeared in a modestly successful concert with some other singers and the reviews were generally good. No mention was ever made of the Riker's Island episode.

But his enthusiasm vacillated. There were a few radio shows and several more concerts. There were the times when he played for drinks and tips in the Village. Franklin came up from Texas to see him one day and was dismayed at Leadbelly's growing cynicism and bitterness. He stayed with them six weeks, found Leadbelly a new job and then had to leave. Martha continued to work at the hotel.

And so the scruffling became more labored. The calendar was suddenly an opponent and he resented it, not knowing one week from the next and having to be reminded of the few engagements he did manage to get. Money was scarce and Martha was now a waitress in a greasy, rancid bar and grill. Leadbelly helped with the war effort, sang for the bond drives, but there was no money there. Help your country, Huddie. Do your bit for the war effort, Ledbetter. Sing for the Red Cross, Leadbelly. Play some music at the U.S.O. Money? Why no, no. This is a war effort, you see.

So "The King o' the Twelve-String Guitar" washed dishes and felt the steaming, soapy water dissolving his guitar-strumming calluses. In 1943 he worked as a shoeshine boy. In 1944, he worked as a janitor. And when the war was over, nothing had changed for him. Nothing, that is, except his age.

He and Martha were still living on East 10th Street in the Village, and there were still only the occasional radio commitments, the spots in a stage show, the rare personal appearance at a decent club in Harlem or the Village. Those who saw him perform went away with an image they would never forget: lavender collar and rolled-up shirtsleeves, emerald green bowtie, brilliant crimson suspenders spilling down the white shirt front, and checked pants and sparkling patent leather shoes. The reedy, somewhat breathless voice told and sang of lynchings, the KKK, street vendors, Blind Lemon, and the fashionable fancy "high yellers" he once knew.

And there were times when he would just sit by the fountain in Washington Square and play for the children, his favorite audience, all day long. Then he would walk sadly home to his understanding Martha.

There were always the sycophants, the listeners and fellow drinkers his ego needed. Drunk, he could excuse the fights, the trouble, the involvement with women. Playing in front of them, he could excuse being broke, playing the "good nigga," using the broad grin and polite bow. He grew increasingly morose and sometimes, after Martha had gone to bed or to work, he would sit by the telephone and stare out the window until midnight.

There were no middle years for Leadbelly, no mellow middle age to spend with his own children. His youth had gone as quickly and as unnoticed as a puddle of alcohol. One year he was young and strong and famous; the next he was old and gray and drifting into obscurity, and he hated to look in the mirror.

###

Chapter Twenty-Two

They sat in the tiny, three-room apartment on East 10th in Greenwich Village, with the early sunlight streaming through the windows and bouncing off the smoky, powder-blue walls. Leadbelly sat in his bathrobe, newspapers strewn on the floor beside him, fumbling with a large coil of shiny wire. He had started to limp a little, and had been affecting a cane of late. He was making a copper-wound handle.

Jack Franklin sat across from him, idly reading a program from Saturday night's concert, at which Leadbelly had appeared for fifty dollars. Franklin had hardly aged. A score of years had passed, yet Franklin was in remarkable physical shape, and only now were wisps of gray beginning to sprout in his curly blond hair. He was tanned and healthy-looking, quick to smile and eager to help.

Martha was out shopping.

"They did a nice job on this, didn't they?" Franklin said.

Leadbelly grunted. "They always do. 'Cept they still don't pay nothin'."

Franklin put the program down. "You're always saying that. Why don't you just ask for more?"

"They wouldn't pay more. I take what I can get."

"For crissakes," Franklin said, getting up. "Do you want to hear lecture number seventy-seven again? You don't 'take what you can get,' as you put it. You <u>don't</u>!" Franklin began to pace. Perhaps it wasn't the best or most subtle way in the world to get to him. But by God someone had to say it, to drum it through that thick skull. Franklin had been following Leadbelly's erratic career since 1920. He was entitled to say it!

"Huddie, you keep complaining about not getting your share of the money that's floating all around you, and you're right. But maybe if you'd turn down a few jobs! Tell them you don't work for peanuts. They'd take notice. Christ, this is New York! You've been here for five years, now."

"That's horseshit, Cap'n, and you know it. They pay a nigga good only when he's famous. Like Cab Calloway. Now, the other night I give Marthy fifty dollars what I couldn't have given her at all if I didn't go play the concert." Leadbelly found the loose end of the wire and started to unravel the copper coil. He picked up his Malacca cane and laid it across his lap.

Franklin kept pacing. "There you go again. Niggers and coons, that's all you ever call black people. You keep calling yourself a nigger, goddamnit, and they'll keep treating you like one. This isn't Shreveport, for crissakes! How many times do I have to tell you?"

Leadbelly looked up and stopped fiddling with the wire. "It ain't? This ain't Shrevepo't? Then what do you call Harlem? Equal? What do you call the riots back in '43? When's the las' time you read 'bout a riot in Shrevepo't? No, suh. I ain't startin' no riot with no white guys what has some money I can get. When I'se famous someplace else 'sides these piss-hole bars around here, then I'll get up and shout 'bout it and join the Negro Congress and all that. Damn, Cap'n, I don't want to be nasty to the white folks. Alan, he one of my bes' friends."

"Sure, he's your best friend. He's getting you these paying gigs. And so is Woodie Guthrie, and Seeger and Brand. But they're all *white* men."

"Don' make no difference. I know how the niggas feel. It's jus' that it ain't time yet for me to do nothin' 'cept sing a few songs 'bout it."

Franklin grinned at him. "You con-man. I've been saying that for years, and its true. You're just a con-man. You know you're just a King Kong sort of attraction, because of your background. You know that it won't be until one of your songs gets on the "Hit Parade" that you'll be a *real* celebrity."

Leadbelly went back to work on his cane, and chewed the inside of his lip.

"And why *that* piece of phony crap? You think anybody will believe that's gold?" Franklin said. "It's copper and it *looks* like copper."

Leadbelly was winding the wire strand tightly around the upper shaft of his cane, moving it up in glistening spirals. He grinned without looking at Franklin and said, "You got some gold wire, Cap'n?"

Franklin started to argue back, but Martha was kicking at the front door. Franklin got up quickly and went to open it; Martha was staggering under three packages of groceries. She had a letter clenched between her teeth.

"They's a letter here from Hollywood, Huddie!" she blurted out. "It sure look important!"

Franklin looked at the letter as Leadbelly put his half-wound cane down and limped over to help Martha. He grabbed the letter before Franklin could hand it to him and looked curiously at the return address before tearing it open.

"Sweet Jesus!" he yelled as he took the folded sheet of paper from the envelope. "This here's one o' the biggest studios in Hollywood! They finally found Leadbelly!"

He laboriously read the letter, and over his shoulder Franklin read it aloud for Martha.

Mr. Huddie Ledbetter, Esq. 414 East 10 Street New York, N.Y.
Dear Sir:
There are plans in this studio at the moment to do the film version of your life, predominantly the middle years in Texas and Louisiana. Of course, your cooperation and that of your agent will be required.
Needless to say, the possibility of your playing yourself in such a film is a real one. However, we have been unable to locate your manager and/or agent, hence are contacting you directly to determine your own interest in this projected venture.
Should you be in the area during one of your concert tours or some other public appearance, we would welcome an interview with you to discuss the possibilities and whatever problems which would have to be overcome.
Of course, the project is strictly tentative, and dependent on budget allocations for the coming year. We did want to make this preliminary query, however, to determine the availability of performance rights.
I look forward to hearing from you. Once again, please pardon this direct query as we have been unable to uncover an authorized representative.
Sincerely,
Robert V. Zahn
Associate Producer

Leadbelly was wild-eyed. He danced, and pranced and sang around the kitchen, shouting to Martha about how rich they would be now that Hollywood had discovered him. Martha read the letter again, and Franklin took it into the living room, sat down and studied it.

Leadbelly was irritated by Franklin's apparent lack of enthusiasm. "How come nobody's happy?" he asked at last. "What's all this frownin' for?"

"Jus' don' go gettin' your hopes up again, honey," Martha called from the kitchen. "This here letter jus' say they want to talk to you if you ever goes out there. Ain't no contracts sent."

"Don' make no difference," he retorted. "They want me in Hollywood, and when I get there they jus' gonna see how perfect I'd be for a movie. I gonna sing them every song I ever heard, and we gonna be rich, Marthy. Rich! No more of you workin' like you do. An' no more o' me havin' to play for tips an' drinks."

Franklin came over and put his arm on Leadbelly's shoulder. "Now hold on, Huddie. You can't go tearing off to Hollywood. For once let's be businesslike and simply reply to his letter."

"You do what the Cap'n tell you, honey," Martha said. "You jus' let him do the managin'."

They spent an hour composing the reply. Leadbelly wanted to elaborate on his musical talents, but Franklin kept it tightly composed and austere. It gave Franklin's name as Leadbelly's representative.

Leadbelly sat back, grinning happily, and completed the winding of his cane, "You hear any more 'bout that man over in France?" he asked a little later.

Franklin shook his head. "Not a word this week. We can't seem to agree on a date. Something should pan out, though. I know they want you for a concert."

Leadbelly finished the cane and held it up proudly. "Beautiful, ain't it?"

Franklin scowled. "It's just a cheap cane wound with copper wire. Phony as hell."

Leadbelly ignored the jab. He held the cane to the sunlight and twirled it, grinning at its refulgence. He was thinking about Hollywood and how the big chance had finally come.

Only one thing bothered him: his health. It was during the war when he was helping out with the war bond drives that he began to have the pains in his legs. He had finally agreed -- reluctantly, for it rubbed against his fundamental vanity -- to buy the cane and use it. But soon he was sporting it like a baton, swaggering with it, liking its feel and the balance of it.

"C'mon, Cap'n," Leadbelly said pleasantly. "I promised a bunch of kids down the hall here that I'd take 'em over to the square and do some play-party songs for 'em. It's one of them's birthday today. Lemme go get dressed and we'll see what we can do about the afternoon."

Franklin waited in silence, thinking about the kids and how they loved Leadbelly, about the Hollywood letter and the possible overseas trip, about the silly cane. He knew the children were the only people Leadbelly trusted, probably because they laughed a lot and didn't want to take money away from him. Even now, after twenty-eight years, Franklin knew a shot of whiskey or two dollars would have instantaneous precedence over a quiet chat or a serious business discussion.

He got up and walked into the tiny kitchen to pour himself another cup of coffee. How could a man spend sixty-one years without learning a single lesson?

Leadbelly managed to add a jauntiness to his limp as he came from the bedroom and brandished the cane. "Let's go, Cap'n!" he called, picking up his guitar. "Can't let the children wait too long, you know!"

They went through the vestibule and down the steps into the icy outside. As they approached Washington Square, children yelled his name and fell into step behind them. Franklin watched the change. Now a child himself, Leadbelly perched himself on a bench and sang his songs. He directed the children in their games and took obvious delight in being the master of the playground. Then Leadbelly took a piece of paper and pencil from his pocket and began jotting down all the birthdays of the children and the names of their favorite songs.

Franklin waited patiently, smoking a cigarette. He had always been unable to get a firm grip on Leadbelly's ambivalent personality. Sullen, moody, arrogant; then avuncular and delightfully friendly; then capable of sudden violence. Unable to adapt to the big city's confusion of rules and regulations, he escaped into women and whiskey. Franklin often thought Leadbelly should have never been enticed from his quiet, simple Southern world into the mocking, taunting sideshow of Manhattan. And yet no one on the face of this planet could be giving those kids so much pleasure. He ground out his cigarette and jabbed his hands deep in the pockets of his overcoat.

When the kids had dispersed and the clouds gobbled up the sun, a chill came over the square. They walked across town to the Village Vanguard. Inside, the usual late-afternoon crowd was beginning to gather -- hangers-on, has-beens, young hopefuls, transients, socialists, folk music buffs and the curious. A group calling themselves "The Weavers" was attracting some attention among the locals.

Franklin bought glasses of beer, and Leadbelly stretched out and tapped his cane on the side of the chair. Several hours later he switched to whiskey, against Franklin's cautioning, and finally went to the telephone and called Martha.

"Honey, I'se down playing for a while, tonight. You want to come on down?"

"I think I'll just go to bed early, Huddie. But you best not do no drinkin', y'know. Remember what the doctor say 'bout drinkin' only fruit juice and soda.

"Now Marthy, don' you go worryin'. I be home plenty early."

He hung up and went back to his chair. Franklin was talking with Woody Guthrie about how tough it was to get jobs that paid anything. Guthrie, his cap shoved far back on his head, was saying, "Lots of difference between trying to get some job in an apple orchard and this here Rainbow Room. I wrote up a lot of songs for the union folks and sung them all over, from Madison Square Garden to a Cuban Cigar Makers' tavern in Spanish Harlem. Or from CBS and NBC to the wild backcountry and in the raggedy ghetto. But at the Rainbow Room, a job'll pay as much as seventy-five a week, an' seventy-five a week is damn sure seventy-five a week."

"Woody Guthrie." The voice cracked over the loudspeaker.

"Well, I got to go play. Howdy, Huddie."

"'Lo Woody."

"Hang 'round some," Guthrie called back. He prodded the announcer out of his way with the guitar neck. With his conversation with Franklin fresh in his mind, Guthrie sang:

> *This Rainbow Room she's mighty fine*
> *You can spit from here to the Texas Line!*

In New York City Lawd,
New York City
This is New York City, an' I
really gotta know my line!

Later, when Guthrie, Pete Seeger, Lee Hays and Millard Lampell were hunched over their drinks at a corner table, Leadbelly took the stage and did two or three songs. He sang a new arrangement of "Irene," the one he was hoping would be picked up someday by a major label.

The applause was scattered.

That was when Franklin heard it. It started as just an under-the-breath grousing, but as eyes turned in surprise the voice got louder. The man was dressed in a flaming red shirt open to the belly, the ever-present chain and medal around his thick neck. He'd had too much to drink and the words came out in a melodic slurring, not unlike the way he sang. He held a cigarette tightly between his fingers.

"That fuckin' nigger gives me a pain in the ass!" he said.

Franklin tried to stare the man into silence, but the electricity in the air was unmistakable. Several more turned, but Leadbelly hadn't heard him yet. He was singing loud, more moaning than singing, really, and it was the "Bourgeois Blues," one of his songs about the time he and Martha tried to get a room in Washington, D.C.

I'm gonna tell all the colored people
I want 'em to understand,
Washington an't no place,
for no colored man.
Oh, it's a Bourgeois town

The man stood up, swayed and jabbed a finger at Leadbelly. "When are you gonna stop that Uncle Tom shit, you white man's coon! I'm sick of hearin' it!"

Leadbelly slowly put down his guitar. He was perched on a high stool and the copper-wound cane was hung over the elbow of his left arm. "What's that you say, Josh?"

The place was silent and Josh White's voice rang off the walls. "I said I'm sick of hearing that Uncle Tom shit, Ledbetter! When you gonna cut it out and stop giving the rest of us a bad name?"

"I think youse drunk, Josh. I ain't lookin' for no trouble."

"Sit down, White. Knock it off," Guthrie said. White ignored him.

"'I think youse drunk, Josh,'" the singer mimicked, bobbing his head from side to side. "Your ass! It's 'I think you _are_ drunk,' and you know goddamned well it is. Why don't you take that cotton-picking, Uncle Tom Lawdy-Lawdy shit back to the dear old Southland where it came from!"

"I ain't no Uncle Tom. I sing all kind of songs, Josh."

"Bullshit! You're just a shufflin', fuckin' gorilla! Smiling and laughing and kissing every white ass in the city!"

Leadbelly slid slowly off the stool and stood up, glowering.

"Oh, sure," White said. "You make records for all these bastards using you for a quick buck, and you sing 'Bourgeois Blues' and 'this place and that place ain't no place for a colored man,' but you sound like a goddamn slave when you're doing it. When the hell have you ever stood up and shouted down a white for treating you like a trained monkey? Where the hell were you during the Harlem riots? Where did we read in any papers about how the great Leadbelly thought that fuckin' white cop should be shot for knocking down that black woman? You make me sick, Ledbetter! You're just a professional coon and you oughta clear the hell out of New York."

White weaved again. He was talking to the crowd at large now, and waited for signs of support. He got little.

Guthrie stood up. "Hold on, there," he shouted. "You do it your way, White, and he'll do it his. You ain't no stranger to showboating yourself. Leave him to his own style."

"Showboatin'? Man, I'm getting a point across! This sonofabitch is just wrecking all the work we're doing with his Uncle Tom shit. Look at that phony fuckin' publicity picture that went around. All dressed up in a new suit and bow tie and pointin' off to the stars. Kiss my ass!"

"Man, youse askin' for trouble, Josh!" Leadbelly said evenly. "I does those things because that's the way whoever I'se workin' for want it, and it's his business, not mine, what he do with his performers. I jus' sing and play, and he run his own publicity. Shit, I sang my Hitler song and Mr. Roosevelt song and my Jack Johnson 'bout the Titanic. And what you been doin'? Ain't you been takin' the white man's money, too?"

"Damn right," White yelled. "I take the money and say 'fuck you, you condescending white bastard.' You, you take it and say 'why, thank you, massah, suh. Thank you kindly, yeah. I'se you nigga, boss-man, yassah, sho 'nuff.' We've all read your shit in that Lomax book. Where did it say you told him to go fuck himself and drive his own white-ass car?"

"He got me out of prison, and I paid him back. If it wasn't for him and Alan I never would've made a single recordin'!" Leadbelly, fuming, looked around quickly and tried to spot Alan Lomax in the crowd.

"More bullshit! You believed all that publicity crap he built up around you and you still believe it. 'Black killer of the swamplands!' 'Singin' coon gets two pardons!' Well, they're not buying that shit anymore, Ledbetter. Wake up to that and you'll make yourself some money."

White turned and started through the crowd toward the door, but stopped halfway when Franklin yelled, "Hold on! I think you owe Leadbelly an apology."

Several people agreed, and a murmur started to rise.

Some booed White, some cheered him. The battle lines had been drawn, and even White knew it. He edged closer to the door.

"I don't apologize to no white man's coon!"

Leadbelly was off the stool and halfway to White when the place erupted. Glasses crashed and a loud roar went up as men swarmed into the middle of the floor and Leadbelly was dragged down. Men were punching each other and yelling, and a scream sounded from the other end of the room. Franklin was knocked out with a bottle. Leadbelly struggled to get up, but couldn't find White.

It wasn't the old days, now, and he was no longer the superman, the behemoth to be feared. Now he took blows poorly, and there was pain. He felt one shooting up his legs. His head hurt, and he was on the floor. Someone was kicking him. He looked for Franklin but still couldn't find him, and then he heard police whistles and it was all like some gangster movie he'd seen and someone else was thumping him in the gut and then it all went black and the word "coon" kept reverberating through the aging, empty halls of his mind.

*   *   *   *   *

She was a good-looking woman, in her mid-forties, and she came into the bedroom with a cup of coffee and a plateful of donuts.

Leadbelly was astounded. He faintly recognized her, but didn't know where he was.

"Heard you moaning," she said pleasantly. "I thought you'd sleep forever." She was wearing a skirt and sweater and her hair was piled on the top of her head and held with plastic combs. She was white.

He stared at her, then looked around, nervous. He remembered nothing. "Where's this?"

"My place. Don't you remember?"

He shook his head. She could tell he was frightened.

"I found you staggering around the streets down in the Village. You said you were in a fight, but I figured you were just drunk until I saw your face. You don't remember anything?"

He shook his head again, and this time the throbbing started. He reached for the coffee and sat up. He was naked under the sheet.

"Well, you probably don't recognize me, but I've been sort of following you around wherever you're playing. I even tried to get into a few radio stations when you had your programs. Last night I was driving home and just happened to see you staggering around like you were lost. I brought you here because you were babbling about some friends of yours and some fight you'd been in. I called around this morning -- it's almost six o'clock now, by the way -- and found out what happened. Apparently there was a riot down in the Village, and the cops came and threw everyone but a few into the paddy wagons. You and some others got out the back. They had to drag you. Then you just ran away, they say, and then I found you and took you here. My name's Ethel."

It was slowly coming back. "Oh, yeah," he said, and then he told her about the confrontation with Josh White. He felt relaxed with her, somehow, even though she was white.

"I don't blame you," she said, sitting on the edge of the bed. She was well built for a middle-aged woman, he noted, even through his torpor. "You're hard to figure out. Sometimes you sound a little too accommodating, but some of your songs are quite eloquent, in their way. Josh White is a bit too impudent for my tastes."

He tried to puzzle her out. She was obviously a fan of his, someone who knew his music and something about his life.

"Drink that down, there's lots more. Listen, nobody asked me, but I've been around the block a few times in my day and I've known musicians in this rotten city all my life. I don't know who your manager is, but you made a mistake in the beginning when you were getting a lot of publicity. You shouldn't have stayed around here, you should have traveled more. Got with a big band, or something like that."

"Lady, I been scrufflin' all over this place, and they jus' ain't no place for me. You gotta be Sarah Vaughn or Joe Louis to get any financial attention!"

"I don't mean that. I mean like right now, even. You ought to work up a concert tour or something and get yourself out of New York. You know, too many show business people don't realize that letting the New York big shots notice you somewhere else is a lot faster way to make it than having them notice you here. You don't understand that, do you?"

He shook his head again, and frowned. "I got a chance to go to Hollywood, I think. Maybe if I get me a concert out there and meet some movie people..." He shrugged. The woman made him think, but he'd have to check with Franklin. The pain in his spine was back. "I ain't got no manager, but a friend of mine takes care o' that arrangin' stuff."

"Good," she said. "That's what I'd do, if I had any talent."

He started to take another sip of coffee, but almost dropped the cup when he looked up and saw her stand and unzip the side of her skirt. She dropped it on the floor, and quickly removed her blouse and slip. When she had stripped naked, revealing a remarkable firmness, she smiled down at his flabbergasted face.

"Don't worry," she said softly. "We're way uptown now, and I promise you'll never see me again. I'll drive you home later and let you off at the corner, or someplace. But right now, there's something I've been fantasizing about for a long, long time."

###

Chapter Twenty-Three

"Oh, Huddie! You had everybody up worryin' all night! Where you been?" Martha put her hands on her hips and stared down at the hulk in the chair.

"Jus' out wanderin' 'round, that's all. S'pose you know all about the trouble last night?"

"Know? The telephone's been jingling on that table like they was a circus comin' to town! Seems like everybody in the world askin' how you is."

Leadbelly sighed heavily. "Martha, would you call Cap'n Jack for me and ask him to come over? How he feelin'?"

"They knocked him out. The policemen brought him home when the doctor said he was okay. He been callin' all day, too."

She went to the telephone. Leadbelly lifted himself up and limped to the kitchen for a bottle of orange soda.

Franklin arrived twenty minutes later, carrying the copperwound cane, a broken twelve-string guitar and a nasty knot on his head. Morose and sorrowful, Leadbelly made up a story about wandering around the midtown streets all night and day, and although no one believed him, he satisfied himself that he had taken care of the excusing formalities. "I been thinkin'," he said. "Can you arrange for a concert or somethin' out in Hollywood, so's I can get out there and meet with those movie people?"

"Huddie, they ain't no use going out there until you hear---"

"Now, Marthy, jus' let us talk. I want to go out there so I can get us somethin' steady. I'se tired of this one night here and one night there kind of livin'. Now, as long as the movie man says they's a chance of my bein' in the movies, then I want to go out there and let them talk about it some more."

"I suppose so, Huddie. But I don't think it's a good idea, either. Why don't you just wait until those people over in Paris come back with the firm invitation and the money? Then we'll even have some built-in publicity."

"No. I want to go *now*, Cap'n! I want to get out there and sing 'Irene' and some of the other songs I know they gonna like for the movie. Now, maybe they don't like the blues, why then I gonna sing more popular songs for 'em. I'se gonna start singin' whatever they want for the movies."

Franklin got up and looked at Martha. Her eyes told him she was against it, too. "Dammit, this is the sort of thing everyone's trying to get you <u>not</u> to do. It's just not done that way, that's all. This isn't Shreveport, you know. You don't go off half-cocked chasing some half-ass possibility before giving it a chance to develop, They just don't up and hire some folk singer for a movie and give him a million dollars! They *just don't do it*, Huddie!" Franklin fell back, exasperated, and kicked Leadbelly's cane across the floor.

"It's just like this goddamned cane. No matter what you do, you can't make anyone believe it's *gold*, for crissakes!"

Leadbelly stared at him for a long time, and then he looked at Martha. "'sides," he said hesitantly, "as long as I'se out there, I can see all the movie people. They's *one* of 'em gonna want to have Leadbelly in a movie, ain't they?"

A month later Leadbelly finally left, still against the wishes of Martha and Franklin. He'd been able to scrape up enough money for a one-way ticket, and Franklin ponied up enough for the return trip. Although it meant sitting in a railroad coach for three days, he was ebullient when the train left. His suitcases were packed with his other suit and enough sandwiches to last the entire journey.

Every seat in the car was filled when Leadbelly finally settled himself in a window seat and peered out the window. Next to him sat an old man whose wheezes kept him awake most of the trip.

They stopped for a time in Chicago, then clattered across the brown patchwork quilt of Iowa and Nebraska, slanted southward and rolled into Denver. After a night's layover, which Leadbelly spent in the coach car, and after a secondary engine was coupled to the train, they began the long climb over the Rocky Mountains.

They finally arrived in Los Angeles at Union Station on June 18, 1948. It was a Saturday. Tomorrow at the children's hospital, and then a brief, unpaid tour of some orphanages and two military hospitals on Monday. Then he would be free to use his time as he saw fit. On Tuesday or Wednesday he would be signing his name to a movie contract, he was sure.

After he found a run-down place to stay near Angel's Flight, in Los Angeles' Bunker Hill district, he called the studio. No one answered. To while away the afternoon, he took a bus to Hollywood, where he strolled around and saw the sights. The Brown Derby fascinated him: a restaurant shaped like a hat! Then others caught his eye, and as with most visitors he soon grew accustomed to such things as restaurants shaped like Elephants, a Monkey Island, a huge clown through whose mouth one could buy a hamburger. He saw a dazzling movie house built like a Chinese temple and eagerly strode around the entrance façade. He looked at the strange indentations of hands, fists, feet and legs in the concrete, signed by famous and fabulous people whose names represented vast wealth. He wondered whether they'd be making an imprint of his guitar after the tumultuous reception for the film about his life.

Down Wilcox Avenue he walked, looking at the gates and billboard house-ads of the studios, and across Sunset Boulevard with still more hotels and famous names. He walked for hours. He picked up a day-old copy of the *Hollywood Citizen-News* and read the entertainment section with interest. He put the paper carefully into a wastebasket and walked on. Down toward Beverly Hills he tried to buy a hamburger in a small diner, but was refused. Used to it, but a little surprised that it existed in Hollywood, too, he searched again and finally found a small Mexican place where he bought a taco. He didn't like it.

That night he found a black bar in East Los Angeles, and he drank and played until it closed. They liked his music, and several people bought him drinks, but he overslept the next morning and was late at the hospital. He played almost all day for the kids, his favorite audience. That night his lower back was paining him again, so he went to bed early. Monday went well, and the sick and crippled servicemen cheered him exuberantly and made him happy. It was starting out to be a good week in Los Angeles, and he looked forward to the morning. He went back to the same bar in East L.A. and overslept the next morning again.

It was 12:45 when he approached the studio's main gate. The guard brusquely asked what his business was. He mentioned Zahn's name, and the guard made a telephone call. Zahn's secretary knew nothing of an appointment. Leadbelly explained again to the guard, but was turned down. With exasperation he went to the corner and called Zahn's secretary himself. The secretary reiterated the need for an appointment and said that Mister Zahn was busy all afternoon. Leadbelly read her his letter and she softened. She told him Zahn was presently out to lunch, but to return to the guard shack at 1:30 and there would be a pass for him. Leadbelly wasn't sure what all the problem was with just walking into a man's office, but he spent half an hour touring Hollywood Boulevard again.

He was back at the studio promptly at 1:30, and there was a new guard, an old man with an enormous paunch. But the pass was there, and Leadbelly limped through the front lot and went to Zahn's office.

The secretary was a prim, purple-lipped old maid with an upswept hairdo. She looked at him as if he were an alien, and her tone was cold.

"How do," he said confidently, brushing at the lapels of his suit. "I'se Huddie Ledbetter from New Yawk to see Mr. Zahn."

The secretary regarded Leadbelly icily, then said, "Mr. Zahn is still at lunch. Sit down over there and I'll call you when he can see you."

"Why, thank you, ma'am," Leadbelly said, turning to the chair. "Certainly is warm here today, ain't it?" The red bandanna was mopping at his forehead. The secretary made a face and went back to her Underwood.

Leadbelly sat down and studied the room. It was plush, with paintings and movie posters on the walls and a bright blue carpet on the floor. For fifteen minutes he read *Daily Variety* and the *Hollywood Reporter* and *Time*. After that, he looked around the room again, attempted conversation with the reticent secretary and, for some reason, opened his guitar case and studied the instrument. Closing it, he went back to *Time*. Half an hour.

When he'd been waiting for almost an hour, the secretary finally looked up and said, "Mr. Zahn will see you now." She indicated a door at the far end of the lobby. Leadbelly wondered how Zahn could have entered without being seen.

He opened the door and stepped inside. Zahn was reading a thick manuscript. He was a young man, perhaps thirty-two, and had large horn-rimmed glasses. He looked up without smiling, and took the glasses off.

"How do you do, Mr. Ledbetter. This is a surprise." He came around the desk and offered Leadbelly a chair.

"Came soon's I could," Leadbelly said proudly.

Zahn went back to his own seat behind the desk and shoved the manuscript aside. "Well, all we wanted to do, actually, was make our first contact with your agent, you see. There is nothing really definite yet about the project."

Leadbelly was confused. "The letter say you want me to play in the movies. I come right out to see about the details."

"You're probably not familiar with the way we work out here, Mr. Ledbetter. Of course, I'm very fond of your music and I myself have been a great fan of yours for quite some time. I once heard you play at a concert in New York, at Columbia University. A long time ago, of course. But I'm afraid there's nothing we can do right now. Someone else got the part for which we were considering you. You see, a much younger man was needed, actually."

"Jus' a second, suh," Leadbelly said. "How can anyone else play me except me? I'se Leadbelly, not nobody else."

Zahn smiled courteously. "That's very true, Mr. Ledbetter. But here in Hollywood, we play to audiences that we know will pay to see only what they <u>want</u> to see. I'm afraid at, uh, your age, you'll understand that you can't play yourself at twenty-five or thirty. In any case, it's out of my hands now. One of our producers has signed up a very prominent director, and it's now up to them to decide the fate of the film."

Leadbelly didn't understand exactly, but he knew he was being passed over. He reached for his guitar. "Maybe if I plays you a few of the songs…"

"Ah, I don't think so, Mr. Ledbetter. I'm sorry, but this has nothing to do with your music. It's just that the physical aspects of filmmaking take precedence over the sound. We can always dub in the music, you see, but the man who plays a given part must be able to match the role as closely as possible in age. I'm sure you understand."

"Mr. Zahn," Leadbelly said, his voice nearly cracking. "I took some appearances so's I could come see you because you sent me the letter about the movies. And now youse tellin' me it wasn't true." He didn't want to admit he was nearly broke, but he knew that Zahn suspected.

Zahn was shaking his head slowly. "I realize there was a gross misunderstanding, Mr. Ledbetter. I'm truly sorry, please believe me. I'll tell you what, though. There are lots of fans of yours out here on the West Coast. Wait out in the office, would you please? I'll make a few telephone calls and see what I can do for you locally. Will that be all right? Will you be in L.A. long?"

Leadbelly was crushed, and didn't especially like the idea of becoming dependent on this man. But he was in Hollywood…

When Zahn called him back into the office, Leadbelly sat down again and folded his hands on top of his cane. "We give a lot of parties out here," Zahn said, "and we're always looking for new entertainers.

I called a few friends and told them you were in town, and they were quite eager to get in touch with you. One crowd in particular is always looking for...er... offbeat entertainment, and they'd love to have you play at a party this evening. There's a hundred dollars in it for you, and perhaps a few more sessions later in the week. Anyway, it'll give you a chance to meet some pretty influential people."

Leadbelly jumped at the chance. *A hundred dollars!* And then he could always pass the hat around. Further, if he could meet some big shots, he'd surely be able to sell himself into the movies. After all, a director couldn't be much harder to convince than a governor.

The party was at Errol Flynn's palatial house on Mulholland Drive. Although Flynn wasn't present, Leadbelly was immensely impressed with both the name of the mansion's owner and the sheer size of the place. It was, without doubt, the largest house he'd ever seen. Leadbelly was glad Zahn had offered the ride -- he would have never been able to find it by himself.

They entered the foyer and gave their names to a man at the door, obviously stationed there to guard against crashers. Zahn vouched for Leadbelly and they went into the main room. Leadbelly was aghast at the extravagance of the house. Everywhere there were gold fixtures, crystal chandeliers and thick carpets. And from every window there was a magnificent view of either the Los Angeles Basin or the adjacent San Fernando Valley.

They were among the last to arrive. Leadbelly saw famous faces all around him. Beautiful women were standing around holding drinks or sprawled on long couches, their fabulous gowns and dresses furled around them like the garments of goddesses. Men stood, staggered and sat about, talking animatedly, sipping drinks, laughing, smiling, arguing, gesturing. At the far end of the room, at a large mahogany bar, another cluster of people pressed against one another, arms around shoulders, hands interlocked, singing and laughing. From somewhere music filled the room, and every room, Leadbelly later discovered, smelled of exotic incense.

During the ride to Flynn's, Zahn had taken an interest in Leadbelly. He guided Leadbelly around the house, interested to see how the black man from the Deep South would react to the hedonistic luxury of it all. He showed him the pool, the bedrooms, the fabulous kitchen, the Roman-orgy bathrooms with their sunken tubs. At one point, when they came upon a group of men peering through what looked like a peephole, Zahn explained it was a one-way mirror into the bathroom, where one could watch the ladies as they relieved themselves. Leadbelly was mildly shocked, and thought briefly of old Benjamin Capp. He wondered with revulsion whether these rich men, these celebrated stars of the screen, performed the same acts as Benjamin did when he watched the girls at Reverend Parker's school. Zahn ushered him on.

Introductions back in the main room were strained. Although Zahn handled them as smoothly as he could, the introductions continued clumsily and perfunctorily as new people approached. Some refused to shake hands, some merely nodded coolly. Some, though, were genuinely surprised and happy to meet Leadbelly and mentioned their favorite songs of his. Leadbelly smiled, nodded, bowed. Many of the men, especially the older ones, made asides to other friends and then chortled surreptitiously. Leadbelly heard off-handed, muffled obscenities that even he considered offensive. One young lady unabashedly asked him whether he was as good a lay as she'd heard, and Leadbelly's embarrassed reticence seemed to amuse her. He "ma'am'd" and "sir'd" nervously through the first hour, trying to shun the cool ones and hastening to talk to those who seemed appreciative. One drunk asked to play his guitar; a fat, bald-headed man slapped him hard on the back and yelled, "Hey, weren't you in the flick with Charlie Armstrong a few years back?"

Until he played, Leadbelly felt like a sideshow freak.

*   *   *   *   *

It was past midnight when he put down the guitar, to mild and scattered applause. Established stars had stood around tapping their feet and bobbing their heads, clapping after each selection. He'd been a success with those who listened, but it was obvious the group in general considered him just another novelty. Most of them liked "Irene" and "The Midnight Special" and "Shorty George," and Leadbelly gave them the bawdy lyrics John Lomax had often forbade him to repeat. These songs went over well, but the women didn't applaud as loudly as the men, although Leadbelly knew well that they had appreciated the raciness of it all as much as anyone.

The frequent gulps of reassuring whiskey had helped him along, and he headed for the bar again, his guitar resting on the stool on which he had perched for hours. There, as he asked the bartender for another, Zahn met him and expressed his appreciation for the music. He introduced Leadbelly to a prominent agent, who had started to leave the bar but was caught by the arm by Zahn before he could depart.

"Abe, meet Huddie Ledbetter," Zahn said with a thick tongue. "One of the best guitar players in the country."

Abe turned, nodded quickly, and started to go off again.

"Hey, c'mon," Abe," Zahn said. "He's in town for a while and needs an agent to set up some engagements for him. He's interested in the movies, too."

Leadbelly smiled at the man. "Yes, suh," he said. "I hardly know anyone 'round this here town. Gotta get me some work for a while."

Abe laughed out loud. "Sure, Zahn, sure thing." He laughed again and wriggled free. "Tell him to call me at forty-five to nine!" And he went off, still cackling, and the bartender laughed, too. Zahn took a puzzled Leadbelly away from the bar.

Later, Leadbelly told Zahn he wanted to leave and Zahn asked for just twenty minutes more to see some other people. He told Leadbelly to wait outside, by the pool. Leadbelly grabbed another glassful of whiskey and went out.

He found the pool and sat down some distance from it, in half-shadows. There were two nude couples swimming and tittering, splashing around raucously in the fully lit water. Leadbelly watched them intently, fascinated -- he had never experienced such a party. The frolickers ignored him. He sat musing for a long minute, afraid to get up and seek Zahn out again, afraid to get closer to the pool. Some minutes later, a figure suddenly appeared in front of him, holding a glass and wearing a man's bathrobe. Leadbelly looked up and saw the star of a popular musical. She still held her youthful teenage look, but she was extremely drunk. She swayed before him, smiling.

"Leadbelly," she said, as if reading a name from a phone book. "I know you."

He started to get to his feet, but she pushed him back down.

"Don't bother," she said. "I don't go for that fucking black-and-white shit. I should be bowing to you. Y'know, I probably know your music better than anyone here."

Leadbelly, awed at being confronted by this famous girl, was further shaken by her language. "Thank you, ma'am," he said. "An' I know you, too. Seen your pictures many times."

"It's a bunch of shit," she said, slugging down another shot of the white liquid in her glass. "They tell you to sing, you sing. Never get a chance to do what I like, for crissakes. They picked me up when I was sixteen and I had to suck their dicks just to stay in the game. Does that shock you?" She grinned down at him.

"Ma'am, I---" he began uneasily.

"Never mind," she said. "They won't bother you. Lemme sit here." She sat down next to him, lurching as she did, fingering a wooden match with one hand. A cigarette dangled from the corner of her mouth as she talked.

"You want to get in pictures?" she asked. "Don't do it. Get the fuck out of here before they slaughter you." Then, as if giving up the entire subject, she turned to him and curled herself up cross-legged on the side chair. "Hey, tell me something. I mean, just between us musicians. All those stories *true* about you?"

Leadbelly looked at her. Where was Zahn? Where the hell was Zahn?

"I mean," she said, "'bout you fucking all those women down in Louisiana?"

Leadbelly sighed and took another drink. "That's right, ma'am. I was terrible with the wimmins. Gettin' kinda old now, though."

"Shit," she said. "That white hair don't fool me. You're built like a bull!"

Leadbelly gulped another. Zahn!

"Tell you what, Leadbelly. Let's you and I go over to the orchard. Don't you think I'm good-looking?"

"I surely do, ma'am. You very pretty. But Mr. Zahn is comin' for me, and I don't think---"

317

"Oh shit," she pouted. Then she opened her robe for him. "Zahn better'n this? C'mon, Leadbelly. Just a fast one, huh? Don't matter none, you know. I've screwed 'em all."

"Huddie!" At last it was Zahn, calling from a balcony somewhere overhead.

Leadbelly got to his feet quickly. "I'se sorry, ma'am, I got to go." He reached down and touched her on the shoulder, and she grabbed his hand and kissed it. Leadbelly felt sorry for her. Her lips lingered on his hand, and he had to withdraw it forcibly from her shoulder,

The episode made him morose, and on the way back he only grunted when Zahn questioned him. He knew, somehow, that he would not be in a movie, and yet he didn't want to know it. The next morning he awoke on time to try to make the phone call to the agent, having spent several minutes examining the face of a clock to figure out exactly what "forty-five to nine" looked like.

He placed the call at eight-fifteen, and a faceless receptionist at the agency laughed. Forty-five to nine, he was laughingly informed, was a nonexistent time. "A butt-out, buster," the voice said. "In other words, don't bother us."

He hung up the telephone and sprawled face down on the smelly bed. It was the final blow, the salt in the wound. He moaned for Martha and thought of her sitting worried in the kitchen, maybe with Franklin or Woody or Pete, and the whole bunch talking about him and wondering how he was and asking Franklin about the Paris concert.

Paris. He rolled over on the bed and stared at the ceiling through tears. By God, the Paris trip would show them! When he was an international musical star, that agent would come looking for him.

It would be just like that January with Lomax so many years ago. They'd hound him for appearances! Hound him! But he and Martha would refuse politely, ask Captain Franklin to organize his next tour and take care of his business affairs. They would spend the winter in Shreveport, where he could build a school for the local kids and help fix up the churches and buy his family presents.

"Oh, Lawd. Please let those crowds in Paris like my music."

And that afternoon, when he telephoned Martha in New York, she told him that the concert overseas was now a fact. Franklin had received confirmation from the *Foundation des Etats-Unis* at the *Cite Universitaire* in Paris that the concert was scheduled for three weeks from then. They had cabled the plane fare for two people. Jack Franklin was keeping it safe in his own bank.

As he got on the train that evening, he looked back out the dusty window, toward Hollywood, and promised the palm trees that he would be back. After Paris, he would be back.

* * * * *

When Leadbelly arrived home, he refused to discuss the events on the West Coast. He suppressed his own hurt, but everyone else's willingness not to bring the subject up only reflected their tacit understanding of what must have happened.

He sat by the window in an old khaki shirt, reading his three favorite papers: the *Daily News*, the *Daily Mirror* and the *Daily Worker*. The sun shone through the frosty window and glinted off his copper-wound cane. Martha was at work in the kitchen, cooking his breakfast on a flat-topped gas burner. He finished an article about the United Nations and closed his eyes.

So many of his friends were politically active, but the farthest he'd gone was to join a union of progressive songwriters formed down on West 42nd Street. They were all there: "Arkansas Hard Luck Lee"

Hays, Betty Sanders, Bernie Asbel, Alan and Bess Lomax, Tom Glazer, Charlotte Anthony,

Seeger, Guthrie, others -- all trying to work the little union, called "People's Songs."

The union printed its own songs and books, and Moses Asch was recording everyone he could. Leadbelly told them all about his life, about the knee-high mud at Sugar Land, the bitter fights in Shreveport. To the men he told of drinking pure alcohol mixed with river water, of black girls on soggy mattresses, of field fights and knifings on the cracked cement of moldy basements. To the women he would tell of the rich taste of flour gravy and red beans, and of the rich flesh of fried crawfish. To the children he would tell of jump-rope rhymes, game songs and jack stones.

The parade of faces through the Ledbetter apartment was a history of the era itself. Gun Thug, Goon, Gink, Fink, Stooge, Stoolie, Sneak, Greasy Dick, Bull Stud Duck, Billy Club, Sap, Brass Knuck, Billy Stick, Car Knocker, Stem Banger, Side Wheeler, Brass Railer, Three-Way Rider, Wheeler-Dealer, Harker, Barker, all were there. Men called Slicky Fingers, Ace-Hole Johnny, Sledge Sanders, Hard Card Harvey, Hard Rock Muldroon, Four Leaf Clover, Whiskey-Headed Driver, Cotton Boll Sli, Cigar Shorty, Muley Ike, Horse Collar Katie, Suit Case Gertie, Dim Light Daisy, Splinter Legs, Satchel-belly, Blockhead, Hambones, Highpockets, Google Eyes, Talcum Stick Snooker, Flat Tire Floogie . . .

They swarmed about him like flies, hanging on every word and story. Many would try to pry him loose, but Leadbelly had stopped drinking in preparation for the Paris concert. He knew his future depended on it. He was content to sip from a bottle of orange soda.

He'd grown angry with Moses Asch because he claimed that Asch had taken a lot of tapes and never paid him. Other singers had "trimmed the balls" off of "Irene," and were recording it in their own manner. One friend in particular, Oscar Brand, stuck by him through it all.

New York had been cruel to him, he thought bitterly. Would Paris be better? He was tired of just scrufflin'. Tired of picking up the pennies. Tired of scrambling for the long green, the shug, the sugar -- anything to pay the rent and buy the food. He thought of the bitter-cold mornings in Central Park singing under a sky filled with craggy white clouds for the children playing on the monkey bars.

He remembered the advertising executive who handed him a dollar and requested him to sing "Springtime in the Rockies." The man didn't even hang around to let him finish. And now his back was sore every morning, and Martha urged him to see a doctor. Maybe she was right. Maybe it was more than a touch of rheumatism.

Well, he decided, no matter. With Cap'n Jack's guidance and business sense everything would work out. Paris, the City of Lights, would catapult him into international fame.

He looked down at his right hand. It was trembling and he couldn't stop it.

###

Chapter Twenty-Four

Spring in Paris in 1949 was spectacular, and Leadbelly was surprised that the local weather was less sweaty and enervating than New York's. As they disembarked at Orly and walked toward the terminal, he thought again about the concert. Three weeks of hard practice were behind him -- weeks of no drinking, no carousing, no late nights. He wondered, on the plane, why the pains were still shooting up from his foot to his thigh and wrapping around his lower spine like a whiplash of white-hot wire, when all he had been doing of late was resting and practicing. He thought it peculiar that he should feel better after a late night of drinking at the Vanguard than he did after three weeks of healthy living.

But Paris made him forget his pains and intoxicated him with new customs and a new tongue. They were met at the airport by a Professor Andre LeBec, who spoke English well enough but whose accent was as novel and fascinating to Leadbelly as Leadbelly's had often been to provincial Yankees.

LeBec chatted amiably about how happy he was to finally have the opportunity to meet Leadbelly, and politely told him how popular his singing was in France. Leadbelly drank in the accolades, and Franklin nodded in appreciation.

The light blue Renault crossed the Seine, and M. LeBec informed them that Leadbelly was to meet in the morning with a reporter from *Le Monde*. They would meet at the *Cafe des Deux Magots*, another name Leadbelly's spinning brain refused to register.

After dinner that evening, they were driven to their hotel, and Leadbelly played his guitar as he watched Paris fall asleep under a crescent moon. He tuned and retuned the guitar nervously, watching the lights of the Arc de Triomphe scintillating in a golden glow. At last he stretched out on the bed, but he was too tense to sleep. He chatted with Franklin for a few minutes about the impending concert. Franklin yawned once more, and Leadbelly's head bobbed. Finally they said goodnight and went to bed. A tiny ripple of pain danced down Leadbelly's spine and through his bones, and he threw his arm across his eyes and waited for it to pass. When it did, he slept. Franklin was already snoring.

The *Cafe des Deux Magots* was crowded, but finding a table was unexpectedly easy. No one stared, and several recognized him. Leadbelly's ego swelled within seconds like the reaction of those peculiar blowfish one finds puff-stiff on tourist shop walls. The broad black man in the red bowtie and pearl-gray hat sat down along the boulevard and basked in a dozen smiles. His cane shined in the morning's sunlight, and his highly polished shoes reflected the filigreed legs of the fragile little table.

The waiter came, and Leadbelly ordered juice, half a grapefruit, bacon and eggs, and a large piece of pie. M. LeBec had coffee and a croissant. People passed by, and the heavy traffic flowed hesitatingly along the wide boulevard. It was a typical Parisian spring morning, but to Leadbelly it was a foreign world where the sunshine boasted a different color, and the flowers seemed more vivid as they swayed languidly in the gentle breeze.

The reporter showed up as Leadbelly started on his pie. After introductions, Leadbelly began to chatter: "Yessuh, I love my pie. Got me a sweet tooth these days, since I ain't drinkin' no more whiskey... jus' can't get enough o' this great French pie. No sir!"

"How was your flight across?" the reporter asked, through M. LeBec's translation. "Was it your first airplane ride?"

"Oh, Yessuh," Leadbelly said. "The first one! An' Lawd, that plane did fly! TWA, yes sir! That's the greatest airline in the world. The food was great! The ladies sure was beautiful and the seat was the mos' comfortable I ever sit in. Yes, suh. And that's the truth!"

"I'se doing right nice these days," he lied. "The record companies takin' down lots o' my old songs again, on these new kind of records, and the radio shows want me back on 'em. Yeah, I even wrote one song 'bout one of my darlin' daughters, gal named Irene. Li'l ol' Irene, now, she don't know really what's happenin', but someday she gonna be famous."

"How long have you used a cane?" the reporter asked. "You're about sixty now, aren't you, Mr. Ledbetter?"

"I'se sixty-three, that's right. I reckon I been using this here cane about five years or so, ever since my leg started givin' me some trouble. That's right, about five years, now."

"Tell me, have you had many race problems in New York? There have been several riots in Harlem, and I hear a lot of Negro musicians have taken up the lead in bettering conditions there. Can you comment?"

"Well, lemme tell you 'bout that. I ain't never been in no riots, but I'll fight Jim Crow anytime. Sometimes I get to singin' and a lot of people want me to sing songs what could get a good American man in trouble. But those times is over, I know, and even old as I is, I still think that none o' those Russians goin' to get the same thing what that Jackie Robinson man got. Now, that's what I think, and I guess youse the onliest newspaperman I ever met what's even been listenin' to what I'm sayin' instead of lookin' around for what's happenin' somewheres else." Leadbelly smiled across the table, and M. LeBec rushed to catch up. He was having great difficulty translating Leadbelly's peculiar English. "No sir, they ain't no problems with me except gettin' all the people to know that we's all in the same boat. I got a song 'bout that, except not too many people knows it. Oh, they's been some trouble with hotels and places, special when I first come to New Yawk with Mr. John A. Lomax, but now I ain't had any trouble for a long time. An' I live among the white folks now, too."

"Is your music accepted among the other music circles in America? Say, among the jazz bands or the popular music fans?"

"Naw!" Leadbelly replied gruffly. "They ain't had no chance to really hear me. I made lotsa records what never really got played 'round too much. The ones what did hear me, though, they surely do like it. They know the 'King o' the Twelve-String Guitar' when they hear him." Leadbelly talked on until M. LeBec terminated the interview, and the reporter thanked him profusely and walked off. Franklin breathed easier.

They went on an extensive tour of Paris, and M. LeBec patiently answered hundreds of questions. He translated signs and explained various places and customs, and they even stopped in one Left Bank place to hear Django Reinhardt. Leadbelly decided he would come back to Paris with Martha. This would be the place. This magnificent, shining city, where white girls could walk arm-in-arm with black men, this would be the place where he and Martha would settle some day. But now his leg hurt, and he was getting a headache. LeBec returned him to his room and told him a car would pick him up at seven o'clock.

Leadbelly was ready on time, and by seven-thirty he was seated off stage, tuning his guitar again and humming as M. LeBec peered anxiously through the curtains.

"There aren't many here yet," LeBec said, pacing nervously.

Leadbelly took out his pocket watch. "Don't you worry none, professor," he said cheerfully. "They's plenty of time. They got half an hour yet."

The "half an hour" soon passed. "How's the house?" Leadbelly now asked, the professional, the unworried star, calm, confident.

No one said anything.

"Ce soir, et il sera tres agreable, parce que son musique c'est magnifique dans les Etats-Unis. Voici, Monsieur Huddie Ledbetter!"

It sounded funny to him, and he started to smile, to smile at the world, and at Martha, and at the Lomaxes and at everyone because now maybe he could pay them all back because this was Paris! But suddenly he couldn't hold onto the buoyant mood -- it drifted out of his reach like a child's balloon, a balloon that popped when he saw the audience.

It was Time, he thought -- that's what was giving out on him. Why couldn't Time wait just a little longer, wait for just one more night, one more concert, one more song? How come there were older men, less talented men, who still had their chances and still made good livings? He'd been popular all his life, with women and with music and with the big drinkers, too -- why didn't he get a chance? Damn it all, Lawd!

But he had thought all that before, hadn't he? He prayed for a chance in Mooringsport and in Shreveport, and at Huntsville with the Captain and at Sugar Land and at Angola and then in New York, and even again in Shreveport and still again when he was bouncing around with Alan and the rest of them. It seemed like everyone had more money, except when he was with his own people, who never had any money anyway.

He stood on stage and began his first selection ritualistically, "The Midnight Special," and when they began clapping and shouting their applause, all thirty of them in a hall built for four thousand, he began counting the black faces for the first time in his life. Maybe there was a difference, as he'd heard so many of the whites say. Except, maybe the difference was different from the difference they thought was the difference. Maybe the difference was that the four black faces in this field of thirty were living their own lives, while Huddie Ledbetter never had. Maybe the difference was that he, the "King o' the Twelve-String Guitars of the World," knew goddamn well what the difference was and he was just too sick of it to care any more.

He swung into "Shorty George" without changing expression or tempo, and they noticed it. The hell with them.

He wouldn't come out for the second half of the concert, he knew that much. And as the rage welled inside him, that old familiar swell with the watering of the eyes and the shaking of the lips and the pinwheel-crazed thoughts, he knew that it was over. His last chance had passed, and he'd practiced three weeks to play his best. Now he didn't want to play his best any more, because he knew he'd played his best thirty years ago in a Texas prison. Why had they all lied to him?

He wanted to hit someone, hard, right direct in the face, so that there was the too-familiar crunch and some blood. But he knew it wouldn't do any good. It was too late for that, too.

He gave up. His international debut was also his surrender.

One little child used to get him started, get him playing and laughing and accumulating more kids; now, thirty genuine fans couldn't do it. He felt like one of those World War I photographs he'd seen a long time ago -- maybe there were a few in the last war, too, but he couldn't remember them -- where a young German, frightened and dirty and defenseless, was marching in front of a triumphant coterie of smiling doughboys with bayonets, waiting to be shot but knowing it wouldn't be when he was flinching. It would be when he was relaxed.

"Huddie, you may as well go out and do the rest," Franklin said. "This won't do you any good if it hits the papers."

Leadbelly slapped open fingers into his other palm, shaking his head as he did so. Old as he was, his girth and his harsh voice belied his helplessness. He walked to the makeshift dressing table and back to the two small green lockers, and back again. "No suh," he said, shaking his head because he had said the same two words two dozen times in the last three minutes.

"No suh!" he said. "They ain't gonna treat ol' Leadbelly like they did down at Hollywood! They's only the smallest group I'se ever played for out there, and here we is in Paris, France! No, suh, Cap'n! This is it! They ain't gonna trick ol' Leadbelly no more, I can tell you that right now!"

Franklin started pacing himself. He knew what was going to happen.

"Huddie," he said, pleading once again. "You have to go out there again. They won't---"

"They won't do nuthin'!" Leadbelly screamed, almost in tears. "They won't do no damn nuthin' and you knows it! They's only thirty of them! Now don't you go givin' me that ol' shit, too, Cap'n."

Franklin could see tears collecting in Leadbelly's eyes.

"Don't you go givin' me that same ol'..." And Leadbelly stopped and turned, and picked up his guitar by its neck and started to smash it against the radiator. But in mid-swing he saw Franklin's face, and it wore a new expression. Franklin had been disappointed before, but now Leadbelly saw the thoughts Captain Jack could no longer hide. As he gripped the neck of the Stella and tried to stop its damaging arc, the look on Jack Franklin's face said, *Go ahead -- I don't blame you.*

Leadbelly stopped himself, but as he lifted his arm to bring the crashing swing to a halt, he let go of the guitar and it slung across the dingy little room, over Franklin, who tried to catch it but couldn't. It hit the cinder-block wall and made a terrible noise.

Leadbelly slumped into a chair. "It'd take a hunnerd Angola guards to get me out there, now. That's the truth, Cap'n. I reckon I jus' want to see Marthy again and go back down to Shreveport where they ain't no lyin' white bastids tellin' me how big a star I'se goin' to be. I guess ol' Josh was right what he been sayin' 'bout us."

"Huddie..."

Leadbelly smiled at Franklin. "Cap'n," he said, "do you 'member when I would've gone out and got drunk and maybe broke up somebody's nice ol' place?" He kept grinning, as if he were drunk again, a caricature of a thousand previous Leadbellys.

"Well," he said, and suddenly stopped smiling. "They ain't no use in doin' that no more either, is they?"

He began to steal a glimpse at the broken guitar across the room, but he turned away from it. Do you ask to see the body of a friend you've killed?

Now not even ten times -- *a thousand times* -- the audience could bring him back. He already heard the French cheers and howls and invocations; he heard the requests to do the dance that tortured his bad legs; he heard, but he stopped listening.

They yelled for Leadbelly, and all thirty of them were disappointed. He didn't go back out.

###

Chapter Twenty-Five

He stood in a heavy wool overcoat, and his hands were trembling with anger and sickness. He pointed the cane at Franklin.

"Now, don't you go with all that 'Now, Leadbelly,' shit, Cap'n," he said sternly. He glanced at Martha, who wore a white uniform with wide lapels and her eyes flashed in surprise.

Franklin raised his hands, but let them fall before saying anything.

"You don't know what to say because it's you old friend Huddie Ledbetter sayin' it, right, Cap'n?"

"That's right, Huddie."

"An' they ain't nobody here what's got anything against you, right? And looky here, Huddie, this here man say he gonna pay you some money for a new recordin' and you do as we say now, hear? An' come on now, Leadbelly, sing for the people and let them laugh they goddamned asses off and…!"

He stopped, and his eyes moistened. Martha went to him softly. He put his hands to his face and dropped the cane. Franklin was tortured. What else could he say?

"Huddie, that phone call was *legitimate*! They want you to do 'Irene' for *national* promotion. It could become a top tune *overnight!*"

"No more," Leadbelly said to his oldest friend. "We jus' niggas after all, and we going home to Shrevepo't. They ain't gonna be no more shittin' on the Ledbetter family, Cap'n. You tell 'em to let Woody or Oscar make that song, and I reckon I'll jus' listen to it on the radio."

"Huddie, why don't you jus' go to your doctor's appointment and we'll talk about it over dinner," Martha said. "The record company people can wait, honey." She kissed him and, with tears shining on his cheeks, he went out the door.

When he was gone, Martha collapsed in a chair and rubbed her eyes worriedly. "Ain't never seen him like that in twenty years, Cap'n Franklin. That man ain't the Huddie Ledbetter these white folks brought up from Caddo Lake, no sir."

The doctor wanted him to take a taxi, but he put up an argument about getting fresh air, not wanting the doctor to know that the fare was excessive. Besides, he said, if he had to go to the hospital for a few days and just lie flat on his back, he wanted to walk home so he could take in the fresh air and maybe see some old friends on the way.

When he left the doctor's office, he walked one block and took a bus to Times Square. He really didn't want to see anyone -- and he knew that was just another rationalization, too. There would be no one to see. No one liked to visit sick people because it only made them sad. They'd all be back when he recovered, and they'd all sing again in his apartment, and drink his whiskey and eat his ham.

He hunched up under the heavy coat and limped painfully along on his cane. He didn't care which street it was. He walked wherever his feet achingly took him, and the distance was great.

The coming of winter in New York is a dismal event. People bow their heads on Thanksgiving Day and the next morning they curse the onslaught of Christmas shopping. The hopes of the past year, new endeavors, new dreams, new desires had possibly been fulfilled, but the odds were slim. But this late Thanksgiving afternoon in New York, no one could even see the sun turning crimson and flattening out on the horizon somewhere beyond the chilly gray haze.

In Harlem, a sewer rat streaked through the garbage-strewn streets, frenzied with hunger. In Wilton, Connecticut, a soft drizzle was turning into a light snow, sprinkling well-kept gardens and wafting the salt-smell of Long Island Sound into fire-warmed homes. In New York, as the night grew larger and once again pushed the day into the west, the leaves of tens of millions of plants were long wilted and the brown stubs now absorbed the dew and coming frost.

Leadbelly greeted Times Square at five-thirty. He was outside Horn and Hardart's Automat, watching the parade of tourists heading into the night seeking holiday fun. He walked on another street, looking with interest at the fronts of buildings and passing cars. He stared at the ornate facade of an exclusive social club as he approached. He wanted to be with friends, and he remembered they had never really done up the city.

He found himself leaning on the railing in Rockefeller Plaza, and watched the figures, like toys, skating on the lustrous ice. An old man was teaching two children how to skate. A teenage girl in black stockings was pirouetting, exhibiting her skill to the others. He spied a blonde girl skating with a Negro soldier, and he watched them obviously enjoying themselves. Never see that in Loosiana, he thought. His hands gripped the cold brass rail.

Forty-second Street was a blazing mixture of neon and paint, a vibrating whorl of plastic and pigment. Leadbelly looked through the grimy window of Doc Laff's Fun Store. He watched a wooden, felt-billed duck bob incessantly into a glass of stale water; a hand buzzer; a water pistol; a gaudy sign: "Once a King Always a King,

But once a Knight is Enough;" an Oriental dagger; a crystal radio; a foam-rubber shrunken head; itching powder; a pack of nudie playing cards; a magnifying glass hanging from an old dart board; a rubber lizard; a poorly made model of a P-38; a phony ink spill; an eight-ball; a sign that read, "We Aim to Please" -- under it scrawled *se habla espanol.*

He walked on. Once a king, he mused. Once a King, always a King...

Almost half a century had passed since he'd left home. And amid the cheap trinkets in the window he imagined a smashed and splintered windjammer. He saw faces; Maceo, that pompous old liar; Roy Dickey; the Coleman twins, those bastids; his daughter, Jessie Mae -- where was she now? Even Sheriff Tom Hughes looked at Leadbelly this evening, and waved goodbye.

He bought a copy of the *Daily News* from a toothless vendor and sat down on a torn plastic stool at a corner grill. Even though Martha was now at home fixing dinner for him, he ordered coffee and the "de luxe steak platter." "Rare," he said. "Blood rare." Page 5 of the paper showed him the half-naked body of a woman who had been found strangled in the Bronx. She was in her slip and it was drawn up high on her thighs. Leadbelly stared at the photograph for a long time.

His food came and he was disgusted to find his steak covered with runny cole slaw and sitting on a half-stack of greasy French-fried potatoes. On the side of the paper plate was a huge French roll. He wolfed it down.

Outside again, the color of the street twisted and glinted off his thick cane. His thoughts returned to the photograph in the newspaper and soon it dissolved into a hand-tinted photograph of a blonde white girl with rosebud lips. He stepped back; he was looking at a sign that told him he could dance with the girl in the picture for twenty-five cents. He thought of Edna Mae and of Lethe and of Margaret and of his daughter. And then he thought that he had never paid for a woman in his life. For some reason he thought back to the peephole in Errol Flynn's house -- he had never done that, either.

24 GIRLS 24, the sign said. He was tempted to go up the stairs but instead he just turned away, smiling. He walked down the dismal street in the direction of Washington Square.

Leadbelly agonizingly climbed the front steps of their apartment, pressing down hard on his cane and trying not to twist his face as each shot of pain seared through his legs and upward along his spine. When he entered the tiny apartment, Martha came to him immediately, her face grave, inquisitive. She saw the deep lines, the tightened corners of his mouth.

"The doc say to go over to Bellevue Hospital tonight for some tests in the mornin'. He say not to worry none, but he got to do some more checkin'." Leadbelly fell into a chair and looked at his wife. "Lawd, I'se tired, Marthy."

Martha came and sat down on the floor near his knees. She looked up at him with tears in her eyes and held his hands for a long time.

"Anybody come over today?" he asked.

She shook her head. "Nobody. Captain Franklin called to see what the doctor said."

"Nobody?" he said, surprised, "Guess they's all busy."

After an orange soda and a sandwich, Martha called a friend with a car and they left for Bellevue. No one had much of an appetite for the hot turkey still in the oven.

*　　*　　*　　*　　*

A week and a half later, on December 5, Martha arrived early at the hospital. She had been visiting him every day, staying long hours near his bed, reading, sewing, doing whatever she could to occupy herself. The doctors had explained the nature of his ailment -- just yesterday one had taken Martha and Jack Franklin into the hallway.

"It's the strong ones who get it, Mrs. Ledbetter. Remember Lou Gehrig? The ballplayer? They called him 'The Iron Horse'."

Martha and Franklin merely nodded silently. "Same thing," the doctor said, "Amyotrophic lateral sclerosis -- a form of poliomyelitis. We don't know much about it, yet, but there's always hope. What he needs now more than anything is just plain rest."

As she entered the room, still not understanding what the doctors had said, she thought again about the doctor's words. Rest. Always some hope.

Leadbelly was lying on his back, his upper lip depressed because they had removed his false teeth. His face was drawn and sharply etched with troughs and wrinkles. On his stomach was his old Stella, repaired now, and his arms cuddled it as though he were a child with a stuffed rabbit.

"How you today, honey?" Martha asked. He tried to smile, but said nothing. He was staring at the ceiling.

"I heard from some o' the boys," she said. "They all send their best, and those what ain't been here yet say they'll be along any time. Say to jus' keep on truckin', honey."

At that, he managed a grin. His hand mechanically crept up on the neck of his guitar and formed a chord on the strings, and he weakly strummed it with his right hand.

Late that afternoon Franklin dropped by and took Martha out for dinner. He promised he'd stay with her all night because

Martha didn't want to leave her Huddie. Back in the room, they sat by Leadbelly, straightened his sheets and gave him water. Martha propped his head higher up on the pillow. A nurse came in -- not the one on duty -- and respectfully explained that she just wanted to meet him, to give him her best wishes. Two nuns came by and one explained that she had been a folk music fan for many years. She gave Martha a Mass card and a crystal rosary for Leadbelly. A doctor came by and looked at the charts hung on the foot of the bed. He looked at Leadbelly's eyes, asked him if he had pain and gave him a shot.

At midnight, Martha got drowsy, and Franklin took her to the cafeteria for more coffee.

They were back in an hour. Leadbelly was awake, and asked for his guitar. He held it on his stomach, strumming it slowly. His eyes were only half-open, but he seemed to want to talk. Martha pulled her chair closer, and Franklin sat on the bed next to him, his hand on Leadbelly's shoulder.

"Marthy?" the voice was dim, faint, a whisper. "I gonna keep that promise, now, you hear?"

"I hear you, honey."

"We going back to Mooringspo't soon as---"

He stopped and took a deep breath. "Marthy, you there?"

Franklin had tears running down his cheeks, and Martha turned her head away to hide hers.

"You remember 'Careless Love'?"

Leadbelly kept talking in disjointed sentences. He kept asking Martha if she was there.

"Mr. Ledbetter," the doctor said softly, "You've got to put your guitar down, now. You need to get some sleep."

"Doc," the wispy voice said. "If I put this here guitar down now, I ain't never gonna wake up."

The doctor reached down and gently took the guitar from the bed. He ushered Martha and Franklin from the room, urging them to either go home or sleep on a chair in the waiting room. Before going, Martha went over and kissed him. He tried to hug her, but could only move one arm.

The next morning they found out he had been right. He never woke up.

*   *   *   *   *

Soon after, Alan Lomax organized a Leadbelly Memorial Concert, and every folk singer and would-be folk singer clamored to perform. But it was his friend, Oscar Brand, who electrified the audience when he walked out with his guitar and said simply, "I've just been told that I've got two minutes and that I can either talk about Huddie Ledbetter, who was my friend, or play. In fact, I guess I don't have any more time than to say that considering how many friends Huddie Ledbetter has -- judging by the number of people who wanted to appear at this concert -- I wonder why he died on relief and had so few people come to see him while he was sick."

With that, Oscar Brand walked off the stage.

Six months later Huddie's song, now named "Goodnight, Irene," sold two million copies and made Hit Parade history. At the same time, Martha Ledbetter was applying at the New York State Employment Service, seeking work as a laundress.

She never received a cent.

###

Epilogue

The light crust of snow from the night before is melting away under the constant drizzle of rain. The ice-mushy ground is pocked with tiny brown puddles as the mourners shuffle in silence into the Shiloh Baptist Church. The people do not speak, but their eyes meet in a gesture of bereavement. The church is filled, the faces all black.

The eulogies are delivered by the Reverends Gilliam and Martin. Someone sits at the piano and plays:

> *He has taken my mother's name*
> *and has left me here in vain!*
> *There's a man goin' 'round takin' names.*

Silence; then the sound of the rain again.

In the front pew, Martha Promise Ledbetter, in a long black dress and a wide-brimmed black hat and veil, sits and stares at her button shoes. Edmond and his children gaze blankly at the catafalque.

The mahogany-colored steel coffin, opened, rests in the center aisle, next to the front pew. During the ceremony, the assemblage files by. The coffin has made the long journey from New York, first to Shreveport's Benevolence Funeral Home, thence to Cook's, thence to Mooringsport and now, finally, to Shiloh Baptist Church. Martha has accompanied it.

Another song is played.

The ceremony ends and the entourage trudges solemnly to the rear of the church and into the cemetery. The graves are marked with bits of broken pottery, glass bowls and bottles, unusable light bulbs placed in symmetrical patterns. They pass an old, plain stone marked "Ammie Ledbetter," a distant relative of old Wes's. They pass by two freshly dug graves, each but two feet long. Dead baby twins. The graves are marked only with broken bricks.

The casket is lowered. Reverend Gilliam intones a final prayer. Martha approaches the casket and kneels in the mud. "Goodbye, honey," she whispers.

Then a man approaches with a shovel. He offers it to Martha. She turns her head and Edmond takes her by the arm. The man scoops a shovelful of soggy earth and throws it on the casket. A metallic *thump* echoes through the graveyard like a distant thunderclap.

Edmond leads Martha away from the silent place.

The rain keeps falling.

###

About the Authors

Edmond G. Addeo lives with his wife in Mill Valley, California. Prior to the publication of *The Midnight Special* in 1971, Garvin and Addeo had co-authored two other novels, *The Fortec Conspiracy* and *The Talbott Agreement*, and had collaborated on books in widely diversified fields ranging from sports to archeology to religion.

Addeo has since written seven more books and has had two screenplays optioned. His web site is www.edaddeo.com.

Richard M. Garvin passed away in 1980.

CPSIA information can be obtained at www.ICGtesting.com
Printed in the USA
239445LV00002B/10/P